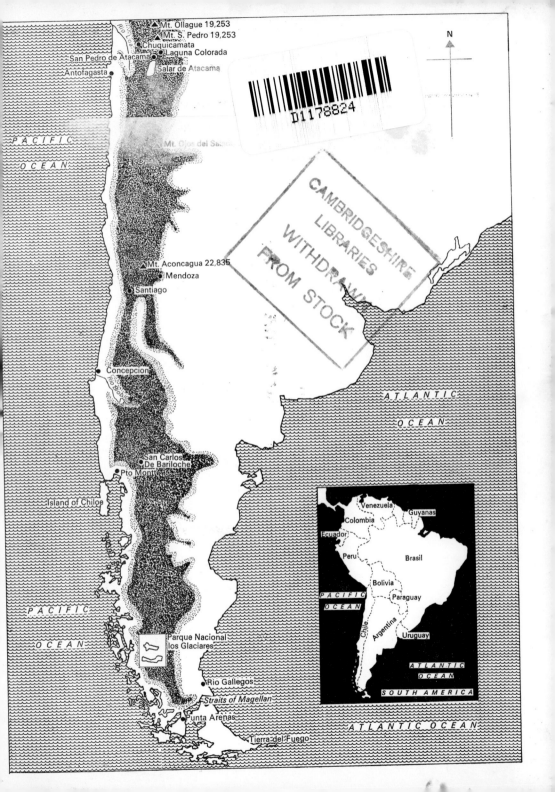

N

▲Mt. Ollague 19,253
▲Mt. S. Pedro 19,253
Chuquicamata
Laguna Colorada
San Pedro de Atacama
Salar de Atacama
Antofagasta

PACIFIC

OCEAN

Mt. Ojos del Salado

Mt. Aconcagua 22,835
Mendoza
Santiago

Concepcion
Rio Biobio

ATLANTIC

OCEAN

San Carlos
De Bariloche
Pto Montt

Island of Chiloe

Venezuela
Colombia   Guyanas
Ecuador
Peru   Brasil

PACIFIC   Bolivia
OCEAN   Paraguay

Chile
        Argentina   Uruguay

ATLANTIC
OCEAN

SOUTH AMERICA

PACIFIC

OCEAN

Parque Nacional
los Glaciares

Rio Gallegos
Straits of Magellan
Punta Arenas
Tierra del Fuego

ATLANTIC OCEAN

Land above the clouds

Survival Books are published in close association with Anglia Television's Natural History Unit who make the 'Survival' series of television documentaries on wildlife.

7/49
£3.99

SURVIVAL BOOKS *Already published*
Edited by Colin Willock

The Private Life of the Rabbit
R. M. Lockley

Birds of Prey
Philip Brown

Living with Deer
Richard Prior

Town Fox, Country Fox
Brian Vesey-Fitzgerald

Birds in the Balance
Philip Brown

Grey Seal, Common Seal
R. M. Lockley

S.O.S. Rhino
C. A. W. Guggisberg

A Wealth of Wildfowl
Jeffrey Harrison

Life and Death of Whales
Robert Burton

A SURVIVAL SPECIAL ON AUSTRALIAN WILDLIFE
A Continent in Danger
Vincent Serventy

A SURVIVAL SPECIAL ON NEW ZEALAND WILDLIFE
Man Against Nature
R. M. Lockley

A SURVIVAL SPECIAL ON AFRICAN WILDLIFE
Ngorongoro: The Eighth Wonder
Henry Fosbrooke

Land above the clouds

Tony Morrison

A Survival Special on South American Wildlife
Edited by Colin Willock

 ANDRE DEUTSCH

To Juan Prudencio
and Lindsay Smith

First published 1974 by
André Deutsch Limited
105 Great Russell Street London WCI

Printed in Great Britain by
Ebenezer Baylis & Son Ltd
The Trinity Press, Worcester, and London

ISBN 233 95737 5

Contents

Foreword by Felipe Benavides 9

Introduction 11

A Naturalist's El Dorado 15

A Long Desert 36

Frontier of the Amazon 56

Adjusting to the High Life 77

The Golden Fleece 87

Folklore and Fauna 110

Lake Above the Clouds 133

Flamingoes and the Red Lake 156

From Deserts to Darwin's Country 176

Odd Men Out 192

Bibliography 211

Index 215

Illustrations

Black and white plates   *facing page*

1   A Coati   32
2   An Andean Hummingbird   32
3   The Puya raimondii   32
4   The resinous *Tola* bush   33
5   Areas where the *Tola* used to grow   33
6   A Black-shouldered opossum   48
7   A Kinkajou   48
8   The Pudu   48
9   A Tamandua anteater   49
10 Black spider monkey   49
11 The Spectacled Bear   176
12 A Giant Coot   176
13 A Tinamou of the high Andes   176
14 The high altitude species of Darwin's Rhea   177
15 A group of vicuñas on the Pampa Galeras   177
16 Shearing alpacas in the highlands of southern Peru   177
17 The forested slopes of the Sierra Nevada de Santa Marta   192
18 An Aymara Indian   192
19 Quechua Indians on horseback   192
20 A Golden Condor   192
21 The arid western Andes of Peru   193
22 The high Atacama desert   193
23 Chipaya Indians of the Carangas province   193

Colour plates   *facing page*

 1   Tony Morrison with very rare caracaras — 64
 2   James Flamingos, Laguna Colorada Bolivia — 64
 3   World's rarest Flamingo, Bolivia — 65
 4   Indian with Alpacas (shorn) — 80
 5   Horned Coots, very rare (*Fulica cornuta*) — 80
 6   Mountain Viscacha (*Lagidium*) related to Chinchilla — 81
 7   Andean Gull — 96
 8   Agouti – Peru — 97
 9   Vicuña Band (*Vicuqna vicuqna*) — 97
10   Andean Goose (*Cloephaga melanopteraa*) — 112
11   Andean Fox — 112
12   Condor (*Vultur gryphus*) — 113
13   Lake Titicaca, Looking east toward the Cordillera real of Bolivia — 128
14   Torrent Ducks with young — 128
15   Condor (*Vultur gryphus*) — 129
16   Tayra (*Eira barbara*) — 144
17   Salar of Uyuni 12,150 feet — 144
18   Andean Caracara — 145
19   Female cock of the Rock — 145

Maps   *page*

 1   Manu National Park, Peru — 88
 2   Highlands of Southern Bolivia and Northern Chile — 134

All photographs by Tony and Marion Morrison

Foreword

The wildlife of South America has been neglected far too long and only in the last five years has the revival of world interest in our fauna made it clear that the problems facing conservationists are enormous. Fortunately, the communications media have publicized the work of researches from Europe and America and now, at last, we can begin to show some results. However, more studies are needed to justify the establishment of reserves and sanctuaries for wildlife, and this work is one of the top priorities at present as Latin American governments have been accustomed to receiving considerable revenue from their natural resources. The demands of local economies will encourage the use of such resources on an even greater scale and will inevitably lead to total exploitation of the forests, coasts and rivers. We hope that such development can be controlled by thoughtful legislation.

Nevertheless some laws – for example, the latest Peruvian decrees to protect the vicuña – are not sufficient on their own and support is needed from the governments of developed countries. In Great Britain and the USA, the import of vicuña products is now prohibited, and help of this nature is bound to be reflected in an improvement of the status of endangered species. Also, help from the governments of the advanced countries of the world will give encouragement to conservationists and leaders of public opinion in the Andean countries, and so we will be able to coordinate our laws through such bodies as the Andean Pact or the OAS which have the power to insist on stringent adherence to conditions.

Today, more than ever before our leaders have a great responsibility for safeguarding our environment and a still greater responsibility when making decisions that will affect future generations. This responsibility is very heavy when one hasty move could lead to irreversible changes. History has a long memory and does not forgive.

FELIPE BENAVIDES
President, Peruvian Zoological Association
Trustee, World Wildlife Fund.

Introduction

By the standards of Africa or Eurasia, South America is not large and yet it can claim some world records. It contains the greatest area of rain forest, and the Andes, the longest continuous mountain chain. Latin Americans are of diverse origin and many races mix with tolerance to create a lively and carefree society, possessing a vigour that surfaces in sheer enthusiasm for fun, sport and politics. Not everyone in the approximate two hundred million population has wealth and some are among the poorest in the world: Indians in the forested regions have a stone-age economy and have not developed even to the barter level. High in the Andes, other Indians, descendants of the conquered Incas, continue to live in much the same way as they have followed for centuries, and their firm, traditional outlook retards progressive ideas. But South America is a continent on the move and we are told that it faces one of the major population problems in the world; the cities will get bigger and at the same time, much of the land virgin today will have to be used in the future.

My first visit provided the chance to see part of the Andes, and was made in the company of a team examining social problems tackled by the United Nations; in fact, I had little time to spare for biology, and anyway one authority had said that the high Andes was not the best place for collecting and I was advised to go to the jungle instead. As it happened the mountains held a quiet attraction. There is something about the vastness and cool, clear air of the highlands which compels one to look again, and subsequently I returned many times and traced their length from north to south.

Later still in La Paz I met my wife who was working on development projects in Bolivia, and we have spent much of the last five years in the Andes, often taking months to reach some of the wildest parts. The wildlife is difficult to find and frequently we had to make long desert journeys by

Land Rover, or in the forests we travelled with mules and guides. On these expeditions, the often trackless Andes were shown as a land for explorers, and some areas we reached eventually were indeed unmapped.

The Andes are young mountains in geological terms and they divide the sub-continent into two unequal parts; from some highland areas rivers flow eastward two thousand, five hundred miles to the Atlantic, as others descend in the opposite direction to the Pacific in less than one hundred miles. In places the summits are snow-capped perpetually, standing in long rugged lines and the scenery is enhanced by glaciers, lakes and volcanoes. A map of the terrain and vegetation shows incredible variety, from absolute desert where rain was last recorded seventy-five years ago, to the cloud forests covering the precipitous slopes facing the Amazon, or the high, cold punas, the home of the llama and the condor.

Finding one's bearings in the literal sense is a problem for the naturalist and explorer alike, and this book is an attempt to satisfy the demands of both – perhaps I should add that inevitably some limitations arise. But none of my work would have been possible without help and this was given by expert naturalists and others whose day to day life allowed them a close contact with the Andean world. It would have been impossible to reach some of the remote corners of Bolivia's southern Altiplano without guidance from Piotr Zubrzycki, a geologist who spent fifteen years there; his precise instructions for driving across water-covered salt flats saved hours of frustration normally accepted in the rainy season. Roy Steinbach, a naturalist from Cochabamba, who, following in a family profession, knows the Chapare better than anyone, gave me much assistance; and from the outset Dr Franz Ressel, with experience of the Beni River and the Bolivian cordilleras provided expert advice and allowed me to use his research papers. In Peru, Hugo Echegeray offered his river knowledge on many expeditions, and on one horrifying occasion saved a member of the party when a canoe overturned in dangerous rapids: fortunately such experiences are rare and yet they form the often catastrophic unknown quantity when treading new ground. Some of the more difficult expeditions to the cloud forest and remote corners of the high deserts were made with Mark Howell who, in the course of other work, helped willingly with the search for rare animals.

The administrators and specialists in all government departments of the

Andean republics were helpful, and when possible they provided information and introductions. Also the British representatives, especially the British Embassy in La Paz and members of the British Mission advising on Tropical Agriculture in Bolivia, who gave time, invaluable assistance and the answers to dozens of problems.

For research, it was necessary to find material from many sources. In Lima, Srta. Nilda Cáceres of the British Council speeded my work in the Bíblioteca Nacional del Peru; and in Colombia, the Banco de la República allowed me to use the superb facilities of the library above the new Gold Museum in Bogota. Frequently the most refreshing and often lengthy discussions have been with students on grants from Europe or the United States; or with those Latin Americans who have found an interest in the natural history of their own country. The universities have been especially willing to offer facilities and libraries, and their experts have given many hours to show me the best collections in each region.

By making observations periodically for several years, I have been able to see the danger that confronts the wildlife of South America, while noticing sadly the absence of any major conservation project. In the early days of this century, the tiny Chinchilla was hunted ruthlessly, and one species probably is extinct in the wild. Now the Vicuña could go the same way together with the Pudu, Guemal, Hairy Tapir and several others. In the past few years there have been great efforts made by a few people and Felipe Benavides, a Trustee of the World Wildlife Fund has managed to capture enthusiastic support in Peru. Other encouraging signs have been the recent moves to establish national parks and Ian Grimwood, with experience from Africa, has seen many of his recommendations accepted in Peru and Colombia. But the balance remains uneven. South American wildlife could be forgotten easily or lost in man's latest conquest of the continent and in the future it could be as elusive as the El Dorado of ancient jungle legend.

A Naturalist's El Dorado

When primitive man first arrived in South America, possibly no more than ten thousand years ago, he witnessed a great change in the fauna. Today the countless fossil records left behind as a picture of animals that roamed the ancient swamps and pampas show that many were truly fantastic beasts which mysteriously disappeared almost as soon as the first hunters arrived. Huge armadillo-like Glyptodonts, with heavily armoured shells, long-necked Macrauchenids classed as ancestors of the camels, and the delicate three-toed Prototheres, one of the earliest horses were among the many representatives of early mammalian types which became extinct in relatively recent times.

The early hunters using spears made of long canes tipped with razor-sharp stones could have been responsible for the slaughter of the last groups of mammoths, though it is likely that the extinction was hastened by an altithermal soon after the last glaciation of the southern sub-continent. As the ice retreated, the land warmed until the great plains reached a peak of desiccation about seven thousand years ago. Without abundant vegetation the enormous herbivores withdrew to a few areas where plants and pools of brackish water remained, until perhaps, with the eeriness of a science-fiction fantasy, the last of the primeaval mammals gathered around failing water-holes where they fell easy prey to the tribes moving in from the north. These sites, now in the extremes of the Patagonian steppe land or on the levels of old plains, are some of the richest fossil-bearing deposits where bones and rock are found in distinct layers.

Now there are no giant mammals, though in the late nineteenth century seemingly recent remains of a Mylodon, one of the giant ground sloths, were found in a cave in Patagonia. The floor of the cave was covered with dung which looked almost fresh, and some pieces of the skin were in perfect condition; in the dark corners of the chambers, traces left by primitive Indians were indications that the sloths might have been kept or stabled like cattle. At that time, a hundred years ago, South America was as surprising as a conjuror's hat, and something new was described by every naturalist who visited the continent; no one knew what might survive in the lost worlds of the Amazon rain-forests or the wild, infernal south, so for a short time a wave of excitement spurred a search for a living Mylodon. Nothing was found, and the only possible explanation for the excellent preservation of the Patagonian ground sloth might be the prevailing conditions of extreme cold and dryness, which would preserve a corpse in a way comparable with the conditions that protected the body of a young Inca noble who was sacrificed over four hundred years ago on a high peak behind Santiago de Chile: the relic was discovered by a climbing expedition. Some thousands of years may separate the death of the prince and the sloth, but in such unique conditions time is unimportant, and now the Inca child will be a permanent exhibit enclosed by a refrigerated cabinet in a Santiago museum – unless a power failure alters the artificial micro-climate.

Any major change which abruptly affects the environment of a species is liable to challenge its survival, though small alterations taking place over a period of millions of years tend to affect the entire fauna of a region and allow very distinctive forms to evolve. South America has both the tell-tale traces of the many extraordinary animals that survived to be contemporaneous with primitive man, but also some living forms which reflect several early ages of development of the sub-continent.

In the early part of the Meozoic era, the southern American landmass was connected with another continent, possibly something like the North America we know today; and at that time the area shared a similar basic faunal stock including early toed-ungulates, primitive bats, rodents, marsupials, primates and edentates. At some time in the early Tertiary, the southern continent became isolated, and for millions of years afterwards it resembled a massive island entirely without contact with the rest of the world. In this period of separation an endemic fauna developed which is well represented by fossil forms of outrageous animals that are uniquely South American. Some families were highly successful and they filled many ecological niches, and have survived to the present day.

For aeons the odd creatures were able to live beyond the influence of the more specialized evolution already occurring in the northern hemisphere, where true carnivores, cricetid rodents, well-adapted ungulates and many others had competed successfully with the older forms. But the sanctity of South American isolation was broken by gradual stages in the Pliocene when a land-bridge formed between the two continents. At first the gap was straddled by a series of islands, though later the entire length of what is now Central America made a connection that allowed an interchange of animals. The invasion was slow: swamps and mountain ranges interrupted the path forcing some species to follow only routes that suited them. Insectivores which are common in the United States are represented only by a single genus of shrews in the northern part of South America. These tiny animals (Cryptotis) have kept to the higher parts of the mountains and range in the temperate high forests of Venezuela in the east and also towards central Ecuador where they have not yet penetrated beyond a warm valley that bars the way south.

A large number of the invaders from the north were well adapted to the conditions they encountered in South America and many of the primary endemic types were forced into hostile environments while immigrants gained dominance. Though the movement of mammalian types was a two way process, the balance was greatly in favour of the more specialized northern forms, and today only a few typically South American species have survived north of Mexico. It was the influence of interrupted contact with another continent and the distinct changes in the climate associated with the late arrival of man at the end of the Pleistocene which has left South American fauna with an individuality only comparable with that of Australia.

Basic patterns of evolution and distribution are recognized throughout the world and within these Central America, the Caribbean and South America zoogeographically constitute the Neotropical Region. It is not the largest region in area though it extends across more degrees of latitude than any of the others and contains the highest percentage and greatest number of endemic forms. Neotropica is frequently referred to as the bird continent and has more avian families than the other regions together; also, insects, reptiles and peculiar mammals abound to produce a riot of biological

2

diversity. The variety can only be credited to the circumstances that once affected the formation of South America and the wide range of habitats existing in the earliest years which have remained to distinguish the continent from many other lands.

A cold current welling upwards from the oceanic depths off the coast of Peru and Chile produces a climate to create one of the driest deserts in the world. Along the narrow coastline over two thousand miles of rock and sand are broken only by occasional river valleys. Then another two thousand miles to the east, the endless jungle canopy stretches three hundred and sixty degrees around the horizon where the trees are briefly forced apart by the great rivers of the Amazon and Orinoco. The forest habitats are a treasure house of species, and the vegetation varies from the sodden Chocó of Colombia, where fifty feet of rain falls each year, to the high gallery forests of Amazonas or the cold, evergreen woods of southern Chile. The tangled 'green-hell' of the Bolivian and Paraguayan Chaco is replaced in northern Argentina by the beginning of the great pampas which extend to the south and the wind-swept steppe lands of Patagonia.

Some of the vast lowland plains are absolutely free of stones, or have a continuity of form only disturbed here and there by old outcrops rising above the surrounding earth, like castles easily mistaken for crumbling cities on many occasions. Perhaps Colonel Fawcett and others were attracted to their death by legends or even the sight of some bizarre geological formations: the answer might remain unknown forever.

The hypnotic sameness of the great central forests is an impression remaining with a visitor for a long time after weeks of canoe travel on the rivers, yet each year the water course can change suddenly when floods cut through the banks and inundate the land. Seasonal flooding continues to cause havoc in some regions like the Moxos plains of Bolivia, but in the past much of the South American eastern land was swampy or permanently under water. To cope with this environment, the terrestrial animals adapted to life in the trees and the prehensile tail is a feature of many Neotropical primates that is never found in the related Old World species. With a tail as useful as a fifth limb, many of the mammals surviving in present times are highly specialized climbers; some of the anteaters, some rodents and even one carnivore cling to the high branches with their tails and perform like highly skilled acrobats. Other species are small and squirrel-like with the ability to scurry in the canopy and live unseen to the casual observer on the ground below. For all the records South America can claim, the animals are not an obvious feature to stand against superficial comparison with the great herds of antelope or groups of elephants typical of safari-conscious Africa.

Rising from the wild Neotropic world, the unbroken line of the Andes mountains form a gigantic barrier that has been called the backbone of South America; the name is apt, but only adequate when describing the geographic location, as from north to south the Andes are restricted to the western fringe of the sub-continent. The mountains of the extreme north in Colombia are exceptional and divide into three ranges, or Cordilleras, that spread fan-like to Darien, the Caribbean and Venezuela: otherwise along the entire four thousand, five hundred miles to the tip of Chile, the range only exceeds two hundred miles in width in Bolivia and sometimes is as little as sixty.

From the wonderful viewpoint in a jet aircraft, the greatest peaks seem only a wingtip away. Flying north from Santiago, pilots point to Aconcagua (22,835) feet on the Argentinian frontier, snow-capped perpetually and the highest mountain in the Western Hemisphere; Bolivia is noted for a jagged two hundred mile long Cordillera Real, with Illimani (21,184 feet), Huayna Potosi over 20,000 feet, and the Condoriri, a Matterhorn-shaped mountain 3000 feet higher than the European version. In Peru, the massif of the Cordillera Blanca has the infamous Huascaran, 22,205 feet with great glaciers which collapse without warning to destroy villages in terrifying swiftness. Over the Equator of Ecuador, the glowing volcano of Sangay casts an evil light into the evening clouds while the other giant cones of Cotopaxi and Chimborazo have been dormant but respected for many years. Looking downwards, this mountain world of harsh rocks and brilliant ice seems totally sterile; even the villages are insignificant smudges and the patchwork of ripening maize fields is the only tangible sign that life of some form must exist.

No generalization can cover an area with such widely different topography: high deserts strewn with volcanic ash are bitterly cold and almost moonlike while only a few miles away the low forested-foothills fringing the Amazon basin have an abundance of species that equals the lowland jungle. Between the extremes, an enormous variety of habitats adds to the Neotropical diversity and some of the unique environments have been occupied by highly specialized forms. In the high south of Bolivia, the world's rarest flamingo is restricted to a group of borax lagoons, and under the cold surface of Lake Titicaca a large frog has adapted to a permanent aquatic life. Some mammals are restricted to the highest levels and chinchillas famous for their valued skins live above 14,000 feet, though on the other hand the widely ranging Pumas (or Mountain Lions) are equally at home in the heights or the warm pampas.

Height, climate and vegetation are related factors which influence the animal population, and the patterns are complicated by the great length of the Andean range, as it extends through 65 degrees of latitude. Similar altitudes in Bolivia and Colombia have a different appearance, and the tough *ichu* grass that characterizes the plateaux of the southern-central Andes is replaced in the north by a more varied *paramo* vegetation. Along the high Puna de Atacama of Chile, the night temperature can fall more than thirty degrees below zero centigrade and only resinous bushes, lichens, and a strange, compressed relative of the parsley can withstand the extreme cold. These conditions limit the food supply and consequently animal life is sparse, whereas on the slopes of the mountains the type of vegetation is related directly to the altitude and so the number of species increases dramatically in the lower, warmer zones. The deserts on the western fringe of the mountains in Peru and Chile are, of course, exceptional, and apart from the oasis valleys, most of the region is almost lifeless. In roughly the same latitude on the Atlantic face of the mountains the forests are an impenetrable wilderness of tall trees, giant ferns and tangled undergrowth soaked in perpetual mist. The level, known as the cloud-forest is one of the least explored parts of the whole continent, and a mile or two from one of the new roads cutting through to the lowlands below, the cloud-forest can turn day into night and adventure into a shivering struggle against the cold. Fallen branches are thickly moss-covered and unusual epiphytes cling tenaciously to the living trees; it is a realm for the hardened collector who is prepared to risk his neck to claim a new species.

For some of the tribes in the lowland jungles the Andes represent the edge of the world. Looking towards the mountains from one of the wide rivers, the cliffs rise from the forest as an immense wall. Heavily forested slopes appear dark and repressive while the summits are lost in cloud. In the same way that the Indians of today find the mountains a barrier, the Cordilleras have limited the spread of some animal types; for example monkeys are not found anywhere west of the Andes in the region south of Ecuador. But conversely, the long temperate region penetrating across the tropics has been the path for many invaders from semi-tropical North America; like the shrews now spreading in the north, other terrestrial mammals including primitive man are known to have invaded Neotropica by this route. Possibly the Andes account for the relatively rapid distribution of man in South America once the first groups had passed the isthmus, and in spite of the difficulty of adaption to the highest levels, some traces of early hunters are known from regions which now are the coldest punas. Ten thousand years ago both the temperature and vegetation were far different to those encountered today and in reaching a workable theory for man's move-ment in South America such factors are particularly relevant. Unusually warm or cold climates place strong demands on man's temperature-regulating system, and to live successfully in the extremes some adaption to the environment had to evolve in the inhabitants of these regions of Neotropica.

The highlands of the Andes represent the most densely inhabited high-altitude region in the world and the Indians who live there are physiologi-cally well suited to the environment. Their ancestors might well have been adapted in advance for the Andean conditions, particularly if they are related to tribes that once peopled the high plateaux of Mexico; such an assumption simplifies the explanation, and most theories postulate highly complex migrations. Certainly man, with ingenuity could fashion rafts and take to the whim of an ocean current. Even the Kontiki adventure across the Pacific, when followed by other similar voyages can be introduced to argue the case for a link with Polynesia, and as an accomplishment it ought to be as effective as a set of space-photographs shown to a meeting of flat-earthists, and yet raftsmen are still greeted with scepticism. Shreds of evidence in the form of pottery designs and styles, linguistic-similarities, and culture patterns are at last beginning to substantiate reasoning for some small migrations from distant regions, though the main invasions were certainly from the north, with man following the Nearctic animals.

For adventurous historians, Colombus Day in the Americas can never have quite the same meaning since it was shown that the Vikings crossed the Atlantic and with research encompassing an increasing range of disciplines such new information can easily disrupt any established pattern. After the first manned satellite passes had been made across the Andes, some photographs taken by the astronauts revealed enormous features previously unnoticed by observers on the ground. In one high region of southern Peru, three craters, altogether covering many miles across, scar the earth. Possibly of meteoritic or even volcanic origin they would have created widespread disaster when they formed. Another photograph included a large Bolivian lake, known to exist, but so new that it is not marked on the maps.

Not much more than four hundred years ago the entire continent was only a legend. Stories reached the ears of avaricious Conquistadores fighting in Darien, and lured by the promise of gold they commenced an exploration which led them to the world's greatest river, most endless forests and the Andes. High in the valleys dividing the cordilleras, they discovered a civilization so rich that the looting continued for centuries and as the last Inca was murdered, his people were turned into slaves. In those same years when the officers of Pizarro's band were gambling away the magnificent ornaments of the sun temples, some cathedrals of Europe were old and a few principles of science had been accepted as fact and not heresy. In Europe the environment was a new challenge to gentlemen naturalists, but discoveries made in the New World by the Spanish and Portuguese explorers only filtered slowly across the Atlantic and even now with all the records we have, some details of the South American sub-continent at the time of the Conquest will never be known. In comparison with one aspect of the political world today, a solid golden wall was drawn tightly around Spanish America for two hundred and fifty years.

When Columbus set foot in the Americas, he opened the way to more than half the world; the Pacific was unknown; Australia and New Zealand with their strange marsupial fauna were discovered almost two hundred years later and Africa, though not an ocean away from Europe was mostly unexplored. Certainly the thought of treasure had urged the Conquistadores to follow the route to the west, and the right of discovery as interpreted in those days was established firmly by a convention between Spain and Portugal at Tordesillas, whereby the 'New founde Worlde' was divided at a point 370 leagues west of Cape Verde. All the territory to the east of the line was given to Portugal and everything to the west belonged to Spain; the agreement was ratified by the Pope and so with his blessing the Americas were closed to explorers from the rest of Europe.

The Conquistadores began the destruction of the golden Andean kingdoms not long after they had crossed the Panama Isthmus. An expedition from Venezuela met in a pincer-like movement with another force from Ecuador and decimated the Chibchas in the highlands of Colombia. In the south Pizarro and his Men of Gallo sacked the Incaic temples of Cajamarca and Cusco, and apart from pockets of resistance that held out for centuries, the entire length of the Andes was quickly in Spanish hands. Santa Fe de Bogota was founded in 1538; Quito in 1534 and La Paz in 1548; by the middle of the eighteenth century, the silver-rich town of Potosi in the Audencia of Charcas was the same size as the City of London of the time. The exploration and settlement of South America moved rapidly; both the University of San Marcos in Lima and of San Francisco Xavier in Sucre were founded before the Pilgrim Fathers sailed from Plymouth; and in 1541 Orellana descended the Amazon from the Ecuadorian headwaters to become the first man to cross the continent. Other adventurers pressed forward in every direction, along the River Paraña into the eastern sierras of Bolivia, or directly from Cusco southwards across the Andean deserts to Chile. There was only one motive apart from the driving force of conquest, and that was the quest for gold.

On their way, the hardy Spanish trekked through terrible forests and over the world's highest deserts, and yet their reports contain few references to the natural life which abundantly filled the new realm they were opening up. Pizarro's men described the 'strange Peruvian sheep' used by Andean Indians as beasts of burden; but these were the llamas or South American Cameloids which are common today in the central Andean highlands, though, fortunately, the Spanish references can tell us that at the time of the Conquest the llama was known also in the coastal desert oasis valleys. Other chronicles give some impression of the state of the Andean civilizations or the primitive tribes of the forests, but the details are often inadequate, and by the time that the finest and most descriptive journals were written the Spanish Empire was established and Iberian influence had begun to override the ancient customs of the Indian peoples. As the course of Spain's American colonies progressed towards an odd mixture of European and Indian civilization, many of the secrets of the enormous wilderness were uncovered. Nearly every possible route was traversed and priests and miners settled everywhere but if they found a dead-end to their searches they left an area, which is an explanation for some of the most heavily exploited places which are now absolutely deserted. Parts of the eastern cordilleras of Bolivia were a stronghold of the Jesuits until the Order was expelled in 1767, but since then the land has reverted to the wild state and has not been thoroughly explored. In the south of Bolivia, the immense semi-deserts were a mining region until the enslaved Indians rebelled in the late eighteenth century, leaving the province without labour until only recently in a good political climate has the inducement been strong enough to revive the industry. Exploration today in South America can seldom cover new territory, but even with the advantage given to the colonists, the field of scientific research remained wide-open and for the explorer-naturalists who succeeded in gaining entry permits in the final years of Spanish rule, the host of new material was like a vast, unlabelled and chaotic museum-collection.

Plants and animals from the New World were returned to Spain, but bureaucracy and rivalries typical of the country at the time prevented any work or classification; specimens frequently rotted at the ports or in the stores of universities; and it was left to men like La Condamine, Humboldt and Spruce to begin the mammoth task of unravelling the secrets of the Andes and Amazon. In 1735 Charles Marie de la Condamine led a group from the French Academie des Sciences to the Equator at Quito, at that time part of the Spanish colonies under the Vice Royalty of Lima. La Condamine's team was the first to be admitted in two hundred and fifty years of rule by the Spanish Crown, and though as a main purpose the expedition was to measure an arc at the Equator for the determination of the shape of the earth, the team included a doctor, a botanist, an astronomer and a map maker. Instructions given to the local officials urged that they should offer every assistance, but the scientists were not to be allowed to probe too deeply into Spanish affairs or the resources of the land. Everything went well at the beginning. The Frenchmen were awed by the massive fortresses of Cartagena, the tropical Darien and the forest-rivers of western Ecuador. All the jungle animals and birds were new to them and they described magnificent herons, egrets, monkeys, snakes and a wonderful insect life that plagued them or fascinated them alternately. Then came the Andes, and the climb to 12,000 feet, to a high cloud-soaked *paramo* below the towering volcanoes of Ecuador.

La Condamine worked for years crossing and re-crossing the Andes to lay a base-line and observation points; the countless triangulations and calculations were made under terrible conditions high on the slopes of Cotopaxi, Pinchincha and Chimborazo. Also, to add to their problems it was inevitable that the Frenchmen should find themselves accused of spying. Their work was quickly mistaken for a form of treasure-hunting: with a fever of suspicion the creoles turned against them and the expedition met the same anti-gringo feeling that flares spontaneously in Latin America today. Within the years that La Condamine worked in Ecuador, he saw his doctor, Seniergues, killed by a mob in Cuenca; he watched his botanist, Jussieu, turn half-mad after losing a plant collection that had taken years to make, and finally the giant markers set up at the end of the baseline were the start of a political controversy. Gradually a tense situation developed that made work impossibly slow, and it was not until 1743, eight years after commencing the task, that La Condamine had some results: the arc was measured and his calculations helped prove that the earth was flattened slightly. But La Condamine's travels did not finish in the Andes; he travelled southwards to the headwaters of the River Marañon and then downstream through to the Huallaga and the Amazon. He studied the depth, the flow and the fall of the river, and mapped its course. On the way he collected *chinchona* seeds at Loja in Ecuador and rubber in the Amazon forests; he saw the sea-cow (Manatee) in the rivers and observed at first-hand many of the natural wonders of South America. His arrival in France was a splendid occasion for the scientists and his material was published in the form of papers and pamphlets which helped to satisfy the curiosity of the natural philosophers of Europe.

La Condamine on his travels down the Amazon had noted the confluence of the Rio Negro with clear, dark water, and the silt-laden mainstream; and he had been told that in the upper reaches of the Negro, the river connected with the great Orinoco system. He took the news to Europe and though the connection was considered, the experts put more faith in early maps, which indicated a vast lake somewhere between the two rivers, and believed to be the source. In part, Sir Walter Raleigh was responsible for the error, for in the time of Elizabeth I, he sailed up the Orinoco and he felt certain that ahead of him El Dorado was separated from him only by the imaginary lake of 'Manoa'. The lake was never seen, but cartographers continued to include it in maps of South America, and it remained for Baron Alexander Von Humboldt to unravel the mystery.

Humboldt arrived on the continent in 1799, accompanied by a great botanist-friend Aimé Bonpland, and they began their work in the Llanos of Venezuela where the main river of the Orinoco flows to the Atlantic. Again the local authorities gave every assistance, and Humboldt's letters of introduction were far more generous than those given to La Condamine. According to the King of Spain's request, Humboldt was to have as much freedom as he required for his researches, and accordingly Humboldt and Bonpland began by ascending the Orinoco, until they discovered the Casquiare canal which links the Orinoco with the River Negro. In the course of the journey, they also discovered another route between the two great waterways where a portage of four miles took them to a stream called Caño Pimichin on the Rio Negro watershed; all these discoveries were carefully described and mapped, and with the work of Humboldt the first highly accurate reports of the land and wildlife of South America began to appear. His travels in the Amazon and Venezuela took only a year, and during that time he described in profuse detail the life of leaf-cutting ants which relentlessly defoliate many trees and shrubs. These ants carry huge chunks of the plant to underground colonies and use the leaves for making a fungus garden in their nest. A close symbiotic relationship has developed in which the ants and fungus cannot live apart. Humboldt noted the uniqueness of this relationship, as well as many other aspects of the tropical natural history of Venezuela; he reported on electric eels and collected many specimens of mammals including a grey-brownish very woolly furred monkey he discovered (later this was named Humboldt's Woolly Monkey – Lagothrix lagothricha-*Humboldt*). His efforts were untiring, and yet after he had finished with north-eastern tropical regions, he turned to the Andes.

In 1801, Humboldt and Bonpland arrived at the mouth of the Magdalena River in northeastern Colombia, a country then called New Granada. The wide slow-flowing river was the route the Conquistadores used almost three hundred years before, and even today it is a major waterway navigable as far as Honda 500 miles from the Caribbean. The delta region of the river is a maze of mangrove swamps surrounding large brackish lagoons or *Cienagas* set between low-lying forests: for animals it is the home of the capybara (Hydrochaerus hydrochaerus), the web-foot semi-aquatic rodent; caymans (South American crocodilians) and a multitude of waterbirds including jacanas, herons, anhingers, limpkins and screamers. Recently more than two hundred species have been recorded in this tiny area and now the Colombian Government has passed a law delimiting the forested Island of Salamanca as a natural reserve.

The journey made by Humboldt and Bonpland took them up-river and over the warm, forested northern Andes to the cool plain of Cundinamarca and Santa Fé de Bogota. Then they went southwards along the rich valley of the River Cauca, which now is one of the finest agricultural and industrial parts of South America. They continued to Popayan and Pasto, small towns in the southern-most corner of Colombia, where deep valleys cut the Andes from 10,000 to 2,000 feet, exposing precipitous cliffs and a home for the Andean Condor (Vultur gryphus). In the highest places the explorers crossed the cold windswept *paramos*, where the vegetation is short, dense and adapted to the altitude and climate; where unique Bromeliads, mosses and ferns are sheltered between many flowering shrubs. This zone gives way to an open *puna* before the snow-line is reached, and the *paramos* lack the harshness of equally high places in the southern Andes. Colombia and Ecuador have green, gentle mountains, overlooked by white peaks which dominate the valleys without the awfulness of the southern cordilleras.

Once settled in Quito the two naturalists began studies of the zonation of plants at different altitudes on a nearby volcano slope, and set down some principles of the relationship of altitude and latitude to climate and the effect on plant geography. Another great accomplishment achieved by Humboldt in the Andes was his near successful attempt on the ascent of Chimborazo, the 20,500 foot high volcano a few miles south of the Equator. With Bonpland, and a Quiteñao, Carlos Montufor, he reached to within 3,000 feet of the summit, and for some time it was a record height for climbing anywhere in the world. (Chimborazo was not conquered until 1880 when Edward Whymper made the ascent, during an expedition in which he climbed many other Andean peaks including Cotopaxi, Illiniza and Cayambe.)

After the high Andes of Ecuador, Humboldt and Bonpland continued into Peru where at Callao, Humboldt checked on the sea temperature and discovered it was far lower than normal for the latitude, and he concluded that the cold current came from the Antarctic and the effect of the cool sea was to prevent precipitation over the warmer, adjacent land. He suggested that a reversal of the usual pattern of coastal climate created the desert, and further researches quickly established the theory, since when the Peruvian coastal current has been known most often as the Humboldt Current: it is a permanent reminder of the highly scientific approach he gave to his work.

Once Humboldt returned to Europe he produced thousands of words to record his labours: his research went far beyond the observations of La Condamine and as Humboldt received acclaim throughout the world, it marked a turning point in South American natural history. His books excited other naturalists at the time when on the sub-continent the colonists were beginning to tire of the restrictions of the Spanish Crown. Revolt spread to every corner until with the emergence of different republics, more trading with other countries was permitted and there was a greater freedom of entry for foreigners.

If any era of the New World can be claimed as a golden age of development, the hundred years from 1830 onwards was the period of greatest advancement. Once Humboldt had commenced the mammoth task of critically examining the flora and fauna, he was followed by others equally skilled in taxonomy and with similar determination. The French naturalist D'Orbigny arrived in 1827 and began work in Argentina and Bolivia, his travels were extensive and covered many of the different zones of the Andes, where he made a collection of birds and mammals – some species continue to carry his name in the classification. In 1831 Darwin began his epic voyage of exploration with H.M.S. *Beagle*, to Brazil, Argentina, Chile and Peru, with numerous excursions inland to the pampas, the forested Andean slopes of the far south and the dry western deserts of Chile. Completing the South American part of his tour in the Galapagos Islands he had enough material to produce an historic account of the natural history of southern South America and of course, his theory of evolution. But in the excitement of Darwinism, many other explorers were forgotten. Von Tschudi in 1838 travelled in Peru, collecting and classifying the fauna; Richard Spruce spent seventeen years in the Amazon and Andes between 1849 and 1886 when he collected and pressed more than 30,000 plants, which was his main scientific achievement, though he is best remembered for his efforts to transfer the seeds of the chinchona tree to India. He lived for some time in Tarapoto, a settlement on the Amazon headwaters in Peru, and devoted a considerable time to the flora of the eastern Andes. Nowadays Tarapoto has changed, and has become a rich site for colonization with some development resources available from government funds. However, in the years when Spruce was there it was a town of crude, tiled houses, built by the Spanish and was a staging point on the way to Amazonas via the River Ucayali. It was from Tarapoto that Spruce set out for Ecuador, to the town of Loja and the woods nearby where Humboldt also had seen the chinchona trees and warned against their destruction. Spruce's mission was successful, at least to the collecting stage, and cuttings and seeds were sent to Madras in India.

Henry Bates and Russell Wallace had preceded Spruce on the Amazon by a few months and produced fine studies of the botany and entomology, thus ensuring that by the middle of the last century far more of the natural history of the sub-continent was available for study and discussion than had ever been known about during the time of Spanish rule.

The naturalists were drawn to South America by the wealth of strange animals. Especially fascinating were the Edentates, a group of mammals found only in Neotropica. In this family are the sloths, anteaters and armadillos. Sloths are slow moving, tree living and apparently defenceless, and yet they have survived. Their main enemy is the jaguar, but the height of their arboreal home is a deterrent, and the Cecropia trees which are the main habitat of the Three-toed Sloths (Choloepus) are home also for a fiercely stinging fire-ant. Anteaters are found as three different forms: the

Giant Anteater of the plains, about five feet from snout to tail, and the two arboreal species, the Tamandua and Pygmy Anteater. These animals found in the tropical regions as far as the lower foothills of the Andes are curiously equipped with long tongues that can reach inside termite nests.

Then the naturalists found the armadillos, which are very tank-like with a hard banded-carapace and live in every type of habitat. One species is common even in the sandy deserts of the high Bolivian Andes. The animals are not related to any other known form, but their history is explained by the ancient fossil forms. Early giant armadillos, the Glyptodonts of long ago have been excavated in the Andes, on the pampas and in some places along the River Paraguay where the fossils stand out in the river bank. Among other ancient Edentates were the ground sloths, the larger ancestors of the modern tree living forms and their remains have been found in the south-western United States as well as in South America. It is in the Mylodon Cave in Ultima Esperanza of South Chile that tourists can see the place where the very well preserved Ground Sloth remains were discovered. The vast ossuraries of Patagonia were visited by Darwin; and fine specimens from this region are now displayed in the Museum of Natural History (Bernadino Rivadavia) in Buenos Aires. Darwin watched guanacos, the wild relative of the llama, as they roamed the pampas, and he collected a species of rhea, a South American ostrich-like bird. Darwin's Rhea and the Guanaco are found high in the Andes as well as in Patagonia, and they are among the largest living animals of Neotropica; by height alone the Guanaco and the Llama would be the tallest mammals, but the tapirs are heavier. Closely related to the Malayan Tapir, the South American species are usually about four hundred pounds, and are known from the forested regions of Amazonas (Tapirus terrestris) north to Central America (Tapirus bairdsi) whilst from the higher forested slopes of the Andes, a rare species, the Mountain Tapir (Tapirus pinchaque) is slightly smaller and is covered with longer, almost woolly hair. These odd jungle beasts, about the size of a small cow, were classified originally as Hippopotamus in 1758 in the Systema Natural of Linné (the Mountain Tapir not being recorded until 1829.)

The South American marsupials of the Family Didelphidae were among the first animals to receive attention from explorers, and when the Spanish arrived in Florida and Central America, they were intrigued by the odd fox-sized Common Opossum (Didelphis marsupialis) with its prehensile tail, and young strangely carried about in a primitive pouch. They did not know at that time that the Marsupials would pose a great zoological mystery, and the first reactions were no more than a passing recognition of a 'strange beaste'. Vincente Pinzón, who commanded the Niña between 1492 and 1493 recorded the Virginian Opossum, and a specimen exhibited in Granada was later described by Trivigiano in 1504. In 1612, the animal continued to arouse curiosity and Captain John Smith wrote 'An opossum hath a head like a swine, and a taile like a rat and is the bigness of a cat'. Two hundred years later, once the marsupial fauna of Australia had been discovered, the obvious question of widely separated distribution had to be answered. Was there an ancient continent in the Antarctic that linked Australasia and South America? Or was there a chance that there could have been a spread of marsupial types throughout the world, but only surviving in isolated continents? As the biological sciences progressed the studies of morphology and zoogeography gained many followers who began to theorize on the problem of marsupial dispersion. The naturalists of the last century sought a linking species and were successful in discovering fossils in South America that represented a Caenolestid type more closely similar to extinct Australian forms than the living marsupials of Neotropica, and it was not until 1895 that a preserved Caenolestid of a living species reached the hands of Oldfield Thomas in London. The first Caenolestids or Rat Opossums to be found came from the forested Andes in Ecuador, and they would have been recognized earlier, if it had not been for a bad classification that included one in a list of Ecuadorian mammals in 1863. Today they are placed in a separate Super-family, Caenolestoidea, while other South American opossums are classified in the Super-family Didelphoidea, though even this classification seems variable, as Ride (1964) gives two Orders; Marsupicarnivora and Paucituberculata with Caenolestids grouped in the latter.

At first, only a few Caenolestids were found and even now they are considered extremely rare. Since the original discovery of the type only three genera have been described and with the exception of the genus Ryncholestes, occurring in the woodlands of south-central Chile, and on the Island of Chiloé, all the other specimens have come from the dense undergrowth of higher Andean forests. Most of the habits and status of these unique animals are unknown, and it is only that they survive in the living form which makes them highly important. Their discovery, as well as evidence of other fossil marsupials in cretaceous deposits in Montana, U.S.A. provides a line of evidence for assuming that the marsupials were spread throughout the northern hemisphere. However, though this is probably correct, the close similarity of the Caenolestids to Australian forms is now recognized as a remarkable example of convergent evolution. When the continents of South America and Australia formed into gigantic islands, the marsupial forms survived in isolation, while mammals evolved elsewhere. A few species of Didelphids occur in present times in Central America and the United States and they probably moved north out of the southern sub-continent when the pliocene land-bridge formed.

Of the other mammalian orders, rodents are well represented and some modern species belong to the ancient families endemic to Neotropica. In the Andes both the Mountain Paca (Stictomys taczanowski) and the Tailed Paca or Pacarana (Dinomys branikii) are rare; they are the size of a small pig and found only in isolated parts of the forest. Agoutis (genus Agouti) and Pacas (genera Dasyprocta and Myoprocta) are similar and slightly smaller, while the Capybaras are the world's largest rodent, and reach as much as 120 pounds. All of these types are included in the Super-family Cavoidea and distributed widely in South America; the Cavids are characterized by the small Cavies (sub family Caviinae) of which the domesticated or Andean Cavy (Cavia porcellus) or household guinea pig, is the best known. *Cuis* as they are called by the Indians are kept for food in many of the sierra houses; the meat is an Andean delicacy often displayed in the street markets and usually garnished with a piquant sauce of *aji*, a local form of hot red-pepper.

On the other hand, many of the mammals can be compared easily with familiar species, and there are rabbits, several weasels, foxes, otters, a bear, several species of wild cats and deer. The birds too, seem to be familiar and there is an abundance of ducks and small waders on the high lagoons; or snipe and ibis in the marshy places. But typically South American are the tinamous (incorrectly named 'Perdiz' – partridge by the Spanish) and the hummingbirds, the tiniest and most active avian form. Sometimes differences are slight, but the Neotropical realm has a tremendous variety of habitats and

Coati – a racoon-like animal typical of much of tropical South America. Several species are found in the ~an region.

~n Andean Humming bird feeding from the flowers ~e Puya raimondi.

3. The Puya raimondi – the tallest flower spike in the world found at 14,000 feet in the Bolivian Cordilleras.

4. The resinous *Tola* bush is typical of the high semi-deserts of the central Andes. It provides good cover many of the animals.

5. In many places the Tola is being cut for fuel and now huge areas are devoid of the plant.

an abundance of endemic species. It is true that none of the mammals are large, and that the greatest number of species are insects, birds and reptiles: in Colombia alone there are over 1,500 different species of birds representing 56 per cent of the species of the entire continent, and more than twice the number found in North America. Many of these are from the Andes or the fringe zones in the foothills, and the higher levels of Colombia have a temperate climate, a condition that tends to extend southwards on either side of the mountain range. Along the Pacific side, the forested zones reach to the southern Ecuadorian border into the Department of Tumbes in Peru where there is a drier scrub-forest at the northern limit of the influence of the Humboldt current. To the east of the mountains the wet Atlantic climate of the Amazon maintains a high rainfall, and the slopes are forested as far south as Bolivia where another change begins between Cochabamba and Tarija; the eastern slope at this point is drier, and falls away into the Chaco scrub-jungle. The far south is different again, with evergreens, Southern Beech and a few Auracanian Pines. Each habitat influences the fauna, and so the Andes can offer an excellent cross-section of Neotropical wildlife, including some species possessing extremely specialized adaptations.

In the early days of exploration the high plains were the focal point of the treasure-hunting Conquistadores, for between the cordilleras the mountain Indians had developed their civilizations. Only relics of the past age remain as ruins such as Tiahuanaco on the southern shore of Lake Titicaca, Cusco in Peru or San Augustin in Colombia and most of the great naturalist explorers made relatively short excursions to the uppermost and coldest areas whilst concentrating their collecting in the lowlands or the warm fringe zones of the mountains. Thus the natural-history of the highlands was left to the observations of anthropologists and archaeologists searching for antiquities or delving into the mysteries of Indian life. Lake Titicaca was studied briefly in the last century, but the first detailed work was not completed until 1937 when the Percy Sladen Trust Expedition visited the area. Also, hardly anything was known of the habits of the Condor until a research student from Wisconsin University set up a project for his thesis in 1968, so in many ways the relative barrenness of the high mountains is reflected in the lack of scientific investigation, and though mountain fauna is listed, very little is known about it.

3

D'Orbigny and Von Tschudi who began the examination of Andean animals were followed by passing observers of natural history; Sir Clements Markham travelled extensively in Peru: Roger Casement visited the Putumayo to report on slavery at the height of the rubber boom and later there was Nordenskiold who discovered Inca temples on summits in northern Argentina and explored in Bolivia and Peru at the turn of the century. More famous among the recent travellers was Colonel Percy Fawcett who before he disappeared mysteriously in the forests of Brazil, spent some time on the River Heath bordering Peru and Bolivia. His mission was to delimit the frontier for the two countries, and his journeys took him from the summits of the Andes to the lowlands through a tough jungle which has remained wild to this day. On his way Fawcett had numerous encounters with dangers close to good fiction and he encountered a variety of animals, nearly all of them being savage. He reported sighting a strange dog-like carnivore said to be 'rare and unknown to science'. At least one small expedition has searched for the animal that Fawcett named the 'Mitla', but so far it has not been found: perhaps it was a weasel or a small carnivore similar to a Tayra (Eira barbara), but for the present the animal joins the legion of unknown or strange species recorded in every part of the world. But the 'Mitla' is not alone in the realm of Andean mysteries, and there have been scores of rumours about Andean wolves, though none of the stories have a basis, apart from second or third hand reports. Now it is accepted that the place of the wolf in Andean ecology is usually occupied by large South American Foxes (genus Dusicyon) which are widespread, and sometimes mistaken for wolves; certainly the first Spanish adventurers confused them and 'lobo', the name for a wolf, has been used as a prefix for many animal names in Latin America.

After more than four hundred years of European influence and a century and a half of scientific accomplishment, the field of South American natural history has been touched only superficially. Entomology and the transmission of disease is increasingly important, ecology and conservation have been forgotten in the rush to develop the land and some animals are on the verge of extinction before any study has shown their position in the Neotropic pattern. The environment is facing tough pressures as the South American republics rush to get into the twentieth century and feed their expanding populations, but on the other hand, the continent retains a romance which continues to attract explorers. The Andean backbone, once the route of the Conquistadores, hides a few virgin regions which, forgotten and almost impenetrable, remain a naturalist's El Dorado.

A Long Desert

From the north of Peru and extending more than two thousand miles southward to Copiapo in Chile, one of the greatest deserts in the world is bordered by the Pacific on one side and the cold heights of the Andes on the other. As Humboldt discovered, it is cool Antarctic water welling up from oceanic depths close to the sub-continent which is responsible for the strange climate; and along the narrow coastal strip the monotonous sterility of rock or sand is broken only by fertile oases valleys carrying rivers from the nearby mountains. Most of the major centres of population are now established in naturally irrigated areas, and Lima, the rapidly expanding Peruvian capital is sited on the River Rimac which provides electric power, drinking water and a drain for industrial effluent.

For many months each year a heavy mist lies over the coast, and though it almost never rains, the light precipitation is sufficient to make Lima miserable for visitors and Limaeños alike, so much so that a local joke says that the Spanish arrived there in the fine summer months and at the suggestion of the conquered Incas, founded the city and built extensively before realizing that the coastal mist persists for half the year. In January 1970 when fine rain fell for nearly twelve hours over Lima, parts of the capital were swamped for the first time in forty-five years.

The desert has preserved many relics of the early coastal civilizations, as the people who inhabited the fertile valleys in Pre-Colombian times made their burial grounds on the surrounding dry fringes and in these places the finest artefacts have been discovered; but many graves have been opened and the contents taken for museums or private collections. It is not known with precise detail how the inhabitants of the ancient towns were living at the time of the Conquest and the remains of each coastal empire with individual characteristics are still desert mysteries. Examples of the fine ceramics fashioned by the people of Nasca in southern Peru over 800 years ago are decorated with stylized pictures of animals existing there today; humming-birds, foxes, scorpions, sea-birds, crayfish and others are depicted in exquisite colours which seem as brilliant as they must have been when they were painted.

Taken from other graves in Chancay, just north of Lima, are woollen toys in the form of llamas which confirms that the animal now typical of the sierras was at one time known along the coast. The skeleton of a 'Chancay llama', the only one of the type that has been found to date, shows slight morphological differences that distinguish it from the species known today, and it is possible that it was a separate breed, used only by the people of that valley.

Though the coast, with the exception of the lush valleys, has been sterile for a very long time, it is equally certain that the sea has always been rich. The cold current carries an abundance of plankton and the food chain culminates with incredible numbers of sea-birds feeding on limitless shoals of anchovies. Guano Cormorants (Phalacrocorax bougainvillii), pelicans (Pelecanus thagus) and boobies (Sula variegata) are the most familiar species, and the Guano Islands of Peru were a byword in the last century when fine sailing ships forced their way around Cape Horn to collect the nitrogen-rich deposits. The guano then existed in beds more than a hundred and fifty feet thick and a fortunate combination of the seemingly inexhausti-ble sea and the dry climate created and preserved the excrement over cen-turies to make fortunes for the traders. At the height of the guano boom in the 1880s, more than forty ships gathered each year around the Chincha Islands alone. Quickly, the guano beds were cut into and worked out. At some low levels of the deposits, ancient silver and ceramics were uncovered, proving that guano had been used before the Spanish arrived: in fact, the Incas are said to have controlled the use of the material. They prevented over-exploita-tion and used the guano for fertilizer in the coastal valleys, but when the boom began a hundred years ago, the government failed to remember the advice of the early emperors. Now the industry is almost dead.

In the far north at approximately latitude 4°S. the cold current swings away from the continent towards the Galapagos Islands and westward into the Pacific. The movement is fast and Gene Savoy, the most recent of the raftsmen to take a chance with the current, said that he was carried along steadily at three to four knots towards the Gulf of Guayaquil, though once abreast of the border with Ecuador he began to rely on navigation and a sail to make any progress as he continued northwards. At about 4° or 5°S. the cooling effect of the Peruvian current is countered by warm water from the north, and the long desert alters within a few miles to dry scrub vegetation and mangrove swamps. The coast in this region is home to a variety of mammals including the Crab-eating Racoon (Procyon cancrivorus), a semi-aquatic relative of the more familiar racoon of North America.

The northern fringe of the desert is characterized by low xerophytic shrubs and the beginning of the deciduous forests. Alongside the rivers at Sullana and Tumbes, the vegetation is dense but these valleys like all the others of the coast have been subjected to intensive farming for many years. At one time there was an abundance of species in the coastal part of northern Peru with many reptiles including caiman, boas and coral snakes; some mammals and a richly varied bird population. Today the wildlife is much reduced but there are Three-toed Sloths, Tamandua Anteaters, one species of Howler Monkey, one species of Capuchin Monkey (possibly Cebus albifrons), the White-tailed Deer (Odocoilcus virginianus) and small numbers of Collared Peccary, Ocelot and Jaguar as well as many tiny mammals.

The edge-effect between the different ecological zones is strong and well indicated by the higher number of bird species. Within the few miles at the fringes there are those species typical of the desert and others characteristic of tropical forests: colourful parrots, hummingbirds, egrets and herons add brilliance between the delicate hues of semi-desert plants. Vegetation is sparse in this region and observation is often an easier task than among the dark equatorial forests. Only sharp thorns and spines on the undergrowth make trekking difficult, or sometimes in the wet season it is impossible to cross the swampy ground of the Zarumilla Province on Peru's border with Ecuador.

South of Zarumilla the land changes to an arid semi-desert of sand and low, dry bushes. Around Talara, the surface is scarred by the complex of roads, pipes and pumping stations of the Peruvian oil industry; but to the south again between Paita and Chiclayo the Sechura Desert projects slightly westward into the Pacific. In this region, the terrain is famous for endless shifting sands, rich phosphate deposits and coastal lagoons alive with many tropical water birds. Parts of the Sechura possess a gentle, timeless quality marvellously remaining in the old fishing villages. The beaches and high surf are some of the finest in Peru and yet they are so remote that they are still untouched. This area has an avi-fauna with a clear-cut difference; many of the water birds are migrants from the north and some of the sea birds are truly equatorial. Frigate Birds (Fregata magnificens) are rarely seen south of this latitude and the Galapagos Albatross (Diomedea irrorata) is an occasional visitor.

The Sechura Desert also represents the widest part of the coastal strip between the Andes and the sea and it is skirted by the modern asphalt-covered Pan-American highway which now runs without a break from Zarumilla to Santiago de Chile. Many of the valleys crossed by this road are served by other routes, sometimes no more than a track, though most are sufficiently good to give rapid access to higher levels of the Andean slopes; even some major roads lead from the coast into the mountains. There is the trans-Andean highway from Pacasmayo to Chachapoyas, or the Central Highway from Lima to Huancayo which follows the Rimac valley and the railway track built by Henry Meiggs – it passes the highest rail junction in the world at 15,800 feet. Other roads lead over the Andes in the south from Nasca and Camana and, though not so finely developed in Chile, there is a good road into the Atacama which is asphalted as far as the great open-pit copper mine of Chuquicamata.

In spite of the barrenness which at first glance is so striking along the coastal plain and narrow piedmont of the Andes, there is a small desert fauna and there are a few exceptional habitats which produce a very specific distribution of some species. In the Peruvian sector, the most important feature is the rich vegetation in the river valleys. The oases are unforgettable and after driving along the narrow, black ribbon of tarmac, often in harsh dry-heat, the road dips suddenly into a green valley with neat fields and white-washed wattle houses typical of tropical South America. Fruit stalls line the streets, donkeys with side-baskets are ridden by men and women in wide-brimmed straw hats, and after the silence of the open desert, the raucous noise from a bar-room with its garlic-tinged scent of *criollo* cooking is one introduction to the way of life of the *costeño* or coastal Peruvian.

Even before the arrival of the Spanish, the coast was highly developed, but now each valley has been farmed with a produce suiting the climate; in the northern oases of Chiclayo, Lambayeque and Trujillo, rice and sugar grow well, while in the south around Ica and Nasca, the cottonfields and citrus fruit-trees and vines form regular patterns across wide flat valleys. Often the cultivation begins at sea level and extends for two or three thousand feet into the mountains, or even higher in some places where carefully terraced fields are built, following the style of the peoples of the pre-Colombian era.

In the river valleys much of the natural woodland has been replaced by other trees and shrubs; elsewhere sugar-cane fields cover thousands of acres. However, animal species seem to survive in this civilized farmland, but face many of the dangers that wildlife encounters when it coincides with the modern farmer. Some types have almost disappeared or have gone completely from districts where they were once common. At one time ocelots were seen occasionally in the Chicama valley, not far from Trujillo 400 miles north of Lima, but now they are restricted on the coast to the forest fringe near Ecuador. Pumas on the other hand have remained in most parts but this is not surprising as they have the ability to adapt to a wide range of habitats; the animal occurs in damp forests, the high frozen cordilleras and the arid desert. Unfortunately, the puma is regarded as a serious danger to farm stock, and when encountered it is killed in all inhabited areas. These animals reach the coastal valleys where their natural predatory instinct takes them to the farms and wild parts of the desert coast where they possibly attack isolated sea-lion colonies or feed on young sea birds. Authenticated sightings are infrequent but Ian Grimwood identified puma tracks on the sea shore at Morosama in the Department of Tacna, when he was making studies on behalf of the Peruvian Government in 1967; also they have been reported by the guardians of the guano bird sanctuaries on the mainland. With this information to confirm other local stories, there seems to be little doubt that the species remains fairly common in the less accessible parts of the coast, and there is a slim chance that the spectacularly rugged terrain will give protection for some years.

The northern valleys and the tropical forest-fringe undoubtedly have the richest fauna and mammals typical of the region are Tayras (Eira barbara), an agile weasel-like carnivore about the size of a large daschund; Cotton-tail Rabbits of the genus Sylvilagus, and the Nine-banded Armadillo (Dasypus novemcincus). These species are found in many other parts of tropical South America, east of the Andes and north of the Sechura, and yet the desert and the high mountain ranges seem to have barred their distribution southwards along the west coast.

At one time perhaps no more than a thousand years ago, some of the mammals might have had a wider distribution than today. Examples of ancient pottery from central-Peruvian coastal cultures include designs in the form of armadillos with each band carefully shaped in the clay. Another more enigmatic relic is the strange pattern of enormous lines and figures drawn on the desert surface at Nasca, over three hundred miles south of Lima. Among the dozens of animal figures is the clear figure of a monkey, and though it is possible that descriptions of the fauna of distant parts reached the early Nascans by occasional contact with other civilizations, the drawing is remarkably like a spider monkey, and perhaps this genus existed in the southern oases at some time in the past.

Within the last four centuries there has been no major lasting climatic change on the coast, though periodic and sometimes drastic variations occur for a few months or even only for days. The Limaeños like to say that nobody wears a raincoat and they will even stare with resentful curiosity at someone with an umbrella or waterproof during days of the strong *garua* or mist which covers the city in winter. Under normal conditions rain is unknown, but occasionally the weather changes, sometimes as a quick devastating thunderstorm. In 1925 the ancient adobe city of Chan Chan, the ancient Chimu capital near Trujillo, was destroyed by freak rainfall which caused considerable damage along the north coast. Even today none of the coastal houses or streets are built to withstand more than the mist, and heavy rain could create a major disaster, leaving thousands homeless.

One of the major factors known to affect the climate is the appearance of a warm sea-current which, forcing southwards from the Gulf of Guayaquil pushes the cold Humboldt water lower, or away from the coast, and at the same time raises the temperature of the desert. Locally, the condition is called the *Niño* (or Child), because it tends to occur close to Christmas, though never so precisely, and only in cycles of seven or eight years.

Occasionally the Niño is unusually strong, and in some years there are very marked effects on the fauna. The sea-birds suffer first, and when the cold water rich in plankton and salts moves away, the birds are forced to fly long distances from their breeding ground for food. Often they migrate to Chilean waters. If the Niño persists, the birds weaken and fail to find the anchovy shoals; then they starve and become susceptible to disease. When this occurs many millions of birds perish and the beaches are littered with corpses washed along the tide-line for hundreds of miles. Pelicans hardly able to walk gather in pathetic groups to flop slowly into the sand as the final stages of starvation or respiratory infections leave them dazed and insensible.

In 1964/5 the sea-bird population dropped from an estimated thirty million to less than three million and there were doubts that the colonies might not recover. Robert Cushman Murphy pointed out that similar drastic decreases had occurred several times in the previous century when the population had built up quickly during the following years. Undoubtedly the extremely rapid recovery is due to the richness of the feeding grounds and by 1970 Dr Murphy's prediction seemed to be borne out to some extent. The sea-birds were far more numerous though there was still a long way to go before the famous Guano Islands would be covered again by the spectacular colonies that have been one of the wonderful sights of the Peruvian coast for centuries.

New factors may have been introduced in the last ten years, as a giant fishing fleet of more than two thousand boats now takes more than ten million tons of anchovies from the Humboldt Current each year, possibly as many fish as a normal bird population would require in the same period. The industry is young and Peru was quick to take a gamble on big profits and leapt into the race to produce cheap fish-meal; by 1965 Peru had overtaken Japan and become the world's number-one fishing nation.

After the initial success the industry suffered from some economic setbacks, but fishing remains one of the top priorities for the country. Because the expansion has happened so rapidly and met with only one serious Niño, it is too early to evaluate the results of local research that could show the effect of the fishing industry on the birds, if indeed it has any. The main work in the field has been undertaken by the Instituto del Mar in Callao, where foreign scientists have worked on many aspects of oceanography and fisheries, but often their observations have been made over a short term and with local friction, some lines of study have been hampered. It is always possible that the results of the work will be revealed too late to prevent a serious change in the ecological balance.

When the counter current from the north is powerful, the coastal fauna is unbalanced and in the simplest form some changes are shown by the introduction of exotic species. In 1891 a particularly strong insurgence of warm water carried debris from the north, down the coast as far as Pacasmayo, where palm trees and alligators were found on the beaches. A similar phenomenon could possibly have occurred some centuries ago, taking a few animals as far as the Nasca river, where startled Nascans probably regarded the arrivals as new gods, to be revered and represented in their mysterious drawings.

The periodic changes in climate, even if not immediately noticeable by some effect on the sea-birds have been known to produce alterations of animal populations in the river-valleys. Among the most spectacular variations are the irruptive increases in the numbers of rice-rats belonging to the genus Oryzomys; sometimes the rapid build-up causes a panic among farmers as thousands of animals appear in the fields almost without warning. The village of Palpa in a valley adjacent to Nasca was the centre of a rat-plague in 1968 (probably Oryzomys xantheolus); local newspapers reported the story in detail and when visiting the area some months afterwards, I was told by the villagers that the peak of the increase had passed, though farmers were still worried over the fate of their crops for that season. These sudden increases occur only very occasionally and in Palpa they could not remember a recent similar plague, so it would be difficult to determine the inter-related factors responsible. Irruptive increases appear in many species, particularly when there is an abundance of food; the effect passes along the food chain and an increase in rodents usually is accompanied by an increase in the numbers of birds-of-prey. One early observation of the phenomenon was made by W. H. Hudson in his book, *The Naturalist in La Plata*, published in 1892 when he recorded a great increase of rodents in the Argentinian Pampas during 1872 and 1873 and predators, both birds and mammals, had a feast.

There seems to be some correlation in south Peru between rat plagues and wet years, but the picture is confused and a consideration has to be given to the warming effect of the Niño as well as the rainfall in the western Andes which, in turn, determines the amount of water in the coastal valleys; or there could be some unknown interaction between these factors. A heavy rainy season in the mountains can have a drastic effect on the rivers flowing to the Pacific across the desert, and once the summer arrives (November to March), none of the Costeños can tell when to expect a flood. The mountain storms occur thirty or forty miles away, and at over 16,000 feet, so that the only warning is the slight rise of a river in early afternoon. In the past, many towns have been inundated and the inhabitants paddle the streets on hurriedly made rafts. Recently, miles of retaining walls have been built along a few river-courses, particularly in Nasca and Ica where disastrous floods occurred in the 1960s.

In some ways the coastal valleys on these occasions are like the *wadis* of the Middle East in a flash-flood, but whereas wadis tend to dry again very quickly, some pools and even small rivers persist on the Peruvian coast throughout the mountain rainy season and far into the dry months. These are havens for many birds, especially waders, and in summertime the migrants from the north pass by on their flight towards the southern part of the continent: some species stay in Peru for several months. Not far from Lima there are many good pools and shallow lagoons, which are excellent places for the weekend naturalist: the Laguna de Villa is no more than six miles outside the city and both Mala and Pisco valleys on the Pan American highway south have excellent swamps. Often, there are brackish ponds behind sand dunes along the sea shore, and from October onwards these are the haunts of North American visitors. Wilson's Phalarope (Steganopus tricolor) appears in large numbers, and they bob around, rhythmically picking at surface larvae with their finely pointed beaks. Clearly recognized by their distinguished bearing as they keep their neck upright, some of these Phalaropes later find their way to the pools of the higher central Andes where they winter. A. W. Johnson in Santiago suggests that the abundance of reports from the Argentinian province of Buenos Aires and other records from Tierra del Fuego and the Falkland Islands points to a main migration along the eastern side of the Andes; this seems possible but the Andes are not a barrier to these birds, and the presence of this and other migratory species along the coast in large numbers shows that the Pacific side of the Andes is an important route.

In Chile, Johnson has recorded thirty-seven summer migrant visitors, and most of these species are recorded also in Peru. On the desert coast the waders and shore birds are especially noticeable; Sanderlings, Greater and Lesser Yellowlegs, Turnstones, Surf Birds and Sandpipers. Also the Osprey (Pandion haliaetus carolinensis) is common on the coast from early summer, though it becomes scarcer in the central Chilean region. Occasionally, as many as a dozen are found close together in some good places, and I have watched them frequently on the Paracas peninsular (170 miles south of Lima) and at Puerto Chala (380 miles south) where the Pan American highway reaches the coast again after cutting inland to Ica and Nasca.

Among other visitors are Least Sandpipers (Erolia minutilla) and Baird's Sandpiper (Erolia bairdii) which are common whilst some, including the Stilt Sandpiper (Micropalama himantopus) are rare and seen only occasionally. Like Wilson's Phalarope, many of the waders are known from the higher parts of the sierra as well as the coast, and once the rainy season begins in the mountains, the climate is equable and shallow lakes abound.

In each region of the coast, the oases provide an ornithologist with variety, and in the northern rice fields, it is easy to find egrets, bitterns and duck. Even the South American Comb Duck (Sarkidiornis melanotos carunculatus), well distributed on the eastern side of the Andes occurs in Chiclayo and Lambayeque, though it does not spread far south.

Among the more frequently observed species is the Prairie Blue-winged Teal, which nests in North America and arrives in Peru during the summer. There are other species which nest in the coastal region, including the Cinnamon Teal (Anas c. cyanoptera) and the Greater Bahamanian Pintail (Anas bahamanensis rubrirostris) though neither of these is commonly occurring along the coast south of the Peruvian border. The Cattle Egret (Bubulcus i. ibis) on its general spread westward is now common in coastal Peru, and reached Lima in 1961, but so far it seems not to have penetrated across the border into Chile.

In fact many of the resident birds of the coastal valleys have failed to pass the barrier of the absolute desert that exists between the River Loa and Copiapo. Over four hundred miles of waterless, scorched sand and nitrate beds separate the only river of the Atacama and the more temperate land of central Chile, and examples like the Groove Billed Ani (Crotophaga sulcirostris), Peruvian White-winged Dove (Zenaida asiatica meloda) and the Pacific Scarlet Flycatcher (Pyrocephalus rubinus cocachacrae) as well as others, are absent south of this arid region.

The River Loa is certainly not typical of the river valleys of the long desert, as it has to cut through the high Atacama plateau in a deep canyon; also it is a small river and the bordering vegetation is sparse. On the road leading from Chuquicamata to the coast, it is hard to see how the landscape could contain a river; the asphalt on the trail is sticky from the heat and parched debris thrown from passing trucks scatters across the desert. Yet in the middle of the road, a brownish shape miraging from ten miles away turns out to be a solitary tree marking a curve in the highway, where the Loa is crossed by a bridge no more than twenty feet long.

In other parts of the Atacama, small springs feed tiny pools in recesses of narrow canyons (the *quebradas*, as steep-sided gorges are named in Spanish). The vegetation, if it exists at all, is limited to the fringes of the waterholes, and wildlife in general terms has a hard struggle to survive the rigours of the habitat. At one time the Chilean desert was vitally important for the famous raw nitrates, but now the industry is dying and the old *salitres* are no more than ghost towns. Exploitation has been transferred to a few mineral-rich sites where copper is produced on an incredible scale, however these industries have not yet affected the minute patches of watered desert and the remoteness has deterred modern man.

Unfortunately, the same is not true of the conditions in Peru, where the coastal valleys are far larger with wider rivers and more intensive cultivation. In an attempt to be self-sufficient in food, the new (1968) Revolutionary Government is pushing hard to develop the coastal agricultural land more than ever before. New irrigation schemes are being given priority and some plans propose turning the raw desert into fields. – Water will be drawn from the Atlantic watershed via trans-Andean tunnels. More people come to settle on the coast each day, leaving their homes in the sierra in exchange for booming towns that act like magnets. Slums hopefully termed 'Young Towns', have grown around every city and this movement daily encroaches on wildlife habitats, – often occurring indiscriminately. Perhaps more disastrously, the farmers constantly are using a variety of crop sprays including DDT and unfortunately Peru lacks trained observers to keep a check on the use of industrial chemicals and their effect on the ecological balance. But notwithstanding these sophisticated problems, which might eventually be solved, habitat destruction is the chief enemy and could force the animals out.

A western profile of the Andes in Peru typically would include one of the rivers starting high in the cordilleras, and descending extremely rapidly to sea level. At 15,000 feet the terrain is classed more accurately with the *puna* or Andean plains, where the climate is affected by rain from the Atlantic side of the mountains. This region extends over the final western ridge of the sierras above the desert and then below this level, there is an extremely dry zone leading down to the sea. Fauna is zoned by altitude, with the exception of a few species which range widely; notably these include the Puma and the Guanaco. Some predatory birds and the Andean Condor (Vultur gryphus) visit the coastal beaches especially in the summer, when there is an abundant supply of carrion from the bird and sea-lion colonies.

At all levels, the true desert is inhospitable and a little favoured habitat; the only mammal encountered frequently is the Coastal Fox, possibly of two species: *Dusicyon sechurae* in the north and as far as at least 12°S., as well as *Dusicyon griseus* from near the Chilean border. These foxes are smaller than the Andean Fox (Dusicyon culpaeus andinus), but belong to the same group of South American foxes which in many ways are almost wolf-like. The genus is peculiar to South America, and as far as the local people are concerned, it is frequently termed 'wolf, wild dog or fox'. Wherever the genus occurs it fulfils the ecological role of these animals and preys on stock and smaller wild animals.

Small foxes are common along the coast, and are often seen at night as they cross the Pan American highway and run for the cliff-edge. Their trails are easily followed in the virgin sand, where the marks frequently show the scrambled retreat of a surprised sea-bird. As predators, the foxes upset the nesting colonies and for this reason, the Guano Administration (Empresa Nacional de Fertilizantes) has built high walls around mainland nesting sites used for guano collection. The barricades extend across the shore into the sea, thereby effectively keeping the foxes out. When there is easy prey, the fox population increases sharply and such a condition occurred after the failure of the Humboldt Current in 1965, when the coast was littered with dead and dying birds. Andean Foxes, though typical of the highlands where they are reputedly a menace to the stocks, are found in the lower foothills and sometimes at very low levels. One specimen, according to Ian Grimwood, was collected at Chosica not far from Lima at only three thousand feet.

Other carnivores from this desert region include the Hog-nosed Skunks (genus Conepatus) which are, in any case, widespread in other parts of the Andes. Cabrera credits *Conepatus rex* as the nominate race found at high latitude, and *Conepatus r. inca* as the form found in the coastal regions of central Peru. Another species *C. semistriatus* occurs in the north of the country and its range may overlap with the race *C. semistriatus quitensis* which has thicker under-fur and a type locality given as Quito-Ecuador.

A marine otter (Lutra felina), the Coast Otter, is rare, and within Peruvian limits is known only along the extreme southern coast. Even there they are in considerable danger as they are persecuted for taking the highly valued fresh-water prawn. On occasions, the otters ascend the rivers in search of this crustacean to the upper limit of its distribution and local fishermen are keen to eradicate the animal to protect commercial interests.

Other mammals found in most of the valleys and well into the foothills of the Andes are insignificant, almost typifying the trend towards small size which is common Neotropical mammalia. Rodents are represented by several species of Rice-rats (Oryzomys), Long-eared Mice (genus Phyllotis); Cotton rats (Sygmodon); South American Field mice (Akodon); the Cavy (Cavia tschudii) as well as various recent invaders particularly the Old World rats (R. rattus and R. norvegicus). Though much of the desert is within the Tropic of Capricorn (Antofagasta in Chile is on the Tropic) there are very few Chiroptera, one Tail-less Bat (Platalina genovensium) is found in Lima; a Smoky Bat (Amorphochilus schnablii) inhabits the Tumbes region in the north, and Common bats (Myotis) are found in some western Andean valleys and around San Pedro de Atacama, 10,000 feet up on the desert plateau.

For a visiting naturalist, undoubtedly the bird-life is the most exciting aspect of the desert fauna. Not only are the sea-birds accessible, but the pools,

A Kinkajou. This mammal has a prehensile tail and lives in the forested regions of much of northern South America; it occurs in the Andes at lower levels.

A Black-shouldered oppossum from the cloud forest level of the Manu National Park. This animal is extremely rare and only a few specimens have been captured.

8. The Pudu, Chilean species, photographed in Santiago zoo. This is the world's smallest deer and is now extremely rare. Photo by Susan Mann.

9. A Tamandua anteater in the dry foothills of the Sierra Nevada de Santa Marta.

10. Black spider monkey. These monkeys occur up to 8,000 feet in the eastern Andes, and at a higher level than most other species of South American primate.

rivers and variety of vegetation introduce a wide range of habitat. In the Department of Lima alone, the late Dra. Maria Koepke lists 313 species and this is only part of the total, for Lima does not include those fringes of forest found in the north. At the lowest coastal level are the waders, some plovers (including the Peruvian Kill-deer Plover – Charadrius vociferus peruvianus): Pygmy Seed Snipe (Trinocorus orbignyianus ingae) and of course many passerines of the scrub and small trees lining the rivers.

Eye catching and often beautifully coloured are the hummingbirds of which at least thirteen species are likely to be encountered in the central region alone. Some are often seen in the fine gardens of Lima's suburbs, while others are remarkably obvious in immense landscapes of the high Andes. Standing out as the Goliath of its family is the Giant Hummingbird (Patagonia gigas) which not only occurs in the western Andes, but from Ecuador to Argentina and Chile. The size of a small dove and easily recognized by slower wingbeats than other hummingbirds, this giant is mistaken sometimes for a 'strange swallow', a confusion that is hardly surprising considering the great disparity between it and the often bee-sized hummingbirds which are among the smallest members of the avian world.

Many of the other birds are intriguing. At one extreme are the Blue and White swallows (Pygochelidon cyanoleuca peruviana), common in the parks and streets of the coastal towns; in Lima they frequent some of the busiest streets, catching insects on the wing, diving madly between passing cars and missing the surface of the road by inches before winging upwards again between the overhanging trees. Some of the tired commuters are daily fans of these tiny aerobats and the endless traffic hold-ups at rush hour are almost bearable despite the summer heat. But out in the desert fringes among the dry quebradas leading into the Andes, though not necessarily too far from metropolitan Lima, other birds well adapted to the arid conditions form the bulk of the species. They nest on rocky ledges or on the ground, or wherever a convenient site is available. One small Spinetail (Asthenes cactorum-Koepcke) builds in the heart of the tall columnar cactus plants characteristic of lonely ravines. At one point almost 500 miles south of the capital where the Andes fall away abruptly towards the sea and high, sloping cliffs are covered with a profusion of cacti, Spinetails are common; also the flowers are visited by other semi-desert species including

4

some hummingbirds and finches. These types live less than a hundred yards from abundant sea-life and present a unique range of avifauna.

At higher levels of the mountains, there is a marked decrease in the number of species; admittedly there are larger mammals, namely the llamoids and some mountain carnivores, but rodents are represented by mice, cavies and the Mountain Viscacha (Lagidium). There are fewer birds and the species are mostly those typical of the highlands. Above 3,000 feet, the green valleys often terminate where the narrow rivers pour down from the high mountains forming small waterfalls. At these levels, often reaching as high as 10,000 feet, Torrent Ducks (genus Merganetta) live in the fastest water; they are uniquely Andean and occur in many mountain streams. In some Peruvian rivers, White-capped Dippers (Cinchus leucocephalus) are fairly common, and instantly recognizable as they bob up and down, moving all the time from rock to rock. They are exactly similar in habit to the Dippers found elsewhere, with their nests built close to the water.

The higher desert slopes of the western Andes are the home of other Spinetails or Canasteros (basket-makers) which are noted for elaborate domed nests of twigs or cactus spines and built with an incredibly small entrance. At the same levels there are Flycatchers and Ground Tyrants and some are particularly good examples of altitude speciation. The Rufous-backed Ground Tyrant (Lessonia rufa rufa) exhibits two distinct forms. In the lower coastal region, the nominate race is commonly occurring from southern Peru across the deserts of the Atacama into southern Chile, while the larger mountain race, the Andean Ground Tyrant (Lessonia rufa oreas) lives only above 10,000 feet in the mountainous regions of southern Peru, Chile, Bolivia and Argentina. Altitude speciation (or the formation of separate races due to isolation of a species at widely different levels of the mountains) is encountered frequently in the Andes. Often the distinguishing marks are only slight–a small difference in size or slight colour variations–but the trend towards producing a distinct species is obvious in most cases, and much attention has been given to this process as it affects Andean birds.

With very few exceptions, most of the wildlife of the western Andean desert region is to be seen in the oases or near mountain streams; the true desert is absolutely dry and cannot support any significant vegetation, though not far above sea level the air contains sufficient moisture to allow the growth of specialized plants. The aerophytic *Tillesandia straminae*, a low silvery-grey relative of Spanish Moss, covers many hillsides. It has almost no root system and absorbs moisture from the atmosphere. The effect when seen from a distance appears similar to a grey, creeping mould, darkening the dull sand, and along the Pan American Highway some local political parties have found it easy to transplant and fashion into slogans visible from miles away. Certainly, after the initial work these advertisements need no attention.

Reaching as far as 1,200 feet above sea level, the wintertime garua or mist creates a zone of extremely high humidity. In years when a Humboldt Current change occurs, the fog is heavier and accompanied by a noticeable precipitation in the morning and evening. For some reason, perhaps involving the flow of minor currents near the shore, some foothills of the Andes close to the sea have a pronounced layer of low vegetation. Often it is no more than a green tinge from tiny plants, but in a few areas the mountain-sides are covered with small trees, shrubs and larger herbs forming a distinctive habitat. It is a complete ecosystem created by the presence of an effective micro-climate and such areas are isolated by thousands of square miles of desert.

Peruvians have given the name *Loma* to describe the many variations of this vegetation and especially famous are the Lomas of Lachay and Atacongo near Lima. In late summer the sand when seen from a distance seems covered with an orange tint which on close inspection is revealed as millions of plants of the Family Amaryllidacea possessing slender green stalks and a delicate tassel of orange trumpets. Above the coastal plains, the lomas woodlands with their scattered groves of trees (Lucuma obovata, Carica candicans or Acnistus sp.) support epiphytes and ferns, while in their shade are slipper-worts, begonias and a Peruvian heliotrope. One botanist collected over sixty species of flowering plants in one Loma, and many mosses and ferns. In a good year the Lomas are incredibly beautiful, with the soft colours of the flowers blending easily with the vivid greens of the forest. On entering the damp coolness between the trees, quiet bird calls are a soft contrast with the ageless, dry world outside and Scarlet Flycatchers, finches, small doves and others find a retreat in the unexpected. A few species are known only from these woods, and the Gray-capped Cuckoo (Coccyzus lansbergi) is found occasionally in the Loma de Lachay during winter months; also the Slender-billed Plover (Oreopholus r. ruficolis), one of the few migrants from the south is found nesting in the same Loma only to return to the sub-Arctic extremity of the continent for the summer.

At present the Loma areas are limited to a few widely spaced and isolated regions, but there is the possibility that in the future a practical application might be found. Already the Ministry of Agriculture in Peru has an experimental station at the Loma de Lachay, and in Chile the University of the North in Antofagasta is experimenting with a small woodland at a site named Tamarugal, near Iquique on the desert highway south of Arica. At Tamarugal there is subterranean moisture, and this has been tapped by the roots of the trees and the research workers. There is sufficient water to maintain a permanently damp zone in the desert at this point, and though obviously it results from different circumstances, the principle of condensation remains the same and moisture drips from the trees overnight. The most hopeful line of experiment follows the establishment of plant communities which in turn form surfaces on which additional moisture condenses quickly; thereby ensuring that the ground remains permanently damp. This effect varies with the humidity and on one visit to the Loma of Lachay, the trees were dripping and shallow pools had made muddy ground; though this extreme is not reached at Tamarugal in the Atacama, a small dairy project is working there with cattle finding enough pasture from the short grass which has now grown between the trees.

It is obvious also, that the entire credit must not go to the agriculturalist of today because the early coast-dwellers discovered the same principle many centuries ago. Near Atiquipa 400 miles south of Lima another fine Loma forest stands almost 2,000 feet above the sea. Not far below the tree-line and covering three large headlands, an extensive system of shallow agricultural terraces has been wind-eroded until the ledges are hardly visible. Each terrace was made with great care, and follows a level course along the hillside; even today they are covered with plants, many of them typical of the nearby Loma. During the heavy winter mists the terracing resembles green, but slightly flattened, corrugated-cardboard and in a few places the local fishermen have grown small fields of corn without difficulty.

These loma zones were once the haunt of Guanacos, the wild and now rare Andean cameloid which has a far wider distribution than its smaller highland relative, the Vicuña. Recently there has been a serious decline in the guanaco population, even in Patagonia where it was an outstanding feature at the time of Darwin's visits. The animal is able to live both in the high mountains or at sea level and in Peru and Chile the small bands are known to make seasonal migrations to the Lomas. Within Peruvian boundaries the guanaco is now very rare: one private reserve in the northern highlands is said to have between four and five hundred animals, and the groups reported on the Lomas of Atiquipa and Morosama are numbered by ones and twos. Chile cannot claim much better conditions, and on the open plateau of the Atacama, the guanacos are shot easily by weekend sportsmen out from the big mining camps. However, one unusual piece of conservation work is conducted by pilots of the Chilean Airforce based at Mejillones near Antofagasta, who are keeping a close watch on a small group of animals which have taken up permanent residence on a large peninsular. Daily practice flights have to be made from the air base and the flying patrol spots the herd several times during each month. Travelling by land no poacher would stand a chance against jet-age communications and the possibility of ultra-quick detection seems to deter them.

Guanacos visiting the coast are dependent upon the few Lomas for subsistence while most other mammals are restricted to the fertile valleys, but one extraordinary instance of distribution and survival is the case of the Andean Spectacled Bear found in the terrible quebradas of La Libertad Province 300 miles north of Lima. Spectacled Bears (Tremarctos ornatus) are South America's only representative of the family, and the distribution though not continuous, is given usually as the forested Andean slopes from Venezuela to Bolivia. In one isolated barren area of northern Peru, the bears live in desert and semi-desert surroundings. The zone is the warm, open country around Trujillo and Chimbote which extends via deep canyons into the high Andes. Vegetation is sparse and consists mainly of tall cactus and other xerophytes that yield fruit and soft leaves for the animals.

This region is the most barren of all the known habitats for the species, and though the bear is known from the northern desert fringe of the sierra where small thickets of dwarf Polylepis trees (Polylepis incana) give them some cover, the range along the western Andean slope is broken, possibly due to the strong geographical barrier presented by the desert. Tracking the bears over the sun-baked rocks of La Libertad is a quick course to death from exhaustion, so local hunters use jeeps or motorcycles for following trails into bear-country. Even with the inducement of a fine status trophy, hunting parties cannot guarantee success, and for the moment in spite of the keen interest in the sport, some of the bears could survive. Few Peruvians know of the existence of the bears in the coastal region, because the eastern jungle is the generally accepted haunt, so it was not surprising when two men emptying a garbage-truck on the city refuse tip of Trujillo fled when they spotted a 'giant' rumaging through the rubbish not far away. The report, which was followed up by the local *Guardia Civil* revealed a large bear which, sadly for the story, they shot. Trujillo is less than six miles from the sea, and the incident became a good reference for the unusual distribution.

All of the desert and its rugged Andean slopes offers intriguing possibilities for fruitful exploration. Surviving from hundreds of years in the past, are the ruins of the old civilizations; giant walls ten feet high and many miles long, cross the deserts of La Libertad: old Inca roads straight for fifty miles pass over mountain spurs without veering a degree from their course. There are old fortresses, outposts of the desert kingdoms, long forgotten but recorded by the few explorers who venture inland today; or the rich grave sites thoughtlessly ransacked in the last few years. But much of the wildness remains and there is abundant space for the wildlife, though pollution from man's efforts is increasing.

Nowadays, a common and repulsively malodorous industry is the fish meal production from anchovies. The factories belch foul smoke, while the sea nearby is blackened and towns are covered with a fine, obnoxious dust. In Chimbote alone, more than thirty factories operate twenty-four hours a day during the fishing season, and the human population has increased ten times in as few years; what was once a honeymoon resort is now a blight that will take a long time to repair. Progress must come to a developing country, and conservationists can do little to change irrigation or mining plans in South America, but perhaps now is the time to consider reserving some of the desert for the future. As the economy strengthens, it will not be long before the need to develop the entire coast becomes of paramount importance. Lima will reach the five million mark within ten years and food can be grown easily if water is applied to the sand. Seeds on the surface germinate for brief days in the damp garua days, and maize from the desiccated graves has been germinated after a dormancy of over five hundred years.

The most accessible supply of water is on the Atlantic watershed, which by a stroke of fortune in some places is less than thirty miles through the Andes by tunnel. Plans are ready and money will be available soon for new irrigation projects; the first is in Olmos in the north and has been surveyed by Soviet engineers. It is an unfortunate coincidence that the region happens to be a coastal haunt of some bears; also, the construction will take roads near the only Peruvian habitat of the Mountain Tapir. Nothing can stop the Olmos project and from the feasibility study it seems ideal. The animals might survive, but the pressure they will be facing heralds another phase in the long history of the desert coast.

Frontier of the Amazon

The eastern fringe of the Andes, extending from equatorial regions to the far south in Tierra del Fuego encompasses vegetation types ranging between perpetually damp cloud-forest and dry tundra. Often, the major slopes are incredibly steep and dissected by canyons which carry the tributaries of the Amazon, Orinoco and Pilcomayo; the rivers tumble downwards to the great plains through treacherous rapids and within a few miles the clear sky over the mountains is replaced by pale light, subtly filtered by trees and humidity. In some parts of Bolivia and Peru, the mountainsides are almost sheer walls of rock from glaciers to the forests, and the vegetation of a single slope reflects the changes found within the entire length of the range from north to south. Obviously, the ecology has infinite variety and there is a great difference between Colombia and southern Chile. Even inside two valleys of Bolivia, a simplified profile from 20,000 feet to the level of the slow tropical rivers can reveal extraordinary variations in the list of animals and plants.

Some of the least explored regions of the earth are hidden in the impenetrable forests of these regions, and even the indefatigable Conquistadores searching for the gold of Paititi and El Dorado ventured only down the open river routes. Orellana discovered the Amazon by starting in the Andes of Ecuador and forcing down the headwaters of the Napo; soon afterwards other adventurers pushed into the Madre de Dios of Peru and the Moxos of Bolivia. One glance at the forests to the east of the Cordilleras is enough to persuade most travellers to keep to the clear trails and in Inca times such routes led only to the outposts of the Empire or rich gold mines, whilst beyond, was the end of the world for the mountain people.

From the point known as Tres Cruces on the road to Paucartambo, not far from Cusco, Inca priests watched the sunrise in June at a time when, for a few days each year, the jungle canopy is clear of cloud, and the immense rivers can be seen clearly winding through forests more than 12,000 feet below. The spectacle is well known today, and a few local tourists sit out and wait for the dawn. Gradually some light reflects from the rivers, and as the sun climbs into the dense lowland atmosphere, there is for a few moments a ball of light which is twisted into crazy shapes by refraction, and the sun rises as an oval or like an hour glass, before beginning a long climb to the zenith of the winter solstice. Far below the Andes the cauldron of forests is covered with thin wisps of cloud, and the greenness reaches without interruption for two thousand miles. It is a different world, and for the tribes of the lowlands, the Andes appear to rise from the jungle as a solid wall, making a barrier between civilizations; the edge of the mountains is also the frontier of the Amazon.

At the end of the last century the fringe zones were centres of rubber exploitation and the slavery well recorded by Roger Casement who visited the Putumayo; since then, roads and small airstrips or powered-canoe travel have helped to open the region to settlers. Some Andean countries give tax concessions to pioneers, and towns along the headwaters of the rivers in Peru are duty-free markets that have attracted a new brand of immigrant. Timber is a valuable export to the tree-less highlands or desert coast; also, fruit and vegetables grow well and are sent to the sierra towns by the truckload. This style of development has changed the eastern slopes of the Andes, and new families are continually moving in and claiming their own land by clearing it. Slash and burn is taken to the extreme and thousands of hectares of forest have disappeared. The destruction of the natural habitat is affecting some species already, but by far the greatest threat to the animals' survival is the profitable trade in skins and live specimens for export. In fifteen years, the size of any black caiman in Peruvian rivers has decreased noticeably, and in some places they have been totally destroyed. Giant Otters (Pteronura brasiliensis) now on the I.U.C.N. Red Book danger list are seldom seen, and it is tragic that the same picture is true for all species valuable in trading centres of the upper Amazon. Only very few parts of the wild no-mans land between the Amazon and the Andes remain in a virgin state and particularly most river routes through the forest are travelled extensively by hunters without concern for conservation.

In 1968 Peru took the first steps to protect a large area of land east of Cusco now known as the Manu National Park. A British naturalist, Major Ian Grimwood, who was in the country to help the Peruvian Government with selection of areas for Wildlife Reserves made a preliminary expedition to the Manu River in mid-1967 and decided that it was one of the finest areas of forest left in a pristine state on the eastern Andes. His report together with relentless pressure from the Peruvian *Dirección Forestal y Caza*, resulted in a Government decree that established the Reserve. In many ways the Manu Park will be unique in South America and the territory covers the *sierra* or highland region, the *montana* (a local name for the forested slopes), and the *selva* which is the lowland jungle. It is an ideal situation for effective protection as the only open access route is along the Manu River that empties into the Madre de Dios system. Thus, by setting up a control at the mouth of the Manu all trading can be stopped. Settlement within the five thousand square miles of the park is almost non-existent and even the widespread Machiguenga tribe has not made much impression because they have been persecuted by a small group of fierce Amahuaca Indians living on the nearby Rio de las Piedras. The reputation of the Amahuacas is responsible for deterring both hunters and settlers from outside and the Manu with its tributaries has been a forgotten and semi-unexplored enclave throughout the first decades of colonization.

The lowest areas of the Manu are just a little less than one thousand feet above sea level, and yet the Madre de Dios River has more than two thousand five hundred miles to flow eastwards via the Amazon to the Atlantic. There is almost nothing to distinguish the Andes at the point where the Manu leaves the mountains behind; the low finger-like foothills are forested and project into the level plains as the river moves lazily between ruddy banks of sedimentary earth. Most of the animals of this region are characteristic of the rest of Amazonas, and an abundance of insect life makes the sunlit clearings alive with colour. While the mammals remain within the cover of vegetation, the reptiles and birds usually are the most obvious fauna. Black Caiman (Melanosuchus niger) and River Turtles (Podocnemis expansa) are found in the Manu though uncommon now in most other Amazon tributaries. There are the other caiman and lizards, or for the unwary, there is always a chance of disturbing a snake. Bushmasters (genus

Lachesis) reach as much as seven to ten feet; the Fer de Lance (Bothrops atrox), a pit-viper, is smaller and extremely venemous and the Corals have distinctive pink and black bands. The largest types include Boas which, like pythons, kill by constriction; and water-boas, the famous Anacondas (Eunectes murinus) which grow to more than thirty feet.

For the wildlife enthusiast the lowlands are a tropical paradise and river banks or treetops are the home of a great variety of birds. In the shallow lagoons formed in old river ox-bows, the heavy-billed Jabiru Storks (Jabiru mycteria) move along majestically and the tiny Jacanas (Jacana jacana) tread gently on the floating leaves of water plants. Many herons and egrets give a flash of white amongst the low undergrowth while some way above them, macaws, parrots and toucans are the most colourful inhabitants of the forest. Everywhere the sounds of birds and insects mingle to form a unique jungle noise changing only at twilight, when the frogs begin a ceaseless croak and parrots screech loudly in flight along a darkening river. Above the water, dense vegetation closes tightly until within the trees, day and night are almost the same; beyond there is the massive upthrust of the mountains well covered by forest and a tangle of lianas which forms a wilderness where the number of species declines roughly in a relation with increases in altitude.

Though the Manu represents what is possibly the finest tropical forest zone of the Andes, other places are still worth consideration and representatives of the basic Neotropical fauna are found in the lower eastern Andes from Venezuela to northern Argentinia as well as the mountain forests of western Ecuador and Colombia. The primary endemic orders of Edentates and Marsupials as well as the distinctive Neotropical rodents are strongly present. Often all three of the anteaters are found in this zone together with sloths, some armadillos and various opossums. One solitary genus of Black-shouldered Opossum (Caluromysiops) is known only from a few specimens found in the upper Madre de Dios valley or near Iquitos, and though these animals are rarely encountered, others such as the Didelphid opossums, Philander opossums and the unusual Water opossum (or Yapok – genus Chironectes) are much more common. Yapok skins are now sold readily in the fur markets and the species could be endangered very quickly. The lowland rivers and forests are well populated with Tapirs (Tapirus

terrestris) which are the heaviest wild animals in South America and belong
to the same ancient order as horses and rhinoceros. Tapirs are browsers, with
a short flexible snout and heavy body; their meat is much used by some
tribes. Another large but fast disappearing mammal is the Capybara, which
is the world's largest rodent and being pig-sized is highly prized for food.
Capybaras have semi-webbed feet, and live in rivers or pools where they
feed both on water plants or nearby land vegetation; sometimes they destroy
large areas of crops planted by the colonists which does little to help their
reputation, and so now some bands of capybara have taken to nocturnal
foraging, and only in places as secure as the Manu Park do they persist in
semi-diurnal habit. On a recent visit, I was able to watch one group swimming
across the Madre de Dios at mid afternoon, and a family of young playing
on the banks of the Manu well before dusk.

Of the more familiar types, the Neotropical primates which are well
diversified are known by relatively few species in the eastern Andes. The
many rivers that divide the territory have formed distinct limits for some
narrowly defined sub-species, though on the other hand some genera are
very widespread. Capuchin Monkeys (Cebus), Spider Monkeys (Ateles)
and Howlers (Alouetta) have the greatest range of distribution, and with the
Smokey Woolly Monkey (Lagothrix cana) which is found at altitudes of
over 6,500 feet, they all have a distribution higher on the fringes of the
mountains than other monkeys. Most monkeys are sought after for food or
for a flourishing export trade and the effect of these depredations is harming
some species severely. Uakaris (genus Cacajao) of the lowland forests are
seriously endangered, but also the Howlers which are found to 4,000 feet
can be shot easily and are disappearing from their known haunts.

Distinct levels of the eastern slope usually contain a characteristic fauna,
though some species range widely through many thousands of feet. Peccaries,
for example (genus Tayassu), the South American equivalent of a wild pig,
inhabit the Amazon region and low forest zone, but in parts of the Andes
they reach the high forest at over 4,000 feet. They are hunted extensively
for food by the colonists and Indian tribes and in some places are on the
decline. Many of the large rodents too, particularly Agoutis (genus Dasyprocta), Pacas (genus Cuniculus) and the rarer Pacarana (Dinomys branickii)
also range well into the high forest. Pacaranas, or Tailed Pacas – sometimes

called Branick Rats, – occur only in the Andes in the forest regions, and were first known by a specimen from central Peru described in 1873. These animals are large, often more than twenty-five pounds, and not very timid, so they are caught easily by the tribes for food. On several jungle expeditions, I have been given Pacarana by friendly Indians, and the most memorable occasion was in the Machiguenga territory of the upper Urubamba, when the meat was rolled in toasted crumbs of dried banana and fried lightly in oil. Unfortunately for the Pacarana, its flesh is far more delicate than good pork.

Both the Machiguengas and Amahuacas from the Manu area hunt with arrows or by simple traps, and for the National Park to be effective the movement of the tribes must eventually be restricted. Machiguengas clear forest land for planting maize and their hunting activities can upset the fauna; sometimes a single family will live miles from the nearest settlement, or several families, together making a small village will work for a *patron* who farms coffee or cocoa. Some Indian ways are changing and though Machiguenga women continue to wear the traditional cotton *cushma*, a thin cloak resembling a long poncho, the men of the larger settlements have adopted trousers and modern shirts. They also have taken readily to guns, which is one development that is producing a drastic effect on the animal population: changes such as these are fairly general for most South American tribes today. Monkeys for sale to the traders are caught by shooting the mother and taking young animals from her back, and many of the jungle cats and caiman are shot at night. At one time all the lower slopes of the Andes were inaccessible and forest tribes had rare contact with the outside world, and though in those days the men hunted the same animals, recent commercial exploitation of wildlife has taken advantage of their primitive skills.

The territory of the Machiguengas and Amahuacas in the upper Madre de Dios or the neighbouring Urubamba river system, is reached from the highlands by narrow mountain trails, or along a river, if raft experts are prepared to venture through the *pongos* or giant rapids formed where the streamway carves through the final folds of the mountains. Travel on the river in this region usually is on a raft made of lashed or pinned *balsa* logs poled by expert Indian boatmen. As the water crashes around enormous cliffs, and swirls through the sharp river curves it forms foul, gurgling whirlpools and the pongo section is the most lonely place on earth. Often many days upstream from lowland settlements, the dangerous rapids deter casual visitors. On the river Urubamba in eastern Peru, the Pongo de Manique is the final barrier before the forest or selva; and cliffs rise two thousand feet on either side of a canyon thirty feet wide at the narrowest, where the river pours through at twenty-five miles an hour. Above the Pongo is the forest occupied by scattered groups of Machiguengas and higher still, the cloud forest is a gloomy wilderness between the lowlands and open sierra. Moving upstream, river travel gets increasingly difficult: tributaries enter the main river, so with every few hundred feet towards the watershed on the high puna, the streams are narrower and more torrentious. Occasionally, the valley opens to a wide floor between high mountains – this type of feature is clearly evident on the Upper Urubamba (or locally called Vilcanota) – and the extensive areas of flat land existing there gave the Incas a chance to develop their agriculture in a temperate climate. Among the higher levels of the forest, above five to six thousand feet, the vegetation types intermingle and no single form is dominant: tree ferns, evergreens, parasitic and epiphytic plants are abundant; and for the orchid-hunter this region provides a tailor-made collection. Perpetual mist shrouds some of the valleys, and the trees are packed closely together, with a thick impenetrable undergrowth filling up any unsuspecting gap. Mosses, ferns and lichens cover everything, and yet this part of the Andes is home for some of South America's rarest animals; perhaps their rarity arises from the difficulties of exploration, as in some cases only a few specimens of each have been recorded.

An easy first in this category are the Rat Opossums of the Family Caenolestidae, which were not discovered until the end of the last century. Only a few other examples have since been found and usually they come from the equatorial Andes, often high in the densely covered slopes. One species is known from the sides of the volcanoes of Chimborazo and Pinchincha (Caenolestes fuliginosus) and another single species of a separate genus (Lestoros inca) is found around Torontoy, not far from the Inca ruins of Machu Picchu in south-eastern Peru; it is so rarely seen that little is understood of its habits or status. These curious, tiny opossums quickly aroused the interest of morphologists by their close resemblance to the ancient fossil Caenolestids earlier discovered in South America. The toe and dentition arrangements differ from other living opossums. Such characteristics as diprotodont teeth, with the first incisors greatly enlarged, and hind feet with all toes separated have given the Caenolestids a controversial position in the Family. Now considered as an excellent example of convergent evolution as some of their features are similar to those of smaller kangaroos, the Caenolestids are partially forgotten. Studies in the wild are absent, but an examination of stomach contents indicates a varied diet of insects, eggs and small birds, but as the animal is nocturnal detailed work is extremely difficult.

The fossil record of South American marsupials starts in late Palaeocene and continues to the Pliocene with animals that possessed massive skulls and thick, crushing teeth. Borhaenids of ancient South America have some similarity to the Tasmanian Wolf (Thyalacinus): almost hyaena-like and known from Argentina, these mammals were carnivorous, and the main flesh eaters of the southern continent during the tertiary period. The tail of the modern Caenolestid is not prehensile but its diprotodont incisors are suggestive of some Australian Phalangeroids. The hind feet however have no trace of phalangeroid syndactylism of the second and third toes (i.e. the fusion of the digits of the hind limb, which makes a comb for cleaning hair. Australasian diprotodonts and bandicoots have the syndactylous comb-like condition). Much could be read into the similarities with Australasian forms, but modern thought points to an early Marsupial type which developed in the northern hemisphere and eventually spread to continents which became isolated from the rest of the world. The opossums survived on the island continent while true mammals evolved in the north and though in part the question can now be answered, it still leaves many mysteries; while Caenolestids continue to be one of the world's rarest animals.

The search for other species continued long after the first discoveries and early in the 1920s, when the other specimens were found in south-central Chile. Their habitat is impossible to search thoroughly and to make matters worse, the animals are insignificant. Even the sharp-eyed Indians of the equatorial forests seem unable to distinguish Rat opossums from the large numbers of Marmosas – Mouse opossums – so other species could remain undetected in the thick cloud forest today. In several years of travel in Peru and Ecuador, my nearest encounter with a Rat opossum was to see a mounted specimen in a Quito taxidermist's shop in 1968.

The anteaters like opossums are some of the original inhabitants of Neo-tropica. Of them all, the Giant Anteater (Myrmecophaga tridactyla) of the plains is the most familiar. Complete with a preposterously long snout and an erect bushy tail like an enormous wind-vane, this odd beast was at one time fairly common, but is becoming rare now: shooting, forest clearance and other influences of man are having a slow but certain effect. Other genera, both widely distributed in northern South America, are arboreal and have prehensile tails to serve as flexible fifth limbs. Tamanduas, or Collared Anteaters (Tamandua sp.) are about three feet long from snout to tail, and the Pigmy (Silky) Anteater (Cyclopes) is smaller, seldom reaching more than ten inches, including a stubby snout. These species are found in the Andean forests, often as high as five thousand feet, where they climb to ant nests in trees, ripping through the tough walls with powerful claws on the manus. Characteristically, the anteaters possess long mobile tongues which can be flicked in and out of the nest galleries to gather insects by the thousand; a busy, hungry anteater tackles a meal regardless of irritating ants which cling to its short fur, and apart from a few desultory swipes with a free limb, the feeding continues unabated. Anteaters are some of the oddest mammals in the world, and fortuitously the arboreal species are fairly secure from most potential enemies; however a small export trade is beginning which in addition to habitat destruction could be a signal for protection.

Often some of the South American racoon family are confused with the Tamanduas because of a similarity between their snouts; but the differences are soon evident. Only the Coatimundis (Nasua sp.) and (Nasuella sp.) are long nosed and they live in many parts of tropical South America, as well as into the higher regions of the forested Andes; occasionally they are reported from the uppermost zones of the vegetation locally known as the *ceja de selva*, literally meaning the 'brow of the forest'. The racoons belong to the Family Procyonidae, all of which are American except for the Asian Panda. In Neotropica the family representatives are descendents of invaders that arrived after the Pliocene land bridge had formed, though some fossil species arrived earlier by 'island hopping' as the southern continent became connected along the Central American isthmus. Coatis are known by several species and sub-species and their size is variable, though only rarely do they reach the size of a European fox; the females and young travel in bands of

ny Morrison with very rare Forster's Caracaras

mes Flamingos Laguna Colorada Bolivia

World's rarest Flamingo Bolivia

ten to twenty animals and despite the size of individuals they are extremely aggressive as a group, showing a fearless co-operative behaviour. They are omnivorous and feed on roots, fruit or small mammals, birds and insects which they hunt, using their highly sensitive sense of smell and mobile snout. The tail is banded, which is a peculiarity of other racoons notably the Ring-tailed Cat or Cacomistle (Bassariscus astutus) of the Southern United States. Another North American species is the Common Racoon (Procyon lotor) and it has a very near relative, the Crab-eating Racoon (Procyon cancrivorous) found along the banks of swamps and rivers in much of northern Neotropica and they could be present in the newly important Manu Park, though not above the lowland section. The family is charac-terized by the exceptional climbing ability of some species. Coatis often take to the branches when after food or when they are surprised, and old trunks or hollow logs are favourite resting places; they use their long tail for balance or adding their notable agility. Other forest Procyonids found in the lower Andes are Kinkajous (Potos flavus) and Olingos (Bassaricyon sp.) Neither genus has well-known habits as they are nocturnal, tree-top in-habitants, but the Kinkajou has a prehensile tail which singles it out as a unique Carnivore and the feature is equalled only by the Binturong Civet (Arctictis binturong) of Assam and Borneo. Kinkajous are tiny and locally they are often classed as monkeys, or given the name of Honey-Bear; their fur is close and brown to golden, with eyes that are typically large. Olingos are even more retiring and seldom seen in captivity; they have bushy tails used for balancing and, like the Kinkajous, they are expert climbers.

Within the forests of Andean slopes, many small carnivores are common, though some of the species are widely distributed in other South American habitats. The Tayra (Eira barbara) is the only species of the genus and is found in many areas, including the Andes to heights of 10,000 feet: they are otter-like and fierce, coloured brown with a lighter part on the chest. The Tayra belongs to the Family Mustelidae which includes the badgers, stoats, weasels and others. There is also one Andean weasel of the genus Mustela, and in nearly every recorded case the Andean species (Mustela frenata) is known from the highlands, though infrequent reports show that it occurs in the ceja de selva and very occasionally at low level on the arid western slopes of Andean Peru. Another genus includes the Grisons or Hurons

5

(Galictis sp) which are recognizable by an extremely long neck and fine weasel-like body; they occur in many parts of the continent, and in the Andes the distribution of *Galictis cuja* reaches the *Altiplano* near Lake Titicaca, though they are more typical of the nearby warm eastern valleys, reaching down to the Beni River.

Of the mammalian fauna of this region the Carnivores are perhaps the most familiar types. As well as the racoons and weasels there are the typical South American foxes of the genus Dusicyon, and Hog-nosed Skunks (genus Conepatus). Skunks occur in the Andean region along the ceja de selva, and are particularly common in the warmer intermontane valleys where they live among the low xerophytic vegetation; usually nocturnal they are seen frequently on the dry mountain roads at night. Almost completely omnivorous they feed on insects, eggs, fruit and small rodents or reptiles and true to tradition they use a powerful secretion of their anal glands as a defense. The fluid, unusually obnoxious, is blinding, and can be squirted for over ten feet; so it is not surprising that they are not threatened by man or other animals, and the best treatment for a skunk is to leave it alone. Even when driving past a flattened skunk on an Andean road, the odour seems to cling to the vehicle – it must be hard luck to be the assassin.

Typical of the lower Andean forests are larger Carnivores and neither the Jaguar (Leo onca) nor the Ocelot (Felis pardalis) are permanent inhabitants of the slopes above 3,000 feet though they possibly make seasonal migrations via low altitude passes. In the upper forests and ceja de selva, smaller Felidae fill similar ecological niches, and the Pampas Cat (Felis colocolo) has a range extending downwards from the highlands into the forest. Another, the Margay (Felis weidii), an ocelot-patterned small cat is widely distributed from the southern parts of Texas to Uruguay and occurs in many parts of the forested Andes, though south of Bolivia it is replaced by Geoffroys Cat (Felis geoffryi).

One of the most famous mammals of the Americas is the Puma – the Mountain Lion or Cougar (Felis concolor); it is ubiquitous and ranges through all habitats from sierras to jungle and open pampas. So far it has remained fairly common in remote places or in pampas zones around the scattered cattle stations. On the other hand, the Otter-Cat or Jaguarundi (Felis yagouaroundi) is little known and is a retiring inhabitant of dense undergrowth beside jungle rivers. It often reaches a length of fifty inches and weighs about twenty pounds; it feeds on a variety of small mammals, birds and reptiles, though little is known of its habits. The species has a wide range from central America to Paraguay and there is some confusion in the taxonomy because the animal exhibits two distinct colour phases with a uniform pelage varying from dark grey to deep russet. A litter can contain young of both colours which is an indication that the colour differences are not features of two separate species but Cabrera lists five sub-species with a note on pelage. As the animal is shy and seldom seen there are only limited reports to establish an accurate distribution for the Jaguarundi in the Andes, but some specimens (Felis y.melantho) have been shot in the montana of Peru at heights of 5,000 feet, and it is fairly certain that they occur at higher levels, possibly as far as the ceja de selva in some places.

Slight colour variation among the small cats is not uncommon and adds to the problem of determining the species for a region. Another confusion is the general term *Gato* or *Gato de Monte* given to most small Andean cats by the local people. The status of many species is hard to assess and though the family is highly successful, no doubt accounting for the large quantity of skins that pass through trading centres, it has to be assumed that the Jaguar, Puma and Ocelot face serious danger. On the Amazon market an Ocelot pelt fetches £15 and a good Jaguar is worth more than £35. Even the smaller Andean cats have a price in the sierra, and Margays are sold frequently under the guise of ocelot, so it is inevitable that most species will decline in settled and well hunted areas.

Andean Spectacled Bears are common also in some parts of the mountain forests, and such areas are well known by local hunters. The species has a wide distribution east of the cordilleras from Colombia and Venezuela to Bolivia, usually ranging from the foothills to near the ceja de selva, with particular preference for the warmer valleys where food is plentiful. In the Sandia Province of Southern Peru and near Chulumani in the Yungas valley east of La Paz, there are frequent reports of groups of bears making raids on the ripening corn crops, and though a bear in the wild could well appear as twice natural size, and seemingly in greater numbers as well, there is no doubt that the Spectacled Bear does raid crops, and has been observed at this activity. Unfortunately the reputation gives the farmers some reason for retaliation and there is a strong possibility that the species is on the decline in many areas; however, in parts of the Manu Park, there are known to be undisturbed populations, and there is a chance that conservation will be successful. The bear is the number one sportsman's trophy in South America, and hunting for pleasure is another serious threat, so it is fortunate that the strongholds of the species happen to be the dense eastern forests or a few of the grim desert quebradas facing the Pacific.

The presence of the larger Carnivores in the mountain forests, from foot-hills to the ceja de selva, is a reasonable indication that there is an abundance of smaller mammals and birds in the same region, and as well as the many medium sized rodents of the lower forest levels, smaller rodents such as Cavies (Family Cavidae) begin to appear in higher parts. The true upper limit of trees is difficult to define in some areas, and dense cloud forest gives way to a drier, almost xerophytic vegetation mixed with a few tough ever-greens and low deciduous shrubs, which in turn open to the puna – a grass-land of tough resistant grasses with areas of soft high altitude bogs. At the highest level of the forest, the short scrub gives excellent cover to some small communities of Pudus (Pudu mephistopheles), the world's tiniest deer, which is only thirteen inches high; they are coloured light brown to grey and are extremely quick and nimble, but despite this, they are being reduced by hunting and forced out by settlement and habitat destruction. The genus occurs sporadically from Colombia to Peru, and then again to the south in Central Chile and Argentinian Andes where another species (Pudu pudu) is established at a lower level in forested land.

Two separate genera of Cervidae occur in the upper levels of the Andean forested slopes and they have a wider altitude range and distribution along the mountain chain than Pudu mephistopheles. In Peru both the White-tailed Deer (Odocoilcus virginianus) and the Dwarf Brocket Deer (Mazama chunyi) are found in the Manu National Park and the former is reported occasionally from the lowest levels among the dense wet forests bordering the low selva, yet in Colombia the White-tailed Deer occurs on the open areas above the paramo vegetation at 14,000 feet. In spite of the obviously exceptional range of this deer, the variation helps to emphasise the problem of defining distinct faunal zones on the eastern slope of the Andes. In the fifteen hundred miles from Colombia to central Peru, the differences of temperature and rainfall at equal levels are considerable and accordingly there is a variety of conditions that do not fit easily into categories. However, a transect taken of the slopes shows that there are similarities and the zonation of animals is often similar, with a shift dependent on the latitude. Generally, the fauna of one area matches the fauna in a similar ecological zone of another latitude.

The dramatic changes of climate on the slope primarily have an effect on the vegetation and insect life at one end of a food chain, so that there is a zonation of small mammals, birds and reptiles closely related to the food supply. In the warm valleys parrots, macaws, toucans and oropendolas are some of the most colourful birds, while in the slightly higher subtropical forests, the brilliant Cocks-of-the-Rock (Rupicola peruviana) is one of the highlights of the Andes. Hardly anything in the jungle can compare with the flash of bright scarlet between the dark leaves, which jerks the eye as a male Cocks-of-the-Rock glides through a clearing. Another species (Rupicola rupicola) is known in the Guianas and Venezuela, but is not so bright, being mainly a rich orange. The male of the Andean species is mostly scarlet with a flattened crest of feathers over the head, covering nearly the entire bill. Some of the secondaries are grey and the rest of the wings and tail are black. Darker colours with distinct maroons and maroon brown distinguish the female. Cocks-of-the-Rock occur on both sides of the Andes in heavily forested regions, and in their typical habitat close to rocky streams and cliffs. The most striking behaviour of these birds is the courtship lek-display when they make a clearing on the ground and the males dance to attract the females. Usually the nests are not far away and in one mile-long length of river gorge in Bolivia I discovered ten nests, averaging eight feet above the water level. The shallow saucer-like nests were of mud and grass, stuck in crevices or on rocky ledges. Each contained two white, brown-flecked eggs which were observed until hatching. With my wife covering the territory on alternate days, I was able to photograph much of the life of the Andean Cocks-of-the-Rock, including the nesting and feeding of the young, a chore left to the female. The Cocks-of-the-Rock are found only in Neotropica: there is a single genus classified in the family Rupicolidae, and they are well-known to many of the forest people; one usual local name is *el Tunke* and large numbers are caught for sale to local zoos and pet dealers. Unfortunately, they are easily recognizable in the trading centre of Iquitos, in Pucallpa and in the north at Barranquilla where the northern species is collected.

Neotropical avifauna is the richest in the world, with about two-fifths of all bird species being represented. Eighty-nine of the hundred and fifty-five families, and more than three thousand five hundred species have been described, and with the Andes offering a wide variety of habitat it is not surprising that there is immense variety in the mountains. The majority of the birds are found in the tropical and sub-tropical regions, but a typical New World family, the Hummingbirds (Trochilidae) is widely distributed. Some species are found in North America, but most of them occur south of the border with Mexico, and they live in all climatic conditions. In the highest parts of the Andes, I have seen them on flowers of the cold puna, particularly feeding from the hundreds of inflorescences of giant Bromeliads, but they are few in number compared with the abundance of species occurring in the warm eastern valleys. Hummingbirds are incredibly beautiful, with vivid iridescent colours: flashing reds, emerald green, or violets that glitter, changing shade as light falls on the feathers from a different angle. The birds have exciting names: Grey-chinned Hermit (Phaetothornis griseogularis) described as a 'coppery green, back bronze green, tail coverts rufous', which is found in the tropical zone east of the Andes in Colombia and from parts of Ecuador, Peru and Brazil. A brown Violet-ear (Colibri delphinae) from the eastern Andes of Colombia or the Spangled Coquette (Cophormis stictolopha) from both slopes of the Andes in Colombia and southwards to Peru. The list is endless, and perhaps the most wonderful of them all is the Magnificent Hummingbird (Loddegesia mirabilis) from the Chachapoyas region on the Utucubamba river in eastern Peru. It was discovered in the early nineteenth century by Andrew Mathews, an Englishman living in Peru. Later he gave a specimen to a botanist, George Loddiges, who in turn took it to Britain where John Gould, the renowned wildlife artist, painted it for his famous work on hummingbirds. The Marvellous Hummingbird of Peru is exceptional not only within the family but among birds because it possesses a very small number of tail feathers; there are only four, and two of them are extended as long filaments with a raquet-shaped feathered section at the distal end. The tiny flags make the Loddegesia very distinctive and the filaments are two or three times the length of the body: it is thought the male uses the decoration to attract the female in nuptial flight and though the females are not uncolourful, they lack the fine tail feathers and some brilliant patches of blue and emerald which decorate their mates.

Other hummingbirds present a great variety of colour, size and embellishment; some have long thin bills or some straight and others finely curved. Each is well adapted to the flowers of the habitat. Some of the birds have crests, plumes or tiny raquets which stand out clearly in hovering flight. Usually the nests are small and made of soft mosses, fibres or other fine material and they are sited in low bushes or tree-forks where they blend well into the cover.

Of all the South American families, Hummingbirds have attracted some of the greatest interest from physiologists, naturalists, painters and collectors. The colour and delicacy of these birds has caught the inspiration of many artists and in the past the feathers were in demand for fashions or the tourist trade. The island of Trinidad which boasts a large variety of species was forced to introduce a law to protect hummingbirds when at the end of the last century the trade in feathers threatened some of the most colourful forms. Colombia with over one hundred and thirty-five species on the national list, was also a centre of the hummingbird trade in the last century and Bogota trade skins were famous and now form a basis of many collections.

The work of Padre Olivares OFM in Colombia has led to the establishment of an excellent skin collection in the National University in Bogota where leading studies of taxonomy are conducted. Padre Olivares is nationally famous and he has made expeditions to every region of Colombia from the snow-fringed paramo to the *tierra-caliente*. Sometimes he has encountered difficulties and by an amazing instance of parallel evolution he found that he was collecting specimens of an insect which had exactly the same habits and food plant as one of Colombia's smallest hummingbirds. Such tiny birds with their rapid motion and ability to fly backwards or up and down like a jump-jet or to hover in one place must possess the most fantastic development of avian mechanics we know. Even their position in the ecology of a biome is not fully understood though it is possible that they are important for effecting cross pollination of some plants.

Another Neotropical family – the Steatornithidae 'Guacharos' or Oil-birds is represented in several parts of the forested Andes. There is only a

single genus and one species (Steatornis caripensis) which occurs from Trinidad to Bolivia. Usually the birds live in flocks, nesting as colonies on ledges
in dark canyons or in caves. They resemble a large nightjar and have a
wingspan of two and a half feet, the adults possessing a lean body of between
thirteen and seventeen inches. These birds have had a long and in some places
continuing relationship with the primitive forest-tribes, and the common
name has arisen from the use of the excessively fat chicks which are taken
from the nest and rendered into oil. The adult birds feed on succulent fruits
which they pluck from the tree when in flight and the floor of the nesting
cave is normally deeply covered with the remains of soft nuts and berries.
Probably, the most interesting feature of the oil-bird is its nocturnal habit and
gregarious nature. A visit to any haunt is impressive particularly at dusk
when the birds become restless, flying skilfully in the high vaulted roof or
low tunnels. After accustoming oneself to the eeriness of a tropical cavern,
the night sounds slowly change. Parrots return to roost on the rocks outside,
the bats move into the dusk and then suddenly the first harsh click-click
of the awakening oil-bird echoes through the chamber. When several birds
are flying together, the intermittent clicking is believed to be a form of sonar
location similar to the sense possessed by bats. Oil-bird caves are often home
to other night birds and mammals and the detritus-covered floor sometimes
seethes with millions of insects. Some caves should be visited with caution, as
the detritus and guano support a variety of delicate fungi. It is far too simple
to inhale the featherweight spores and the pulmonary disease of histoplas-
mosis can be contracted. One cave near Tingo Maria in eastern Peru is
infamous for *mal de cueva* or cave sickness, and most visitors only venture
into the humid outer cave where the floor is firm. Caution and a fine mask
are advised if any extensive exploration is contemplated.

Caves in the sub-tropical level of the eastern and western forested slopes
are likely to hold a colony of oil-birds; the birds are also found in parts of
Colombia's Sierra Nevada de Santa Marta, or near the border with Ecuador
and Peru, with a southern limit probably around the River Heath on the
Bolivian frontier. Again, in Trinidad, West Indies, the oil-bird suffered
extensive exploitation and legislation was needed for ensuring protection
and, like the hummingbirds, the colonies have recovered; but in the wilder
regions of the Andes a natural balance seems to have been established long

ago, and man continues to take the young without a serious effect on the population, though a new threat comes from the colonists, and the Guacharo Cave at Tingo Maria is now a reserve.

High in the narrow and torrentious sections of Andean rivers, Torrent Ducks (genus Merganetta) are especially adapted to feeding in fast-flowing water; the birds cannot be mistaken for any other species, and there are six races between Colombia and Chile. Usually they occur at levels between 3,000 and 10,000 feet, and are easily identified by their habits. Living in pairs, they rest on boulders in the river and dive into raging water to feed on insects and larvae; the spate does not worry them and they swim powerfully against any current. Sometimes they seem to remain absolutely stationary though they are able to move upstream rapidly underwater. To cope with these conditions they possess a long and stiff tail which appears to have the function of rudder as well as hydrofoil to divert the pressure of the current; their bills are long and thin, their body is small (usually fifteen to sixteeen inches) and the webbed feet are large. The tail and feet are exceptionally well developed in the very young birds and are completely out of proportion to the size of the chicks, which are able to swim strongly. Habits of Torrent Ducks have not been studied completely, but A. W. Johnson of Santiago watched a pair at a nest in southern Chile, and found that they used a hole in the river-bank about six feet above water level.

In Peru, I was able to follow the life of two adults and four young over a period of a month as the chicks were leaving the nest and beginning their river life. Their reaction to danger was exceptionally interesting: at any sign of movement on the steep bank above the family, the female would dive, heading upstream and the young birds would cease swimming and allow themselves to be washed downstream quickly. The river was not far from Cusco and very steep, so the family was divided instantly; often the youngsters would be separated from the mother by fifty to a hundred yards, and they came to rest under over-hanging rocks or behind tiny waterfalls. During the dispersion the male kept watch from a central rock or a vantage point beneath the bank, and once the danger had passed, the female followed her chicks downstream; slowly she collected them together again, being led to their hiding places by their high-pitched whistling call. The stream was close to a mountain path and disturbances averaged over eight times a day, but in the four weeks of observation the family number remained constant at four chicks; not one was lost in spite of the powerful current.

The male can be distinguished easily by the white head and neck, which has a black stripe running across the crown, and laterally along the neck to the body. Blacks merge with sandy brown on the upperside, while ventrally the bird is white, streaked with grey. Only a touch of green on the wing speculum, and the bright orange bill give any strong colour to both sexes, though the female is almost completely orange rufous and has a darker back. There is a carpal spur on the wing, and this is larger in the male. Only slight colour differences separate the six races.

Water temperature seems to be an important factor governing the altitude range of these ducks, and it seems likely that the main reason is the influence of temperature on the food supply of the habitat. They unquestionably prefer extremely fast flowing water and this factor strongly limits their territory in a length of river; sometimes two or three pairs will live close together along a mile of tumbling water with each pair specifically keeping within a short length of rugged streamway despite extensive level water above and below the waterfalls. Torrent ducks are not confined to the eastern slopes and occur in many rivers on both sides of the mountains; on the Amazon headwaters they are found from above the ceja de selva to the uppermost tropical zones.

These are not the only ducks found in the Andes, and Tree Ducks (Tribe Dendrocygnini) live in the low selva zone and throughout much of tropical South America, while in the highlands there are tiny Puna Teal (Anas versicolor puna), Ruddy Ducks (Tribe Oxyurini) and other species characteristic of mountain lakes such as Titicaca and Lago Junin. In nearly every way however the Manu National Park will give a perfect cross-section of the fauna of the eastern Andes. Most families common to the Andes are present inside the boundaries and species are plentiful. The richness of the lower zones is evident and clearly contrast with the cold sierras and their sterility – an image which is more typical of the giant mountain range.

The cold climate presents serious problems for agriculture in the central Andes and with such plentiful land only a few miles away to the tropical east, some attempts at colonization are proving successful. Local government plans involve the removal of entire communities often against the present wishes of the people: for example, entire villages of Altiplano Indians have been moved from the Bolivian highlands. In some cases the pioneers have died, but of course often the transfer is successful. Parallel schemes cover road-building, new towns and hydro-electric projects, but sadly the development is certain to upset the ecology.

Parts of the fine Yungas valleys east of La Paz have been opened for many years, and the warmer slopes are the centres of coca production; the leaf of the plant (Erythroxlyon coca) is chewed almost universally by the highland Indians of the central Andes, possibly to alleviate many of the physical effects of their high altitude life, and poor diet. Coca plantations existed in Inca times and old paved roads descend from the sierras through the warm valleys. Not far from La Paz, an Inca road remains clearly at 16,000 feet, where it clings to the vertical mountainside, twisting downwards for thirty miles to the Yungas jungle. This region of the cordillera is the most precipitous of all, and the cliffs are more than five thousand feet in one giant step from the snow to the cloud-forest. Looking back between the creepers and tangle of plants, the snowfields of the flat-topped Mururata are fantastically clear against the indigo Andean sky; glaciers overhang the forests and freshly melted, they pour over cliffs in a thin lacework of cascades. Modern engineers have followed a slightly different route for the new Yungas roads and, by blasting along the precipice, the highways to Coroico and Chulumani descend through 11,000 feet in less than thirty miles.

On either side of the road below the six thousand foot mark, settlers have cleared the trees, and in most accessible valleys the ecology has changed completely. Close to the towns, there is nothing for the wildlife and many species are absent. Settlement is continuing and as the human population increases in this wonderfully rich area, habitat destruction will ensure the total loss of some species. Almost everywhere along the range of the Andes the same pattern is developing. Tarapoto, home to Spruce for two years is a government-aided centre of colonization, while immense tree-felling machines are clearing land for eventual cattle grazing on the edge of Peru's Amazon. Colombia is well advanced with agriculture and settlement of her sub-tropical Andean regions, and there are places like Tena on the Napo River in Ecuador intended as the nucleus for future exploitation. With these new efforts to diversify and develop somewhere other than around their capital cities, the Andean Republics hold the responsibility for destroying great tracts of unexplored forest, and only the foresight of preserving places like the River Manu in Peru or the Sierra Macarena in Colombia can prevent an irreversible total disaster for the fauna. Unless these conservation attempts are successful, the magic of one frontierland will be lost forever.

Adjusting to the High Life

Most of the high Andes to the north of the Tropic of Capricorn is habitable. On the one hand the equatorial regions are fertile and valleys are warmly scented with tropical fruits grown in tiny farms tucked between steep hillsides; on the other, the south around Lake Titicaca, the Altiplano of Bolivia and Peru which averages 12,500 feet is cold, sterile and uninviting but home to more than four million Indians, who struggle with subsistence level harvests. One source gives a world total of twenty-five million people living at more than 9,500 feet above sea level, with the majority being Andean: Bogota has two million inhabitants at 8,569 feet; Quito approximately four hundred thousand at 9,375 feet; Cusco, the ancient Inca capital of Peru has eighty thousand people at 11,440 and La Paz, the world's highest capital has over four hundred thousand at 12,400 feet.

La Paz 'El Alto' airport is the highest in the world, and the terminal and runways are at 13,300 feet. Passengers arriving from sea level are advised to avoid exertion, and to drive into the lower level of the main city as quickly as possible. Cusco is a great tourist centre, and the best hotel gives visitors a note suggesting that their first few hours at the altitude should be spent in bed, followed a little later the same day by gentle excursions around town. 'If you feel unwell, call the hotel doctor – oxygen is available': – a thoughtful gesture but not a recommendation to anyone elderly or with a weak heart. On the other hand most sports, particularly football, are followed without danger by the inhabitants of many of the sierra towns, while recently the organizers of a motor rally around South America warned international competitors that many of the roads were at extremely high altitudes rising to nearly 16,000 feet. A note in the rules stated that 'Competitors must take medical advice as to their ability to withstand sustained effort at such altitudes'.

Among the world records La Paz can claim is certainly the highest ski-lift and at over 17,500 feet on Mount Chacaltaya behind the city no un-acclimatized ski enthusiast can hope to enjoy an afternoon on the slopes. Even the Paceños are unenthusiastic and find a few hours at the increased altitude are exhausting.

From personal experience driving a car or even a Land Rover is relatively light work, though on my first journey over the high passes I noticed a slight 'light-headedness', excitement and apparently increased perception. But without acclimatization any sustained effort, including car repairs or 'digging out' when stuck in the highland bogs, leads even a fit individual towards the symptoms of mountain sickness or '*Soroche*', which in simplest terms is due to a lack of oxygen. Sometimes the effects are severe, with headaches, nausea and fainting; some visitors to Cusco have died; also, well-fed businessmen tend to avoid La Paz, though if they happen to go there they usually spend their time in bed before leaving on the next flight back to sea level.

It is clear to any tourist walking slowly up the steep streets of the high capitals that the Indian who overtakes him is at home in the rarified air. Often smaller in stature and loaded with enormous bundles, the Indian takes the hillsides in short, quick steps and manages to prolong the effort for many hours in spite of a poor diet said to contain less than 1,500 calories per day. So apart from the effects of instant arrival at high altitude, experienced by passengers arriving at El Alto, there are two main branches of physiological research. Firstly the acclimatization of a visitor to the highlands for a short or long period of time, and secondly the adaptation of man and other animals that have lived in the mountains for hundreds of generations. Some effects of altitude have been known for many years, and the Spanish Conquistadores were the first to notice that they lacked sexual potency when reaching the high sierras. Certain individuals are affected seriously, with a few cases of complete infertility being recorded. The usual change is a sharp drop in the sperm-count for the first few days, followed by a gradual return towards the normal level that seems to be related to the degree of acclimatization acquired.

The ability of man to acclimatize to high altitudes probably has received the greatest public attention in recent years. Studies have revealed not only how mountaineers react to the heights of Everest and other Himalayan peaks, but also the Olympic Games of Mexico 1968 gave a first-class opportunity to examine the results of a large number of athletes working at different tasks with one hundred per cent of their available physical ability. Results, in general terms showed that there is little difference in athletic performance between men performing at sea level or the high altitudes when the exertion is practised for a short time, though when continuous effort is needed over a longer period some results indicate a decline in the performance. Perhaps running up a long flight of stairs gives the most vivid example. Both in La Paz at 12,400 feet or in London (at sea level), the average person can take the first flights at the same speed, often with two or three steps in one bound (always assuming that he or she is motivated sufficiently) but while the energetic Londoner might succeed in maintaining a good pace for several floors, the unacclimatized man in La Paz fades quickly after the first all-out effort. Afterwards, the recovery period is longer for the man at the high altitude and in some cases severe exertion in the highlands is accompanied by unpleasant sensations that are symptoms of the low oxygen pressure or lack of the ability to acclimatize, a condition which is termed hypoxia. However, the reason that a high rate of muscular effort is possible for a short period is due to the anaerobic activity of the muscles. That is to say, muscles can work without oxygen but require oxygen for recovery afterwards: in fact a form of oxygen debt is built up in the tissues and it is this which determines the degree of fatigue.

The basic reason for the difference in the athletic performance and the unacclimatized man's inability to work hard at high altitude is described as lack of oxygen; but more correctly the cause is twofold. Firstly the air pressure at 12,000 feet is roughly half the pressure of the atmosphere at sea level, though the relative percentage of the main constituents of the atmosphere retain almost the same proportions, and it follows that any given volume of air at 12,000 feet contains less oxygen than the same volume at sea level. The lower pressure affects the rate of oxygen transfer in the lungs, and the decreased quantity of oxygen per given volume of air requires that a greater amount has to be processed to support any activity. People normally living at sea level can acclimatize to living high, and this was demonstrated to me quite dramatically in the days when Faucett (a Peruvian domestic airline) flew to Cusco with unpressurized aircraft. Once past the edge of the Andes, oxygen tubes were handed to passengers and it was essential to suck the gas to avoid blackout in the high stages of the flight. Yet on the return journey after two or three weeks in the Andes, roaming between 11 and 17,000 feet, it was possible to make the flight without resort to the oxygen supply.

The human body compensates with obvious changes. More red cells with a greater total weight of oxygen-carrying haemoglobin are formed during acclimatization (this exists already in the highland native), and some reliable figures for this roughly indicate a 2·3 per cent increase in the cells per three thousand feet of altitude.

At the same time a so far unexplained increase in the uric acid content of the blood has been noticed in those people who move into the high altitude environment. Visitors to La Paz have a clear increase of uric acid which levels off within a few days of arrival. Sets of results show the following factors:

    on arrival at 12,000 feet: factor 6·8
    8 days after arrival: factor 8·3
    30 days after arrival: factor 7·8

It seems that this change is related to the change in the number of red blood cells and an alteration in the plasma volume.

Additionally there is an increased pulmonary volume available for oxygen transfer, which results from a greater alveolar surface being opened for transpiration. Highland people have relatively larger thoraxes (possibly an indication of greater pulmonary volume) and the acclimatized man probably calls upon more of the available alveolar surface than utilized normally at sea level. Acclimatization is helped also by an increased ventilation rate – an increase in volume of air breathed per minute – and this is brought about, not by the usual stimulus of carbon dioxide tension in arterial blood affecting the respiratory centre of the brain, but by other receptor organs sensitive to oxygen tension. Regulation of breathing and the change when a man moves to high altitude is a slow process and sometimes unnerving spasmodic breathing is experienced. However, an acclimatized man is able to live at altitudes frequented by Sherpas and Andean Indians, and

Indian with Alpacas (shorn)

Horned Coots (*Fulica cornuta*)

Mountain Viscacha *(Lagidium)* related to Chinchilla

impairment is suffered only by the unfortunate individual who fails to acclimatize or is introduced to the highlands too quickly. At one time it was thought that the mountain people were inferior. Joseph Barcroft who worked in Peru in 1924 said that 'all dwellers at high altitudes are persons of impaired physical and mental powers', but recently this view has not been upheld, and the apparent backwardness of Indian peoples probably is due to closely related social and nutritional deficiencies which will be overcome in future.

Despite the apparent simplicity of the problem much research is needed to solve the deeper secrets of the mechanism of acclimatization and if such a thing occurs, the inheritance of adaptation. Some workers believe that at the tissue-level where the oxygen is used by the body, an alteration in enzymic action might be responsible for the more perfect utilization of oxygen. Also, the adapted man is known to possess greater capillary circulation, which means, in effect, that blood can reach the tissues more easily. These ideas serve to illustrate the problems of investigating acclimatization and inheritance of adaption and separating them.

Much of the work is carried out in Peru, Bolivia, the United States and Great Britain, but the Andean countries are concerned with man and in high altitude, mountain environments. North American research inevitably covers the sophisticated techniques of high flight while British physiologists have studied acclimatization at very high altitude, particularly on mountaineering expeditions.

In 1927 an Institute of Andean Biology was organized in the Faculty of Medicine of the University of San Marcos, Lima, under the direction of the late Dr Carlos Monge, one of Peru's most distinguished scientists (in 1961 this was reformed as the High Altitude Research Institute). Several years earlier Monge had recognized the existence of the chronic mountain sickness of 'mal de montaña chronico', an illness not uncommon in the high sierra. Unlike the Soroche which is experienced for short periods before acclimatization is reached, the chronic sickness is due to the loss of acclimatization, or the inability to acclimatize. Most of the early work on this problem was carried out in Lima (500 feet above sea level), or in Huancayo, an Indian town roughly 100 miles east, but more than 10,000 feet high in the mountains. In 1951 a laboratory was built at Morococha at nearly

16,000 feet, and other research facilities exist in the Hospital of Cerro de Pasco, part of the mining complex of the Cerro Corporation. Bolivia has one high altitude research programme organized by the Medical Faculty of the University of San Andres, and another run by the Institute of Occupational Health (joint Ministry of Health and USAID), which studies occupational diseases affecting highland people. As many of the disabling illnesses affecting the Andean miners are pulmonary, such as silicosis, tuberculosis and pneumonia, the relationship between high altitude, the incidence of the disease, effective cures and other factors are of the utmost importance to the mining industry of the Andean countries. As the world demand for minerals increases, greater extremes of mining conditions have to be faced; and now many of the deep tunnels in the Andes present difficulties of dust and extreme heat, while on the Bolivian frontier with Chile, the world's highest mine is at over 19,000 feet and the workers are living at an encampment only 1,500 feet lower.

Since these Andean biological institutions were founded, more than six hundred papers have been published and many of them have appeared in overseas journals and magazines. Occasionally Peru and Bolivia jointly hold a symposium, and frequently send representatives to international conferences; thus establishing the two countries a world-wide reputation in the field. (During the border war between India and China, Indian troops had difficulty at the high altitudes and India sent doctors to Peru to study the Andean research.)

Some of the most significant results have come from studies of men born and raised in the high altitudes. It has been demonstrated that they have the most efficient degree of acclimatization and comparisons show very little difference between the first generation of men born at high altitude and the Indians who have been there for centuries. Acclimatization begins at the foetal stage in high altitude populations and at birth it appears that the adaptation exists already. Undoubtedly there are differences in stature and thoracic capacity between Indians and European settlers which seem to indicate genetic differences or certainly racial variety, but both groups lose their acclimatization when brought down to sea level for some time. Other discoveries are even more surprising and it has been stated that the highland people suffer less from some common diseases. Heart attacks are infrequent, leukaemia and cirrhosis of the liver are almost unknown, and surprisingly, the proportion of duodenal to gastric ulcers is totally reversed between men of sea level and the Andes. However, some authorities are more cautious when interpreting these statistics, and it is well recognized that some of these diseases can be related to the pressures of life in an advanced society, and sierra Indians, though on a poor diet, perhaps benefit by not overeating and missing the worries which affect the city-dweller.

Unfortunately, it is not only the different ways of life that confuse the results, but also there is the tremendous range of environmental factors to be taken into consideration. Cities like New York or London with their box-like offices and fume-filled streets have to be compared with the crystal-clear air of the Andes; there are different ozone levels, different degrees of bombardment by cosmic rays; and recently there has been a difference in the exposure to radioactive fall-out. All these factors and their effects will have to be investigated and related to results in any branch of high altitude study. Even Indian lore might be taken into account, as some Indians refuse to walk through parts of the mountains reputed to induce the 'mal de montaña'.

Some of the most recent work in Peru has been aimed at the process of ageing at high altitude compared with the same process at sea level; and though concrete results have yet to be published, the line of research illustrates the general way in which data of high altitude life could be of use to general medical studies. Another case with wide application is the complete study of hypoxia. Because the condition is not unique to the highlands and is met with when some diseases affect men living at sea level, Andean biologists believe their work will help with a better understanding of the problem and lead to advances in therapy.

The field of physiology within the study of Andean wildlife is almost untouched and probably the paucity of information is due to the extreme difficulties encountered with any field work of sampling in the high sierras. Also, once the initial museum-collections were made for taxonomic purposes, most naturalists seemed to devote their efforts to morphology and attempts to place the new Neotropical animals within the scheme of the world's fauna. Recently the behavioural sciences have been given more attention as a field of research which is important in population control,

Game-park management or the preservation of endangered species. The fact that a vicuña can run at thirty miles an hour for several miles without tiring has been overlooked; the condor, probably flies higher than any other bird and yet comes down to sea level; likewise the guanaco and puma range from the Andean heights to the coastal deserts with apparent ease, and many migrant birds pass from the coastal lagoons to high altitude lakes during the course of their annual movement. This field is wide open for research and there could be exciting new discoveries of specialized adaptive mechanisms.

One line of research has examined the state of torpor which humming-birds pass into at night or under cold conditions when the ambient temperature falls. Most diurnal birds exhibit a slight drop of body temperature when they are inactive overnight but the temperature of the hummingbird has been known to drop to 18°C. and lower in Andean species: for example, Jaeger who studied the hibernation of the Colorado Poorwhill also observed the Andean Hillstar Hummingbird (Oreotrochilus estella) and found that the body temperature fell to within 0·5°C. of the ambient night temperature. This represented a fall from 39·5°C. to 14·4°C. Andean Hillstars occur in the high puna country of the Andes of north Chile, southern Peru, Bolivia and northeast Argentina, and are one of the commonest high altitude species in this region. Though the torpid state is a generally accepted adaptation by which hummingbirds cope with widely differing day and night temperatures, the adaptation is especially essential in the Andes, where night temperature even in a sheltered spot can reach freezing point or below. The torpid bird with its metabolism reduced to as little as one twentieth of the daytime rate is able to conserve energy and pass the night without starving or having to move to a lower level. Sometimes these Andean humming-birds have been discovered in a torpid state in rock crevices or old mine shafts though other species have been found in snow or very frosty conditions and have become active with the warming sunlight.

The thin Andean air warms quickly so that in La Paz in winter a tropical suit is adequate on one side of a street but in the shade more than a sweater is needed. Hummingbirds have evolved so that they can cope with these conditions, also other high altitude animals are able to survive the rigorous climate. Tiny Altiplano lizards are active once the sun is up; small rodents survive at very low temperatures and a few arthropods, particularly Altiplano scorpions move about at night when the ground temperature is well below zero C.: on one occasion we had to move camp away from a sandy, scorpion infested area when our thermometer registered minus 15°C.

The central Andean region from Titicaca southward to the high deserts of the Atacama and Lipez are cold and dry for most of the year. Plants have a short alpine life, or are toughly xerophytic to survive desiccation. A spiky grass, Ichu (Stipa ichu) is common, and between the large tufts, other plants find shelter: dwarf compositae, a few gentians, madders or even lupins. A few species have evolved as hard compact forms, a feature especially clear in the Yareta or Llareta (Azorella glabra). Also water conservation is vitally important for the high-living fauna. The Andean Camelidae, grouped in the sub order Tylopoda with the Asian camels, possess water cells in the stomach rumen and the animals can survive in desert or semi desert regions. For man too, water is an important factor, and at very high altitudes water loss from the lungs is increased, because of the dryness of the air and increased breathing. Maintaining a high intake of fluids is an essential for mountaineers and if a deficiency builds up when working in a high altitude weakness and tiredness ensue.

Though not specifically related to living at high altitude and possibly far more accurately associated with the climatic variation at different heights in the sierra, the quality of the mammalian fur is a feature that follows a rule-of-thumb improvement with increase in altitude. One pioneer sheep-farmer from Britain, John Revie of the Illpa Stud Farm in Puno, says that the wool of his Merinos is finer when he keeps them on high ground. His results have been borne out by his wool topping the London sales on several occasions. Some very fine Merino (30 microns diameter) is very similar in size to coarse vicuña (28 microns) but of course cannot compare with the finest vicuña – 10 microns. The highland habitat seems to have induced the development of particularly fine wool or fur, and alpaca, vicuña and chinchilla pelts are in great demand. The last two examples have suffered tremendous depredations by skin traders. However, despite their scarcity in the wild, attempts are being made to farm vicuña in the Andes and chinchilla breeding stations are now well-established in many parts of the world.

For this market alone, any studies of adaptive mechanisms, e.g. in reproduction, would be useful and might lead to greater profits or perhaps the eventual re-establishment of these species in places from which they have long since disappeared.

The Golden Fleece

Some of the wildest puna country in the central Andes reaches westwards from the pass of La Raya between Cusco and Lake Titicaca as far as the province of Chumbivilcas. Most of the land is well above 13,000 feet and short valleys dissect gently curving mountainsides where only an occasional rocky scarp breaks the continuous yellow cover of ichu grass. In this remote land, some Indian life continues almost unchanged by the approach of civilization and Santo Tomas, the centre of the province, is noted for a *Fiesta de Toros* when, until a year or two ago, condors were tied to the bulls in a crude, pagan ceremony. Territorial rights in Chumbivilcas have never been settled and each year some communities battle before the planting season: in the fights a serious injury or a death is heralded as a good omen for the harvest so the struggle is hard without pulled punches.

The country life of these Indians is isolated and a burden nearly impossible to absorb into the sophisticated pattern of the present, and though some policies of west coast republics have inched slowly towards a small degree of highland development, places like Chumbivilcas seem destined to remain linked to the past. There the year is divided conveniently into seasons for planting, harvesting and animal husbandry: each day has a significance deeply rooted in ancient lore.

For the highland Indians of Peru and Bolivia, the Llama (Lama glama) is vitally important within the simple economy and the animals are common throughout the lofty sierras. In Chumbivilicas, some of the finest flocks number in thousands and when herded from the open puna or between widely separated villages, the beasts are decorated with bright tassels and colourful packs, in much the same way as the tribes of the east dress their camels.

Llamas are classified in the ungulate sub-order of Tylopoda which

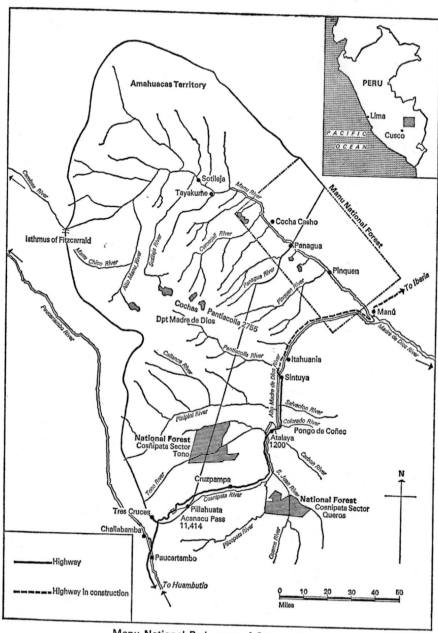

Manu National Park, east of Cusco, Peru

includes all the modern camel-like forms. These animals evolved from the same basic stock during the Tertiary in North America, and by modification they developed as two distinct branches; the camels of the old World, and the llamoids of Neotropica. Some basic similarities clearly link the two groups, but the Andean llama and the three other related Neotropic species are all humpless and much smaller; a fully grown llama seldom exceeds three hundred pounds and is tiny alongside a large dromedary weighing almost a ton. Other features are useful for making a quick and superficial distinction: all the llamoids have short tails, deeply cloven feet and normally the body is without the typical calluses that camels have developed by kneeling on their knees, hocks and sternum.

The Llamas are the most commonly occurring of the few South American species and have been kept by Indians since some distant time in the history of South American man. Alpacas are another domesticated species, while vicuña and guanaco have remained wild in spite of many attempts at domestication. At some stage in the Pleistocene all the Neotropic llamoids had an extensive distribution within the limits of the sub-continent, and their remains have been discovered from the warm pampas of Argentina to the Andes and north coastal Ecuador. With the exception of the guanaco which is able to live both in the heights and low foothills, or even southward into the steppes of Patagonia, the llamoids are restricted in present time to the higher levels of the Andes.

Physiologically, both camels and llamoids are well adapted to survival in extremely dry conditions: some bands of vicuñas roam in parts of Bolivia where the ground is frozen most of the day and the scant vegetation gives only a green tinge to the earth for many months of the year. Possibly metabolism of stored fat in long periods of drought is one of the mechanisms that enables the animals to survive and there are also the special water cells in the complex rumen of the stomach. Llamas can make marches of three or four days across deserts: long 'caravans' of the haughtily graceful beasts accompany Indians making an annual migration from the high saline-flats of the Andes to the warm valleys of northern Argentina. Each animal loaded carefully with two blocks of crude salt for trading against maize and sugar, moves in a long file across a desolate landscape of the same hazy endlessness as the plains of central Asia. Three hundred years ago similar caravans carried silver to the Spanish fleets and before that the caravans carried the gold and harvest of the Incas.

Our knowledge of the early distribution of the llama has been confused by the domestication of the animal in pre-Colombian times, and the diffusion of highland culture that followed the expansion of the Inca Empire. Some Spanish chronicles record 'a beast of burden' said to have been described by an Indian chief in Panama who made a drawing of a camel or possibly a female elk. It is unlikely that llamas were taken by the highland tribes as far as Darien, but southern Colombia does contain a region called the Paramo de Guanaco and there is a possibility that some early contact was established between the tribes of Panama and northern South America, enabling a vague description of the animal to filter northwards.

Some llamas were kept in the oasis-valleys of the coastal desert of Peru at the time of the Conquest, but they are absent from this region now; possibly they were a different species and able to withstand the unusual climate, though it seems more likely that they were maintained from special breeding-flocks kept in the Sierra. Today, the distribution of the llama extends from Riobamba near the Equator to the northern provinces of Argentina and Chile, with only a few gaps in north Peru where it has been replaced effectively by sheep and cattle. Throughout their modern range llamas are restricted to the highlands and do not thrive below eight thousand feet; some are kept in zoos without too much difficulty, but specimens in the warm climate of Lima for example seem to lack the fine pelage of sierra animals.

In its homeland, the llama is the most valuable possession of the traditional Indian; transistor radios, galvanized iron roofs for homes and new bicycles might have assumed some importance in the communities near main urban centres, but outside these places, the llama is the most important animal of the sierra. In the first Spanish reports from the New World, were noted the strange Peruvian sheep kept by the Indians and the mistake was due possibly to some parallels that can be made between the flocks of Europe and the Andean llamas. For the Indian household, their animals give wool, transport and sometimes meat, but they are not used for milk. Within each flock, colours can vary from black to white, with many intermediate shades of brown, particularly the darker tones, and occasionally yellowish-orange.

Any animal with a pure colour is prized, and the commonest specimens are variagated, but with one or two predominant colours; sometimes a beast with as many as a dozen shades in small blotches stands out like a gaily-painted clown, though seemingly unaware of its comic quality. From the excellent range of colours, the Indians shear and select the wool at the beginning of the summer. Each of the colours is separated and the fine hairs are teased into a soft mass to be spun by hand. The spinning usually is a feminine craft, though men and boys of some regions are adept; on long journeys they carry wool and a simple distaff, so they can spin along the way. Homespun yarn lacks strength until woven, but is turned into crude garments or typical ponchos that serve both as a coat and blanket in even the toughest Andean conditions.

At one time, all Indian clothes used only the shades of raw wool, or simple colours from mineral or herbal pigments, but with the introduction of bright organic dyes, the Indian women were prepared to change the fashion and particularly the Aymara around Lake Titicaca are now wearing costumes that brighten the bleak landscape with splashes of vivid red, blue and green. Perhaps the careless appreciation of brilliant hues and an indiscriminate use of such combinations as fluorescent pink and primrose yellow is an upsurging creative rebellion against centuries of repression and life in a harsh climate. Their ancestors did not have the opportunity for experiments in colour and yet examples of the ancient Peruvian weaving using cottons and wool are certainly the finest of the type known to the world. The Paracas peninsular on the desert coast of Peru, about two hundred and fifty miles south of Lima was the home of a culture that existed several centuries before the Conquest, and in a series of excavations, archaeologists uncovered a burial ground of hundreds of well-preserved mummy bundles. Some of the finest Paracas bindings are eighty-four feet long and over thirteen feet wide. A few are patterned with exquisite figures of warriors or trophy heads, while others have stylized animal designs or strangely ornate demons. All the colours are naturally occurring browns, reds and yellows, with rich touches of indigo – at least one hundred and fifty hues have been counted – and artistic and technical ability of the Paracas level has not been retained. Today a synthetic gawdiness has replaced the techniques of the traditional Indian craftsman.

Alpacas (Lama pacos) are smaller than the llama, with longer and finer wool giving the animal a status of increasing importance. Many wool and skin products are sold through the centres of Cusco, Sicuani and La Paz; and fetch a high price in the European and North American markets; often the fine skins are made up of two or three pelts from young alpacas which come available in reasonable quality from young that fail to survive more than a few days after being born. The fine quality of alpaca wool is sometimes used as an argument for a hybrid origin of the animal and the possibility that either accidentally or by design of primitive man, llamas and vicuñas were crossed to provide the raw material for better clothing. Alpacas are well-adapted to high level conditions and they have a high respiration rate as well as an extremely high red-cell count. Some alpaca-like remains have been found in the pampas of Argentina, but today, alpacas have a restricted distribution from southern Peru and north Bolivia to a few isolated pockets in the Andes of northern Argentina and these areas are both high and cold.

Another theory more generally accepted is that the alpacas are a distinct species that was widespread in the Andean regions at one time, and that since the late Pleistocene the range has been limited slowly until they could exist only in a highly specialized habitat. Then at some stage in the past, primitive man realized the value of the wool and began to domesticate the few surviving flocks. Careful husbandry appears to be necessary for the development of the herds and the animals are segregated according to age, sex and intended use: breeding is often aided by Indian farmers who say that their help is necessary for coitus to occur. This, possibly, is a sign of long domestication, though more likely the practice is part of the ritualization of the llamoids in the ancient culture. Some proof for this might be that some wild alpaca herds were reputedly surviving in the nineteenth century.

Most alpacas are pure brown or black, or occasionally pure white; unlike llamas they are seldom multicoloured and the hair is long over much of the body. On the face, the hair is short and thick, but often is covered by long hairs from the forehead: the metatarsal glands that show clearly on a llama are obscured on alpacas. If the hair is not sheared it sometimes grows into a shaggy coat which can reach the ground. Two breeds have been known since pre-Colombian times: the common *huacaya* and the *suri* and possibly a third is *chili* (Cardozo). The true origin of these breeds is unknown, though it is suggested that the ancient Peruvians developed the suri for the fine wool needed for clothing; perhaps the huacaya is the original alpaca and the chili a cross between the two breeds. The Indians are able to select the finest wools for the market and shearing is done with a knife (or shears) every two years, though a few are saved for a further season so the hair has a chance to grow to maximum length. Yields of up to fifteen pounds of fleece from one animal are normal.

Two common hybrids are derived from the alpaca. A female llama and male alpaca produce a *huarizo* and a female alpaca and male llama give a *mixti*. Both crosses are fairly common in regions where the species are kept together and the hybridization between alpacas, llamas and the two wild camelids is almost unknown except in controlled conditions. Llamas and guanacos will cross to give llama-guanacos, llamas and vicuñas have been known to cross to yield a llama-vicuña and alpacas will cross with guanacos to give another huarizo – the paco-guanaco. Male vicuña bred with female alpacas give a paco-vicuña, which has some of the qualities of fine vicuña fur and alpaca quantity. The cross is not entirely successful and by the third generation the proportion of infertile crosses is very high; however since the arrival of the Spanish and perhaps from times long before, paco-vicuña crosses have been tried with the same enthusiasm as alchemists looked for a way to make gold. Several owners in Peru have small groups of the breed, and their experiments continue to be interesting but so far unprofitable. There is no doubt that a breeding paco-vicuña would be a money-spinner, particularly when its fleece is similar to the fast disappearing vicuña.

The late Francisco Paredes at the Hacienda Cala Cala a few miles north of Lake Titicaca in Peru, managed to develop a large herd of vicuña and paco-vicuña crosses. He was perhaps the foremost breeder and his work led to a fine collection of animals grouped according to the percentage of vicuña strain. Obviously, the results were exhibited in the quality of the wool where the fine vicuña wool of six to ten microns was represented in a paco-vicuña wool of fifteen to twenty microns, or even finer dependent on the cross. Unfortunately, much of the Paredes work was an extremely personal research and at the time of his death the recognition of specific crosses in the herd of over six hundred animals could only be left in less skilled hands.

In 1969, the hacienda was acquired by the Peruvian Government, under the Agrarian Reform, and now has been established as an experimental centre; Government specialists will have to start from scratch, and attempt to classify many hybrids mostly resembling vicuñas.

Vicuñas and guanacos are the truly wild llamoids and some taxonomists consider them both within the same genus as their domesticated relatives, while others prefer to classify the vicuña separately. The guanaco (Lama guanicoe) is slightly smaller than a llama, reaching about forty-three inches to the shoulder and a weight of nearly two hundred and fifty pounds: it is slimmer and possesses an almost uniform pelage for the species. They have a rich, tawny brown fur shading to a lighter colour nearly white ventrally; around the eyes the hair is whitish and there are light areas on the chin, lips and ear edges. Slight variations seem to distinguish the animals from some regions, and the high Atacama guanacos have a dusty faded colour that merges well with the dull arid semi-desert.

Of all the llamoids the guanaco has the widest distribution and altitude range in modern times, though in the Pleistocene it is known that guanacos occurred along most of the Andes from Colombia south to Tierra del Fuego, and from the west coast eastwards to Paraguay and the Argentine pampas. High in south Colombia the Paramo de Guanacos is one clue to the relatively recent distribution and a similarly named area extends into the Bolivian Chaco. The animals are absent from these places today, though they are found from north central Peru through parts of Bolivia to southern Chile. Occasionally, bands of guanaco travel down to the Pacific coast along the north Peru desert where they feed on the short loma vegetation, but in the southern latitudes the ability to range between widely different altitudes is more pronounced. From the Andes of Argentina and Chile, where some small herds are found at over 14,000 feet, other groups are known on the pampas of Argentina, and south to the steppe-land of Patagonia where until early this century they were a common feature of the plains fauna. They are even known to swim between the islands of southern Chile, and a small herd has been introduced and is well established on Staats Island in the Falkland Islands.

Like all the Andean camels, the guanaco has a peculiar brand of inquisitiveness. Unless they belong to a group which have been heavily persecuted, they seem to have little fear of any danger and stand and stare, almost motionless for a long time. A Land Rover or lone hiker is permitted to move within a distance of thirty or forty yards before the group walks slowly away: any sudden movement, prolonged attention or attempt to close the distance and the band breaks away quickly. Llamoids seem to eye any intruder with an intelligent stare; their tall necks stretch upwards and with ears erect they give an impression of haughty intelligence which seems to challenge the stranger daring to enter their territory. Though generally they retreat, sometimes they can be aggressive. Llamas and alpacas will occasionally rear up on their hind legs and strike with their forefeet, and their habit of spitting seems universal: usually they eject part of the stomach contents forcibly as a form of defence. One male vicuña was kept at the ruins of Machu Picchu for several years, and it was free to wander along the grassy terraces where tourists could take photographs. After a couple of seasons the animal developed an intense hate for all female visitors and became notorious for watching them and craftily edging into a position that it would use to make an attack. In the early stages possibly it was provoked but towards the end of its 'residence', the sight of any woman tourist was sufficient to make the vicuña charge. Later a few more docile alpacas were sent to graze there and the vicuña was sent to Cusco.

The Vicuña (Vicugna vicugna) is the smallest of the four species and possesses a superficial resemblance to a small guanaco, though the neck is relatively longer and the body has a slender build. No other Neotropic mammal has the same grace and delicate beauty as the vicuña, which is exhibited to perfection when the animal is running at high-speed. The ears are forced down and its neck reaches forward so that the body is streamlined like a greyhound on a track. Suddenly the animal is wildlife in action at its best and over level ground a band of vicuñas has been timed at thirty miles per hour, perhaps not a record at sea level, but remarkable at 13,000 feet.

One of my most impressive sightings of this rare animal was in the high semi-desert above Arequipa, behind the perfect volcano of El Misti. The main southern route to Puno traverses the region and for a long time it was thought that vicuñas had disappeared from there. However in 1967 my wife was certain she had seen a small troop at dusk near El Descanso Soltaro and we returned there in late 1969 to check as much of the area as possible.

After a few hours on the plateau, it was clear that vicuña or guanaco were around as we had passed several well-worn animal trails; and some of the distinctive communal voiding places. We then drove to a slightly lower level, around 14,000 feet, and entered a desert bathed in wisps of mist and dappled sunlight: not too surprisingly we found the vicuña – only a tiny group of four – but exquisitely coloured in the gentle, unreality of a ghostly wasteland.

It is the fine vicuña fleece which is so highly prized and in great demand for the luxury fur market, unhappily to the detriment of the species. The colour is soft, creamy brown shading to white on the ventral side, with white patches on the chin under the eyes, the underside of the tail and the flanks. Each of these areas has a value, and the trade uses every section, with the result that a fine bedcover can be made of a dozen large lateral pieces with the fine gradation of colour; or shin pieces from two or three hundred animals are sewn together to give a blanket of lesser quality. All of the richly coloured wool is silky-fine and there is very high density of fibres – an adaptation to its high altitude environment.

At present the vicuña has a distribution range from about latitude 9° 30′ S as far as the high mountains of northern Chile, south Bolivia and northern Argentina – about latitude 24° S. Until this century the zone occupied by the species was continuous, but recent persecution has been disastrous and now only pockets of the animals survive – even in the most typical part of its distribution range, the highlands of central Peru, the species has all but disappeared between 9° 30′ S. and 13° 30′ S.

Armchair conservationists and the recent governments of Andean South America cannot be criticized harshly enough; their attitude has been to neglect the problem or to turn the situation to political advantage. Such a sweeping generalization would be unfair in most countries, but only recently one minister of an Andean Republic was unable to estimate, even approximately, the vicuña population within his country, and the trusted guards on the only reserve were willing to sell the animals at not much more than a dollar. From Inca days, the vicuña has received some measure of protection, and for the peasants of the ancient highland civilizations, killing or molesting a vicuña was a crime punishable by death: Simon Bolívar continued the tradition with similarly strict laws, but the present international trade

ndean Gull (summer plumage)

Agouti: Manu Park, Peru

Vicuña Band *(Vicugña vicugña)*

together with the availability of automatic weapons could soon force the extinction of the animals in the wild.

A lone battle for the vicuña has been fought over the past few years by Sr. Felipe Benavides Barreda who in his native Peru is an active conservationist as well as a member of the country's oldest family. Don Felipe is also a Trustee of the World Wildlife Fund and on visits to Europe he has attempted to explain the difficulties that impede conservation work in South America. Unfortunately when he visited London he had to make it clear to the Press that the most serious problem was the unrestricted import of vicuña products into Britain and that as the export of any vicuña material was technically prohibited from Peru, Bolivia, Argentina and Chile, the British dealers were trading openly in contraband. Don Felipe tried to put his case to the Board of Trade; initially he was unsuccessful and as well as receiving the usual courtesy of an offer of an investigation, a representative of the Board suggested that Peru should tighten her own laws and prevent any illegal export. Though the suggestion was illogical, Don Felipe returned to Peru and with immediate help from the Revolutionary Government a new Vicuña Law (Decreto Supremo 17816) was signed by President Velasco. Hunting vicuña – prison for one to three years; trading in vicuña – prison for three to five years, with, additionally, severe fines for possession of vicuña fleeces and obstructing game wardens or police in their duty.

In 1970, Don Felipe's efforts were rewarded. The United States included vicuña on a list of animals and animal products that by law were not allowed to be imported into the U.S.A. Later in the same year Britain also banned the import of vicuña skins and hair; the announcement was made to the press jointly by the Fauna Preservation Society and World Wildlife Fund. The success of the British campaign was largely due to the enthusiastic support given to Sr. Benavides by conservationists who managed to put forward a strong case to the Board of Trade.

With new legislation in Peru, Britain and the U.S.A. the Peruvian vicuña population seemed safe, but there was a loop-hole. In Bolivia, the revolution-wracked neighbour, the laws were not so clearly defined, or if clear, could be circumvented. In La Paz, vicuña products were on sale openly even as late as early 1971 with one of two legal reasons to protect the dealer. Either the pelts were said to be old stock or it was claimed the pelts came from

7

animals found dead. In each case the law would protect the trader and in the Andes a slight chink in the armour is enough to make a farce of any judicial action. Adding to Don Felipe's problems was the convention signed by Bolivia, Argentina and Peru which fixed a joint policy for the defence of the rare animal, and which Bolivia had failed to comply with. The agreement was signed by General Rene Barrientos who was killed in a helicopter accident in 1969 and succeeding presidents were too occupied with domestic problems to follow-up the vicuña problem until Don Felipe made a personal visit to President General Ovando who promised to act. On the face of it, there is not much of a problem in the Bolivian sector as the vicuña population was seriously low by the end of the sixties, but a well recognized trade has long existed across the frontier: animals from Peruvian reserves are killed and their skins smuggled to the neighbouring country. The extent of the trade was so great that there was some doubt about the survival of the species outside a few reserves. A great part of the Andes is wild and many areas are ideal for vicuña, but the small Andean camel has disappeared: shot, trapped and skinned, the vicuñas have been reduced from half a million twenty-five years ago to less than ten thousand today – in fact the figure is likely to be less.

It is a sad truth that the fine quality of the fur of the vicuña is responsible for the near extinction of the species. Until recently in La Paz it has been easy to purchase a bedcover made of the pelts of a dozen young vicuña, totally in the luxury class of Hollywood film mogul appeal, and the price a mere £100. At a New York store or in London, the same article costs between four and five times as much, while back on the cold Andean puna, the Indian asks just one dollar, or roughly 37 pence, for a salted skin. Bedcovers, coats, fashionable-wraps made from smaller pieces of vicuña cost only slightly less and then additionally there is the trade in wool.

Each vicuña produces about one pound of wool annually, but much of the wool on sale is from animals trapped or shot for the trade. Usually the fibres are between six and eleven microns, roughly seven times finer than human hair, though guard hairs are somewhat coarser. Even fine merino is almost three and a half times as coarse as vicuña, and so the high prices paid for vicuña knitted or woven cloth are easily understood. A fine scarf for evening wear is light, warm, soft and so fine that it can be drawn through a wedding ring: by this test a shopkeeper in the Andes sells a scarf for £20. In London, in 1970, vicuña cloth was selling at £115 per yard.

Not many people can afford to pay these prices, though the demand is high enough to keep the trade moving. However, now another problem enters the already murky arena. With only about 10,000 vicuña left in the Andes and a quarter of that total in reserves and three-quarters widely scattered, how does enough vicuña wool reach the market to satisfy even a small demand? So far investigations have failed to answer the question, but fine alpaca wool can be as little as fifteen microns, guanaco roughly similar and there are the paco-vicuñas with very high quality fur. Most of these animals occur in colours very close to vicuña and so 'pure vicuña' wool fetching astronomic prices in world centres of good life, is likely to be from another camel – possibly not even one from the western hemisphere.

The status of the species in highly accurate terms is difficult to define: vicuña territory is often wild, remote and not always within reach of a road. Since 1961 my own travels have followed not only the trails into the Peruvian central sierras, but to some of the distant corners of vicuña distribution in the southern provinces of Bolivia. Some bands have been thinned out from fifteen to less than five or even three and the situation is desperate. At this moment, the only hope rests in the success of one reserve in Peru, at Pampa Galeras in the Department of Ayacucho. Only fifty miles from the desert town of Nasca, the reserve is at over 13,500 feet and covers six thousand five hundred hectares (16,250 acres) where approximately seven thousand animals (1973) are guarded by wardens of the Dirección Forestal. Another concentration of vicuña occurs only a few miles eastward near Puquio where as many as three hundred have been counted. Bolivian officials state they have 'about' one hundred and fifty animals at Ulla Ulla near the Peru/Bolivia frontier north east of Lake Titicaca, and another 'unconfirmed' three hundred animals near Jesus de Machaca in Carangas, south of Lake Titicaca. Elsewhere, the groups are small, seldom seen, and data cannot be revised to keep pace with the poaching. Ulla Ulla has come under Bolivian reserves legislation, though any scheme of this nature has the in-built problems which face conservation in Latin America.

The most detailed recent study of the status of vicuña in Peru was the work of Ian Grimwood who studied the sierra regions in search of a site for a national park: his report has been the basis for the latest conservation measures. Other vicuña research was undertaken by Carl B. Koford, whose monograph is the leading reference work at present, though a doctoral candidate from Utah State University, Bill Franklin was studying group behaviour and inter-group relationships from 1968–1970. Franklin's efforts could lead to better management and eventually to establishing breeding groups from reserve stock re-settled in areas where the species has been lost.

Apart from the conservationists viewpoint, there is a strong argument for saving and studying the vicuña. The fine wool is established already as a luxury; expensive, yes, but highly marketable and there is an excellent case for commercial breeding of paco-vicuñas of high vicuña strain. Wool production would be higher than from the pure vicuña (roughly four to six pounds of fleece come from a paco-vicuña) and there is little difference in the quality. With the same colour and almost the same texture paco-vicuña wool would be accepted, as indeed it probably is already.

These are the weapons that Don Felipe Benavides is using in his campaign, and he is making headway. His main battlefields are widely separated. In Peru he has to see that bales of alpaca wool for export are checked – often vicuña has been smuggled out in the centre of alpaca consignments; and in other countries he has to prevent trading. The difficult task is not ended, but if he gets his way Don Felipe intends to slowly substitute legally produced fine wools for vicuña and save the species at the same time.

Vicuñas are not alone and the guanaco also is endangered: in parts of the central Andes it has almost vanished and in Patagonia the large herds have been decimated. The situation in Peru is more serious for the guanaco than for vicuña, and few animals are found in the wild. There are small bands in the south around Tacna and some in the central regions of Apurimac and Ayacucho; another reserve is the private land of Hacienda Calipuy near Santiago de Chuco where the owner had almost one thousand animals; they are culled frequently and an epidemic in 1969 cut the number to around two hundred and fifty. However the situation is controllable under present conditions, though a change in ownership could be disastrous. The guanaco of the central Andes are considered as the race *Lama guanicoe cacsilensis* by Cabrera, while he places the southern species as the nominate form, *L. guanicoe*. To the south distribution is patchy with small numbers in the high Atacama and northern Argentina and a similar sporadic pattern extending southwards nearly to the tip of the sub-continent.

Unhappily, the extreme isolation of some regions where vicuña and guanaco manage to survive is no limitation to the resourceful hunter and in the desolate southlands of the Bolivian Altiplano bands of vicuña are so intensely nervous that they begin to run for cover at the sound of a distant jeep; when a band is feeding the male leader gives a high pitched whistling cry as a danger signal and all the females run as a group along the shortest line to the crest of a hill, while the male stands alone before racing away behind. If the male is isolated, or shot the females often stop and appear confused; sometimes they can be caught easily in such circumstances but the usual reaction is some attempt to escape and they disappear within the security of the high valleys. Social organization of vicuña groups follows two forms; there are small bands of up to fifteen females with an adult male, and leaderless troops of males. The bands are strongly territorial, but troops range widely; if an alien male enters the territory, then the male leader breaks from the band and vigorously chases the intruder – this behaviour is easily observed at Pampa Galeras where many groups are close together. Females tend to move away from the approaching male, almost bowing to the male dominance, and also, adult females dislike the close approach of other females in the group: interference leads to a display of aggression with kicking and spitting. Peacefully grazing vicuña become highly emotional with any of these intrusions, and they react quickly. Chasing or butting suddenly disturbs the placid groups, only quietening as each provocation is resolved.

The male of the band is clearly sure of his territory and intruding males can only enter to a well-defined limit before there is a reaction from the resident male. In his research at Pampa Galeras, Franklin divided the area by means of stone piles at intervals: and with trained assistants, his observation of groups in daylight was continuous. One line of interest was the attempts of non-resident males or females to join established bands. Females of neighbouring bands are not allowed to join an established band, but unattached females are admitted without concern – a not unreasonable attitude for the male to take. On the other hand, the encounters between males are more aggressive and if a roaming troop approaches, the resident male rushes out and takes a stand, posturing before the invaders; the action is often repeated two, three or even more times, gradually moving the male troop away. Sometimes, the fights between males are prolonged, often occurring between male leaders of bands on neighbouring territory. At these times the kicking and biting is accompanied by high pitched shrieks which carry for miles across the open puna.

The vicuña, being so fast over open territory, has few natural enemies: Andean Foxes, the mountain cat (Felis colocolo) make the groups wary. Possibly pumas might attack them, but the vicuña can outpace everything in the Andes, and only determined hunters can run them down. Often working from horseback with dogs, or from a pair of four-wheel drive vehicles, poachers have taken a great toll. One other problem faces the remaining vicuña, particularly those in the Pampa Galeras reserve. Vicuña and livestock frequently compete for pasture and the reserve is still in part claimed by the community of Lucanus, nearby. Llamas, a few alpaca and sheep are allowed to graze on reserve land and this is an inhibiting factor; the domesticated animals favour the same soft puna grasses and broad-leafed herbs that are eaten by vicuña. At present not much can be done; Lucanas farmers need the land for their animals – it is just another matter for Don Felipe to solve.

A fully grown vicuña weighs not much more than one hundred pounds and many of them are slightly less: like the other llamoids, metatarsal glands are present but completely covered by heavy short hairs and the skull also has some distinct differences. The lower incisors are ever-growing, parallel-sided and rootless with enamel on the labial side only, whereas those teeth of the other llamoids are rooted. Some features make the simple classification of the vicuña impossible, and similarly the origin of the llamas and alpacas is questionable. Most probably the guanaco and vicuña are the wild representatives of two distinct genera, and both llamas and alpacas are sufficiently distinctive domesticated species to be considered as members of the same genus as the guanaco. However, counter arguments are cited readily by taxonomists who oppose the two genera system. It is simple to point out similarities between the alpaca and vicuña such as their continuously growing lower incisors, their short snouts and concealed metatarsal glands; they are of almost the same size which is a feature that also can be used to relate the llama and guanaco. But by taking the simplest criteria, colour similarities would more readily associate a guanaco with a vicuña. This riddle is likely to remain with zoologists for a long time and so leave the vicuña as either Vicugna vicugna or Lama vicugna according to the choice of the writer.

The habits and reproductive cycle of the four species follow the same pattern, though the domestication of llamas and alpacas must be taken into account. Rutting is usually late in the Andean summer, and the single, or rarely two precocious young are born about ten or eleven months later at a time when vegetation is best in the arid highlands. They wean quickly within half a year, and vicuñas are mature in twelve months while the guanaco takes between two and three years. Indian herdsmen give considerable attention to the selection of their animals in the domesticated species and older beasts are taken from the herds for meat, and in recent years for sale in the large fur markets. Llamas are usually considered as beasts of burden and meat producers; alpacas are kept for wool and rarely used for carrying cargo.

Communal voiding places are typical in llamoid country and the wild species have particular areas in their range where they feed, find water and defaecate. On the high southern deserts, the area favoured by a band of guanaco or vicuña can be traced, firstly by any positive geographical limitation – hills, good water and shelter – or by the obvious patches of dung that permanently mark the open surface of the ground. Each bolus is tiny and hardly an inch in diameter, like that of a sheep, but the Indians collect llama dung for fuel because other material is scarce. The same areas have favourite wallowing grounds which are used frequently, possibly to remove irritating ectoparasites. On one occasion, along the sandy eastern shore of the Laguna Colorada in South Bolivia, a group of seven vicuñas went about their dust bath ritual and one after another they rolled and writhed in the shallow depressions they had made after long use of the place. Their cleansing was carried out with great enthusiasm and each one contorted vigorously, twisting over on to its back and working fore and hind limbs with the frenzy of a worried escapologist. After a good scrub in the earth, the vicuña would get out of the pit and join the rest of the band watching unconcernedly nearby. The small dust storm was the only indication of this powdery-sauna, and the trace was visible for almost ten miles across the clear Andean hillsides. Llamas and alpacas roll in dust in a similar way to rid themselves of lice (llama mallophaga louse Trichodectes breviceps) and a small mite (llama itch mite – Sarcoptes scabei aucheniae) which is probably the carrier of a mange that occasionally sweeps through the herds. A liver fluke is a common parasite in some areas, though there is no certainty that the alpacas are more prone to infestation in spite of their preference for high marshy ground. One Indian belief is that they must not let their alpacas drink from stagnant pools which are considered to be the source of a severe intestinal malady. Another disease is referred to (in Bolivia) as *Karachi* or the Alpaca syphilis (Pyosepticemia) is specific to alpacas, which suffer a chronic fever and an inflammation in the genital region. The attack is accompanied by outbursting pustules that quickly develop into serious lesions; an Indian cure is often effective, and they rub the area with a pomade of lard and oxide of mercury. The age-old story that the spirochete syphilis disease of man appearing in 1493 in Italy was introduced to the Old World by the Spanish, after their contact with the Indians or llamoids of the Andes is known to be untrue. Careful research has shown that the syphilis bacteria (Treponema pallidum) does not exist in any of the Neotropical camelids and the Alpaca disease is caused by a coccus.

With their livelihood closely tied to their animals, the Indians are afraid of many evil spirits that they believe must enter the body of the beast and cause ill-health. For some epidemic conditions where the hundreds of animals owned by a community are in danger, the villagers call upon the local witchdoctor to perform magical rites to release the illness; at other times the Indian family will attempt a simple cure with wild herbs or heavily minera-lized earths; even the pounded carapace of crabs or cray-fish are burnt in the corral as part of a simple magic that highland people continue to respect.

After centuries of domestication, vicuñas, llamas and alpacas are asso-ciated inseparably from the life and religion of Andean Indians. One high-land saying

'No vendas tu tela antes de esquilar tus llamas'
is translated
'Don't sell the cloth before shearing the llama'
obviously means much the same as one of our own proverbs. Older and from the *Quechua Indians* of Peru is a reference to their god Viracocha

Purun wikkuna
Qaqa wiskkacha
Uywaman tukun
Paypaj qayllanpi

The vicuña on the high desert
The viscacha among the rocks
Make their homes
Around him.

Garcilaso de la Vega, a chronicler who wrote soon after the Conquest said 'there was only one deity which all the Collas united in worshipping and holding as their principle god. This was a white sheep, for they were lords of innumerable flocks. They said that the first sheep in the upper earth – heaven – had taken more care of them than the other Indians, and that it showed its love for them by leaving them a larger posterity in the land of the Collas than in any other land of the whole world'.

The Collas were the ancient tribes which lived around Lake Titicaca and the part that now is north Bolivia; they were the ancestors of the modern *Aymara Indians* who continue to have great reverence for the llamas and alpacas in the face of an imposition of Christianity by the Spanish priests. To the north in the Inca land, the heart of the Peruvian Quechua territory, the Indians worshipped the black llama or alpaca and in some places today a black alpaca is sacrificed at the ceremony of *wifafa*. Folk-tales and magic survive everywhere in the mountains, but the Indians are seldom willing to discuss their beliefs; after four hundred years of Catholicism with the widespread distrust of any stranger, it is hard to uncover the truthful details of the traditional practices. Sacrifices were common in pre-Colombian times and a monthly slaughter of a hundred animals would be made at the command of the Inca; on special feast days a thousand or more beasts were sacrificed in Cusco at the principle temple, and the *Inti Raymi* at the mid winter solstice was a festival that has continued in one form to the present day. Such large scale sacrifices of llamas are no longer common and the Indian has developed a great fondness for his livestock; he offers a beast only when some disaster seems imminent, and most minor sacrifices are made with sheep or the household guinea pigs. However, some communities cling to the ancient lore and resist any change: in Peru the high puna of Chumbivilcas is a region where the people continue to adhere to customs, and in Bolivia, both the cordilleras to the north east of Lake Titicaca and the great southern Altiplano are strongholds of magic and Indian lore. The Chipaya Indians of Carangas, a province west of Oruro, sacrifice a llama before building a new home, and fresh blood is splashed across the walls leaving deep brown stains to ward off bad luck. In the same area, all the Indians gather their flocks of sheep and llamas together in May; herding them into large corrals where they hold them overnight before making at least one sacrifice at sunrise. The villagers of Jesus de Machaca, near the River Desaguadero, have for years killed as many as four hundred sheep on the same day, afterwards they cut the meat into strips for drying in the sun which gives *charque*, a meat that keeps for many months.

When animals are killed the females might hold a foetus and this is particularly prized. Along market rows of the Altiplano villages, or in one narrow street of La Paz, buxom Aymara women have baskets of herbs and medicines as well as several assorted foetuses dried carefully and stored. A week or two after the month for killing, the baskets are filled with these weird fetishes of half-formed animals, and the suspicious vendors cover them quickly with a cloth to escape the evil-eye of a camera. Of all the Aymara magic, the symbol of unborn life, an image of the ancient Colla supreme deity is retained as the most powerful magic. The foetus is buried in the foundations of a house, or carried to hilltop shrines by the strongly conservative Indians whose faith has been confused so much that they carry a picture of Christ in their pocket and put a cross on their roof.

Beliefs surrounding llamas and their relatives are extremely numerous, and apart from sacrifices to counter evil spirits, the animals were used for divination in Inca times, when the priests would examine the entrails of a slaughtered beast and give a prognosis from the things they saw. Clay images of llamas are buried in the present day under the puna where the flocks are put to graze; with the certainty that the animals will live unharmed for a year. This practice was more extensive in pre-Colombian times when tiny llama figurines, or woollen llama toys were buried with the dead in the highlands and on the coast. Wool from llamas is dyed and used for magic, and the closeness of the Indian to his animals is apparent from other Aymara witchcraft. In one spell, an Indian will take strands of hair from a llama owned by his victim. The wool is twisted into a miniature rope that is tied around the neck of a frog or small mammal and the creature is in turn tied to a bush or stone near the victim's house: if it dies the owner of the llama is believed to die at the same time.

Like other ruminants, the Andean camelidae have hard concretions in the stomach: these are bezoars or bezoar stones. For the Indians, the presence of these objects gives another method of divination. They look at the number, the shapes and the relationship, then the witchdoctor gives his advice – bezoars can be good and bad luck, and most Indians carry the lucky ones in their pouches.

Many llamas are decorated with coloured tassels and this custom is practised in an extreme around Chumbivilcas while elsewhere only simple tufts of wool are tied to the furry ears. Such adornments are intended for several purposes: they help by identifying individual animals, especially those of good parentage that will be useful for breeding and among the regular herds also the tassels take the place of amulets intended to bring good luck or fertility. Before the introduction of other livestock by the Spanish, far more care was taken in dividing the llama herds; the young of four to twelve months were the *unakuna*, from one to three years *malta una*, with other names and divisions for sterile adults, load-bearing adults and the different colours. In those days the llamas were the property of the Inca and his princes. Individual beasts and sometimes small herds would be given as presents to officials of special rank, and shepherding was work for many peasants. Laws of state controlled the movement of flocks and their care. Bestiality was recognized as an unnatural act and even in Colonial times the communities had rules to prevent a lone herder taking animals on a journey. Forbes, one of the foremost scholars to study the Andes in the last century, commented 'It is well known however that such unnatural intercourse is common and that under the Incas severe laws were enacted against it. Even after the Spanish conquest, an old law not permitting the llama drivers to start on their journeys unless accompanied by their wives was retained in force; and this regulation was intended to safeguard against such abuses'. ... Possibly this ruling has never been repealed formally and is now lost within the disruptions that changed Colonies into Republics, but the Indians are seldom alone with the llamas and much of the shepherding is left traditionally to women and children.

Llamas graze on the march, or on rough puna pasture and at nightfall they are driven to villages or isolated homes where they are corralled for protection against the wily fox or rare attack by a puma. With the change of season, the herds are moved to better ground in the bottom of high valleys for the coldest months, and for this migration which might only be a short distance, a few shepherds and their families build simple huts from puna grass to provide shelter while they guard the herd. Often the corral in these places is made from a low wall of stones, and even a single rope around each group of llamas is enough to keep them together at night. Their occasional low bleat, almost a moan, or the sudden shrill cry of a tinamou is the only sound to break the total silence of the high sierras. Life of all kinds has changed little in the centuries of civilization and the constant care of the herds will assure the survival of llamas and alpacas for a long time.

For the two wild species, the story may be different and as both vicuña and guanaco are declining quickly, something has to be done. Until the arrival of the Conquistadores, the rules of the Inca and his princes across the Four Quarters of the Sun Kingdom were enough to protect the animals and some ancient customs helped to retain a balanced and healthy population of the species. Great hunts – *chacus* – were held every three or five years and some provinces were established as reserves specifically for this purpose. At the command of the Inca, as many as forty thousand Indians would be gathered together and formed into a circle encompassing entire mountains and valleys of a radius more than ten miles. Gradually the vast ring of beaters would move across the land, driving all the wildlife in front of them towards a large corral built in the neck of a valley or ravine. The animals retreated into the trap: hundreds of vicuña, guanaco, some frightened pumas, the unwary bear and a host of tiny foxes, deer and game birds. The task was enormous, undertaken amidst great shouting, an operation that was guaranteed to provide vicuña wool, as well as the skins of older animals and a vast supply of pelts from other species. Once the chacu was completed, the stocktakers are said to have made counts of live animals and their condition and recorded the numbers on ancient string *quipus*, a form of primitive mnemonic device that has been discovered but never diciphered.

The majority of the animals were released and their royally protected status was accepted by everyone. In the palaces and halls of the Sun Virgins, young girls were set to work making some of the finest cloth garments ever used and only the Inca and his chosen lieutenants had the privilege of wearing the magnificent golden fleece. Always soft to the touch, and naturally a perfect insulation against the biting sierra coldness, the vicuña cloth was a respected mark of rank. Today, anyone with a good cheque book can buy the skins of a hundred animals; fashioned to order by the skill of a modern craftsman they are eventually worth many times the original price. Only a few animals survive today after the almost ceaseless trading of the past years; and at last the considerate intervention by enlightened governments seems to offer a chance for the species to recover. But, if the traders of contraband discover an outlet in a country where import restrictions are not in force, then the vicuña might disappear forever from the wild fortresses of the Incas.

Folklore and Fauna

In a distant corner of the Bolivian Cordillera Real, to the east of the high inland sea of Titicaca and between the precipitous hills of Charazani, a group of villages nestle in the security of the mountains. Hidden with these isolated settlements is a school of learning as old as the first sierra empires: an association of Indian men, eminent in the understanding of native medical science. Even today from Ecuador to Argentina, along the entire length of the Andes, *Kallawaya* doctors from this tiny region are traditional consultants to the highland people. For a small fee they will recommend a live dragonfly under your hat as a cure for a headache, or for other illnesses they carry in their shoulder bags an array of love-charms, potions and weird fetishes. As modern surgery progresses to the transplant, some simple Indian remedies have an almost laughable quaintness but not quite: some of their cures work and are now world-famous.

The Kallawayas live on the edge of Aymara territory and as well as the Aymara language, they speak Quechua, Spanish and a strange dialect of their own which is believed to be similar to the tongue of the ancient Colla tribe which occupied the southern quarter of the Andes long before the Inca Empire expansion. No reasonable explanation has been suggested for the existence of this highly individualistic clan though it is possible that they developed through the good fortune of living in a place half way between the cold, sterile Altiplano and the warm, eastern lowlands which gave the group access to knowledge and contact with two types of culture. The climate of the narrow valleys also is ideal for the cultivation of wild herbs now known to be the natural source of many drugs. Quinine from the chinchona bark, cocaine, curare, hallucinogens, abortificaents, contraceptive agents and more; all these change an average herbalist into a competent pharmacologist and the Kallawayas have the knowledge to use each substance correctly, though simply in the native form. Schooling takes years, and their early days at collecting would make any naturalist particularly envious as they spend months in the forests searching highly inaccessible regions where generations of patient study has located specific plants and insects needed for their pharmacopaeia. Once the medicines are prepared, each is listed in a locally-held directory and the men can begin to practise wherever they are accepted. Often they are away from their home villages of Curva and Charazani for two or three years continually travelling up and down the Andes, calling at the small adobe home of the Indians, and even the doors of some wealthy city-dwellers who are traditional customers. The craft of the Kallawayas is based on science and beliefs rooted in the earliest days of South American civilization; alongside the witchdoctor or *yatiri* whose abilities cover witchcraft and psychology, the Kallawayas help to perpetuate a tradition of extremely close contact with the living world of the Andes. A large percentage of the magico-medical folklore is related to ailments and evil-spirits, with a tremendous range of cures, mostly herbal, though by virtue of the limited numbers of high altitude species, much of the native fauna also possesses a significance.

In the central Andes of Peru and Bolivia, some armadillos are common and their hard carapaces serve as fetishes or are used on the back of small guitar-like instruments. All armadillos are Neotropical and belong to the order Edentata which includes sloths and South American anteaters; the order is one of the major groups that existed in the days when the sub-continent was a great island, completely isolated from the rest of the world. Like many other strange or remarkable animals they have been used and depicted by cartoonists as highly mobile, tank-like beasts which roll quickly into a ball and then either roll out of sight or defy the challenges of every assailant. Only one genus is true to this form: that is the Tolypeutes found in the lowland regions of Bolivia's Oriente and eastward to the Atlantic. Tolypeutes has a carapace well-shaped to allow the armour covering the head and tail to fit into the main shields as the animal curls up. Once in this position it is safe from most predators and even a dog is unable to grip the smooth 'sphere' and usually leaves it alone.

The defense of other species of armadillos rests with their fantastic ability to dig quickly and by using well-developed and powerful forelimbs and their hind feet as 'shovers', one of these incredible animals can disappear into the soil in less than a minute. Even a few seconds is enough time for them to escape below the ground level, and they cling to the inside walls of the tunnel protected at the sides by earth and by their carapace from over-head attack. The different genera have distinctive armour and the number of sections dividing the carapace has given the simple names of nearly all the species. A Nine-banded Armadillo (Dasypus novemcincus) that reaches three feet including a foot long tail is one of the most widely distributed; it occurs from the southern United States to north Argentina. In all sections of its range it is persecuted by Indians and peasant farmers as a source of pro-tein; after turning the meat into a meal, the natives use the carapace as a household container. A distinctive form is the rare Giant Armadillo (Prio-dontes giganteus) which can be as much as five feet long and weighing one hundred pounds: it is an inhabitant of lowlands east of the Andes and is fast disappearing. On one occasion in Bolivia, a friend telegraphed from a jungle town with news that Indians had arrived with two of these rare animals. At that time, local communications were chaotic – the normal state of affairs in semi-revolution days – and our cables passed slowly. After asking for photographs, an almost indignant reply came to La Paz with the information 'photography difficult, armadillo best mechanical excavator have seen'. The news made me even more determined to fly to the jungle and get some film and with plans ready for the following day, only a quick round trip, I went to bed. At seven next morning, the radio announced the Peoples Revolution and advised everyone to remain in-doors; by five in the afternoon the aircraft I should have returned on had crashed and forty-eight hours later the armadillos had been eaten. The chain of incidents left me wondering whether armadillos were lucky or not.

The Fairy Armadillo (Chlamyphorus truncatus) just five inches long is found usually in the Andean foothills around Mendoza in the westernmost province of Argentina. Locally they are called Pichy Ciego – 'the blind pichy' – and in the family they are exceptional. They have a tiny jointed carapace that is no more than a flattened semi-ossified shield attached only along the dorsal mid-line, and supported away from the body by long light yellow hairs. Within their range they were not uncommon at one time, but

ndean Goose *(Cloephaga melanoptera)*

ndean Fox

Condor *(Vultur gryphus)*

since the beginning of this century urban progress has cut into the native habitat.

Armadillos are found in many different regions of Neotropica, from the hot dry valleys in the south eastern Andes to the wetter, forested slopes astride the Equator, or even on the lowland pampas. The Nine-banded Armadillo is found in the tree zone as high as ten thousand feet and a species of another genus, the hairy *Chaetophractus nationi* inhabits the deserts of Bolivia's southern Altiplano and is the highest-living example of the family. However, most species are known from the lowlands of Brazil, Paraguay and Argentina where they are a familiar feature of the fauna of the pampa or open woodlands. In their feeding habits they are almost pig-like and they busily tear up the earth with the claws on the fore-limbs and use their snouts to search out the insects, earthworms and grubs in the soil. Sometimes, they favour a decaying carcass and on the pampas it is usual to find at least one armadillo settled, almost in idyllic retirement beneath a dead cow. They make a burrow under the animals and scramble to the surface every time they need a meal; the flesh and the grubs that collect on it provide easy rations for a week or more. Although they are classed with sloths and anteaters as Edentates, the 'true' Edentate type did not have teeth, and of the forms existing today only the highly adapted anteater conform to the strict pattern; sloths and armadillos do possess simple teeth and the peg-like dentition of the armadillo is about the most primitive known in any mammal. Of the nine genera only Dasypus has a set of almost milk teeth that precede all but the last of the nine permanent pegs; the others have an extremely simple formula characteristic of the order.

The armadillos tend to be nocturnal, though on the pampas they are occasionally seen in the midday, lying on their backs seemingly fast asleep in the sun. Their rosy, armoured life of food and sleep is only upset by the sudden appearance of a predator and they are quick to retreat into the safety of the ground. In the forest at night it is easy to surprise them, and their tell-tale scraping among the debris gives away their position so a flashlight can be used to mesmerize them for a second. If given the chance they can run quickly and the Tolypeutes flees across the pampas on the tips of its toes, moving at high speed with the agility of a dancer. Hunting by farmers and colonists in South America is not always a sport and the threat to a species

8

nearly always depends on the demand for food; though armadillos are noted for their delicate meat, some country people never take any trouble to catch them and only kill one if they encounter it on the trail. Two species are common in the Sierra Nevada of Santa Marta, but life there is good for the colonists and they would rather sit in the nearest bar than risk a night-time foray in the jungle where snakes, particularly the venomous corals and fer-de-lance are numerous. For the Giant Armadillo of the lowlands the situation is different as it is an excellent catch and consequently has become very rare in most areas. The high Andean species generally belong to the genus Euphractes or Chaetophractus; these are characterized by long hairs growing out from between the scutes, and Indians believe that the hairs must continue to grow after the death of the animal, otherwise foul luck will affect the household that owns the carapace. A small industry flourishes in the warm valley of the River Vilcanota below Pisac on the route to Machu Picchu, where craftsmen fashion guitar-like instruments, using the locally found armadillo carapace or '*quirquincho*' to form the body. Similarly, in the departments of Potosi and Oruro in Bolivia, the small *Chaetophractus nationi*, which is covered with long hairs, is in demand for making an instrument known locally as a '*charango*'. Only experts play anything that is recognizable but charangos are part of the Indian dress in the region, and while the puna man might carry a spinning spindle, the Indians of the warm valleys of Potosi herd their llamas along quiet dusty roads and pluck a few notes until the sound echoes faintly from the dull, cactus covered hillsides.

In the Bolivian capital of La Paz, a tiny street not far from the centre is lined with stalls of the witchdoctors' market. On display are boxes of dried starfish, llama grease and other materials needed for Indian magic. Each stall-keeper possesses at least one armadillo shell, usually the Nine-banded or local Chaetophractus: they are kept traditionally as a fetish with the belief that it will deter a thief. Any Aymara villain knows that he must never pass a carapace placed in an Indian doorway as a silent guardian, or he will quickly grow a nose as long and as comical as the pig-like snout of the living armadillo.

From the depths of Aymara folk-science and superstition, a witch's brew using animals, their excrement and vital organs can be concocted for every sierra malady. The heart of a skunk is eaten to help a woman in labour, the human amniotic fluid is taken for diseases of the gall-bladder, the Altiplano snake or *Asiro* (Aym) is eaten to restore male sexual vigour and a host of other remedies are prescribed by the Kallawayas or medicine men. Not all of the prescribed remedies are available from the Andes and some shellfish come from the relatively distant coasts of Chile and Peru; others, especially plant products are found in the jungle and traded at the headwaters of the great rivers.

On the other hand most Indian families keep cavies in their homes. Cavies are exclusively Neotropical Rodents and commonly called 'Guinea pigs'; they are one of the primary endemic forms and are classified in the Family Caviidae with the Capybara, Agouti and the Maras. *Cavia porcellus*, the Indian household *cui* has been domesticated since long before the Conquest, and it was one of the first animals recorded by the Spanish. In some areas pest-control squads have been actively destroying the animals in Indian homes as a precaution against the spread of bubonic plague, and fewer cavies are found in the villages of northern Peru and Ecuador than in the Titicaca region or Bolivia. Such treatment apparently upsets the Indians who have kept cavies for generations. The animals live in the Indian adobe houses where they are allowed to scurry around in darkness, foraging for the occasional scraps of food. Unless children collect some fruit or plants for the animals, most Indians take little care of them until they kill a few to make a tasty delicacy seasoned with hot spices. But the warm viscera can be used on a patient suffering from any intestinal pain and in many respects the cavy resembles our household aspirin and is used for many things. Sometimes as many as fifteen or twenty live with the Indians in a completely uncontrolled state, and the plaintive squeaking 'cui-cui' call has given the local name. All cavies resemble the guinea pig and are small and tailless, though the name is sometimes given to the Mara (Dolichotis) or Patagonian Hare, which is much larger.

Four genera are recognized and the two main groupings are the genus Galea that includes the wild cavies of the Bolivian highlands, and the genus Cavia of the domesticated form, which is widespread through much of the northern region of the sub-continent. The others are the *Kerodon* or *Mocu* of north-eastern Brazil and the Microcavia of the Bolivian highlands, Argentina and Chile. The typical cui is about twelve inches long when fully grown, and though its tail is absent externally, a vestigium of about twenty-five millimetres is present under the skin. Generally they are white, or with mixtures of brown and black; the hair is short and silky though one breed has a long fine coat, like Angora. Recently a large breed of 'super-cavy' has been developed in Peru which is almost twice the size of the average Andean specimen, and there is some hope that breeding these successfully in the sierras could help the Indians in the drought-affected southern highlands.

Attempts at hybridization using the domesticated (C. porcellus) and the wild forms have been partly successful; the crosses with species from the Arequipa region have produced fertile offspring but crosses with species from other regions including parts of Brazil have produced a proportion of infertile hybrids. The evidence for a centre or original domestication, or the homeland of Cavia porcellus is confusing, and though at one time it was thought that the domestication occurred in Brazil, the genetic and morphologic evidence seems to point to the Andean highland area. It appears certain that cavies have been kept by the sierra Indians for several millennia and the greatest numbers of domesticated form are located in the central Andes where Cavia also is found wild; (south of Puno the genus Galea tends to occupy the same niche). Galea species can be captured easily and are not difficult to keep in captivity though the presently wild members of the genus Cavia are difficult to domesticate. For this reason alone it seems strange that the Galea has never been domesticated completely, or even that it was not the form chosen by the early breeders.

The closeness of the Indian cui to the life of the household is quickly obvious to travellers offered Indian hospitality. Overnight, when curled up in sleeping bags in the corner of adobe huts, we were always disturbed by the incessant scurry and occasional squeaking of the tiny animals in their energetic search for food and they would scramble over the bags or through the rough cactus leaves covering the floor, totally unconscious of our presence or the Indian family. Their place in the home is a distinctive part of the sierra culture and occasionally one or two animals are sacrificed when the family believes that a ceremony will help with problems, or perhaps avert a minor disaster. Traces proving the continuance of these practices are to be found outside the villages often beside large rocks or a cairn of stones, even under a cross near a church. The bones of a cui can be seen mixed with a pile of ashes, where the sacrifices were followed by burning the tiny corpse with charcoal, copal and alcohol. Flamingo feathers, or coloured wood are used in some ceremonies and these, together with amulets, are placed carefully on the site. In Inca times, as many as a thousand cavies were sacrificed to the Air, Sun, Water and Frost, yet very few con- temporary ceramics include cavies in the design, and none of the pottery decorations depict an unmistakable cavy form. Unlike the truly Andean llamas, existing today and known also from many bones found in tombs, few cavy remains have ever been discovered by archaeologists, which paradoxically can help the suggestion that cavies were domesticated in the highlands. The Family is spread across most of the sub-continent and always there has been an association between some of the species and man which makes the question of domestication into one of those South American mysteries that may never have an answer.

Indian witchcraft and magic is not easily discussed with any of the tribes and Kallawayas guard their herbal secrets as closely as any other specialist, openly resenting outsiders who pry into any aspect of their life. Sacrifices, libations and the application of cures are performed in secrecy at night, dusk or sunrise, which makes it impossible for even the most careful observer to get a story that is wholly truthful. By offering an Indian a cigarette and matches, or some of his favourite coca leaves, a stranger has the chance to make slight headway in gaining their confidence, but if the tokens are given in the wrong way, then an inflexible barrier is created immediately. At one time the passing of port in the right direction was traditional in our society, and even now for the Indians of the central Andes, the correct selection of coca leaves for chewing is part of a rigid etiquette that must be followed.

Some folklore related to the wildlife of the sierras is easily observable, though arriving on the spot at the right moment is often a matter of luck. At certain fiestas along the eastern shores of Lake Titicaca, the 'hunting of the perdiz (partridge)' is a gay and noisy ritual followed by most of the villagers. True partridges are not found in South America, and they are replaced by the unique Neotropical family of Tinamotidae, the Tinamous. Many of the species are sufficiently similar to the partridges so that the Spanish confused the early nomenclature by calling them *perdiz*, or 'partridge' in Castilian. The family is widespread in South America with some species common to the pampas and lowlands while others are restricted to the punas and tola bush heathlands of the sierras. Some taxonomists and morphologists have defined certain features that indicate a distant relationship with the Rheaforms, the larger ostrich-like birds typical of the open South American grasslands. A more recent view is that the tinamous are possibly very similar to the ancient avian stock from which modern birds developed, and it is thought that being relatively unspecialized they are unique and evolved along the same general line as the ratites – the name given to the giant flightless birds which include the rheas, kiwis and ostriches. Ratites usually lack a keeled breastbone, and though the tinamous' breastbone is strongly keeled, the family possesses other ratite features particularly in the palate structure.

None of the tinamous are large with the Crested Tinamou (Eudromia elegans) of the Argentinian pampas among the largest. Less common and slightly larger, reaching seventeen inches is Pentlands Tinamotis (Tinamotis pentlandii) known from the higher zones of southern Peru and the Puna de Atacama. Another species from the central Andes is the Ornate Tinamou (Nothoprocta ornata ornata) which is about fourteen inches and these are just three representatives of the family which incorporates about fifty species.

Found singly, or in pairs, with rarely two pairs in the same territory, tinamous have simple nests on the ground, concealed only by vegetation. The eggs are unmistakable and despite slight variations in size according to the species, all have the same high gloss porcelain-like surface. Richly coloured in deep olive or purple, Tinamou eggs resemble an exquisite fine china that should rightly be only fractionally more solid than fragile eggshell. A single clutch consists of between five and twelve eggs and soon after hatching the young are able to follow the female. In the high Andes they take 'runs' between the clumps of grass and when disturbed, the guardian bird takes to the air in short flights, sometimes planing as much as two hundred yards down the hillsides after each take-off; later she returns to the chicks, locating them by their shrill, plaintive cries made from cover. All tinamous are camouflaged well and merge with the dull-brown or grey-green plants; or they are almost indistinguishable among the undergrowth of the forest floor. Often they remain motionless and take to flight only when trodden-upon, but the Indians know that noise and movement will flush them, so the traditional hunt in the sierra takes the form of one of the ancient *chacus* or round-ups held in Inca times.

The villagers dressed in bright costumes and wearing masks of animal skins, or cloth painted with a comic face, turn out onto the puna in a great throng. Music from drums and flutes, accompanied by a rattling of tins and weird high-pitched shouting, sets the tinamou on-the-run, and once the hunters have sighted the bird they broaden their front and keep moving at a quick pace; they know that the tinamou is a poor-flier, taking half a dozen short flights at the most before it takes to the ground, running short distances until exhausted. The noise is enough to scare the birds into making a move that is ultimately fatal; and the hunters can pick up dozens in an hour. Once the ritual catch has been accomplished successfully, the fiesta develops with bouts of drinking and dancing lasting all night.

Tinamous are not persecuted relentlessly and ritual-hunts are not a widespread part of the sierra culture pattern; generally the Indians take eggs or catch the birds if they make a chance encounter, though a few sportsmen from urban areas make a weekend party of a 'perdiz-shoot' but such inroads are slight at present in the central Andes. (South in Chile there is a problem, however.) Possibly, the main threat comes from the destruction of the habitat, and in many parts of the Bolivian Andes, great areas of resinous tola bushes are cropped each year for fuel: in what is essentially a treeless zone this practice is leaving the tinamou without cover.

The dominant species of wildlife close to a primitive society often reaches a supreme position in the mythology and folklore and for the Andean Indians both pumas (the Mountain lion or cougar – Felis concolor) and the giant Condor (Vultur gryphus), the largest of the world's birds are accorded a reverence that has withstood powerful external influences.

In early pre-Colombian times, each of the tribes inhabiting the Andes had individual cultures, which were lost in some instances when the Inca Empire developed and diffused a religion as far as Ecuador and north Chile. One of the strongest and most ancient dieties was the jaguar in the tropical areas and the puma in the highlands. Everywhere in the Andes the feline motive is ubiquitous. It occurs in textile designs, pottery, giant stone images and carved into solid rock. At Tiahuanaco, an ancient temple on the shores of Lake Titicaca, there are stone figures of lion-men in a place known as the Puma Punku or Puma Gate. From the same site, zoomorphic pottery has been unearthed, and the design portrays fearsome feline animals. Pumas still roam the Andes, and though not common near civilization, they are reported from the wild places, or areas where farm stock is kept in the open at night. Though in need of protection, the species is widely considered to be safe and not endangered. The position is undoubtedly due to the wide distribution, and the ability of the species to adapt to a variety of habitats. Furthermore, puma skins have very little commercial value and those taken in the Andes are kept on the farms. With the current trend to sport-shooting everywhere in South America, the position could change and there is not much hope that the hunters of today will have the same outlook as the traditional Indians or the ancient tribes. Garcilaso de la Vega, an early chronicler, recorded that the fear of the Puma god was so powerful that any man who encountered the beast on his path fell before it, even if it meant that the animal might kill him.

Puma cults were strong in the Atacama and petroglyphs remain on hard rocks to tell part of the story; in other places llamas were worshipped and the Collas of Bolivia said that a white llama was supreme. In other areas there were condor worshippers and some cliffs are marked with condor designs. Condors are depicted on pots and textiles – even some pre-Inca towns in the north of Peru have condor symbols over the walls. Both the puma and the condor have survived in the tradition of the Andean Indians and their folklore continues to feature the ancient myths. Not all the tradition is confined to the primitive societies and modern coinage of most of the Andean countries is embellished with an image of the bird. Bolivia's highest merit is the Order of the Condor, and along the length of the Andes many mountains and provinces include the name of the bird in local dialect. In Colombia, the central department where the capital of Bogota sits on an 8,000-foot plateau is known as Cundinamarca: literally 'Condor country'; there are also many 'Lakes of the Condors', 'Condor mountains' and some Indians have 'Condor' in their name.

It is not surprising that the bird receives so much attention, as it sometimes reaches an incredible wingspan of ten feet and though not as wide as the giant Wandering Albatross (eleven feet), the total wing area is greater.

With this vast and perfectly aerodynamic surface it is able to soar well above the high peaks until it seems no more than a speck in the purple firmament, even when viewed from a mountainside 16,000 feet above sea-level. The birds have the ability to use very slight current of the thermals and for hours at a time they keep aloft using no more than slight adjustments of their wings or the occasional double flap. Following their flight is one of the most frustrating tasks for a naturalist, and on many occasions I have attempted to keep a bird in sight along a valley, frequently trailing far behind in a Land Rover driven madly around the winding hairpin road. In every case the condor was faster, and could sweep by at more than forty miles an hour, effortless gliding ten miles between the sierras before turning and covering the same ground again. With their flight, they use a head and neck movement, turning the head from side to side and slightly downwards to give a good view of the ground as they watch constantly for carrion.

Darwin made some observations on these birds when he travelled in Chile and he concluded that they located their food by their keen eyesight and not by sense of smell; also he carried out simple experiments to illustrate this. Though the Turkey Vulture (Cathartes aura) which is common in many lowland parts of Neotropica is said to have well developed olfactory nerves, there seems little doubt that excellent sight is the vital factor and whenever a condor or vultures descend to food others follow quickly, even when they are a considerable distance away.

Andean condors are cousins of the almost extinct Californian condor (Gymnogyps californianus) which has been studied extensively in order to further conservation efforts, but little work was done on the Andean bird until 1968 when a research student from the University of Wisconsin began three years field-observation for his thesis. The student, Gerry McGahan with his wife Libby, based his research on a small number of condors in the southwest of Colombia near Pasto, and then extended his field to Ecuador, Peru, Chile and Argentina. Much of his most satisfactory observing was at the well-known desert coast region of Paracas and Laguna Grande near Pisco in Peru, where many condors arrive from the nearby sierra to gorge on the profuse carrion from the sea-bird colonies and seal nurseries in summer. Though it is frequently referred to as a bird of the high Andes, the condor is found at low levels in Argentina and southern Chile where the sheep farms fringe the mountain range, so it is not too surprising to find an abundance of them at some places along the Peruvian desert-coastline. At good times of the year I have counted as many as twenty around a seal carcass and from the six hundred-foot cliffs at Paracas it is possible to watch the birds in flight at very close range. In warm weather when the air currents are playing strongly up the cliffside condors pass by in procession often no more than ten feet away, even when the watcher is exposed. This fly-past place the birds in danger and Sunday sportsmen take their children to practise shooting – not only is the target big but also it is close, so that once a seven year old was able to get a hit.

When condors land to feed they are especially wary and anything unusual near a carcass quickly disturbs them or deters them entirely. On the coast they normally land on a high point from where they can watch the carcass for some time before slowly walking with a vulture-like gait towards the food. In any case they land some distance away before moving close and for the observer this is the most critical period, as the slightest noise or movement can turn them away. Once they have settled to feeding they seem less sensitive and when they are well gorged the condors are slower and find retreat laborious. Either they have to take a long run to get off the ground or they return to a high point and take off with a clumsy glide. On one occasion I watched as three male adults were disturbed from a seal carcass when a fisherman passed some hundreds of yards away. The birds retraced the route they had taken from a nearby cliff and with great difficulty they climbed a steep sandy bank to a promontory where they waited a few moments before taking off. The enormous marks from their feet showed well in the soft sand and the outward and inward trails were so close that it seemed that they had followed their own spoor very accurately – the route taken was not the shortest line between the two points.

Condor nests recorded by those lucky enough to find one were in very inaccessible places, usually high on cliffs, high caves, old mine openings, in fact in places where climbing has to be a subsidiary skill for an ornithologist. Every mountaineering technique in the book is needed to get at some nests and possibly only McGahan has been able to observe the nesting bird in detail. I have had nests pointed out to me in several parts of the Bolivian Andes and in 1967 I thought I had struck lucky in the far west of Carangas near the Chilean frontier but in no case so far have I been able to find a nest with young or egg. McGahan succeeded in finding a nest with a chick which he described as 'enormous' and 'like being face to face with a turkey'.

From earlier data collected by A. W. Johnson of Santiago, the description of eggs and young is given as a single or rarely two ovate white eggs marked with very few fine spots: the shells are relatively thin and the female is responsible for the incubation. Because of the size of the chick and the long period of parental care it is said that condors only lay every other year, the young bird having to wait in the nest for several months until flight feathers develop. Six years pass before the condor reaches maturity and the adult birds are superb and easily recognized. Firstly they are large, not only in wingspan but the body is well built; they weigh about twenty-five pounds and both male and female have bare neck and head with a fine white ruff of soft feathers that is conspicuous in contrast with the predominantly black plumage. The upper wing coverts which are greyish-white are often visible when the bird circles in flight and the male is distinguished by the soft-fleshy crest on the head. In sheer size the condor is impressive and though some people find their feeding habits distasteful, no one can fail to be charmed by the docile and affectionate demeanour of a condor in captivity. Sometimes Indians take them from nests and these birds turn up in zoos of Andean cities, particularly Cusco and Quito: they are even kept as mascots. The Bolivian Air Force usually has one, some football teams have taken them on the field and for the sierra Indians the bird is a powerful and highly respected god.

The sierra Indians believe that condors take young sheep and llamas soon after birth and they have tales of giant birds that sweep down from the heavens and snatch lambs from the flock before soaring again to the mountain tops. During summer when the young animals are born, women and children who are the usual herders keep a wary eye on anything that seems suspicious, always alert for the evil omen of a condor overhead. Though the predatory habits of condors have been watched as they stand hopefully near animals giving birth and even to the point of the female advancing against the bird to protect the newborn, so far no reliable reports of the condors lifting power have appeared. Like other vultures they probably have weak legs and little strength for clutching and these characteristics are not needed as their habit is to feed on relatively large carrion on the ground. Infrequent reports from sources that should be reliable seemingly uphold Indian legend. One helicopter pilot said he had watched a condor as it went past carrying a small lamb and another story from a mining engineer followed the same pattern, but in all personal observations even on the Peru coast where there is an abundance of food, I have never seen a condor carry anything away. Possibly the romance surrounding the condor has coloured most stories and any large bird seems condor-like to a casual observer. Another answer could be that any large bird could be confused by the non-specialist and the sightings refer to the eagle-like Black-chested Hawk (Buteo fuscescens) which is about twenty-eight inches and the largest found in the high Andes. Other names for this species include Aguilucho Grande (Great Buzzard); the Chilean Buzzard (Buteo f. australis) or Grey-backed Buzzard from the ashy-grey wing coverts. It preys on small foxes, viscachas and stock.

In spite of the paucity of evidence to substantiate the legendary predations of the condor, these habits feature in some mimes performed at Indian fiestas around Lake Titicaca. In May, at Huata, not far from the Straits of Tiquina, two groups of Indians perform, one dressed as condors and the other as young alpacas. All the costumes are made up of entire skins of the animals and the condor-men have wings supported by a simple framework strapped to their arms, while the long, bare vulture neck is strengthened by wire and forms a bow that bends upwards over the head of the dancer. The Indian's face is concealed by gauze while the lower half of his body and legs seem incongruous in short trousers and shoes showing beneath the incredible disguise. The Condor-men are silent, except for the tiny bells attached to the wing-tips, and these are tinkled incessantly. Baby alpacas are represented by dancers dressed in outrageous costumes of bright ponchos and strangely decorated headgear, while each man wears an alpaca skin over his back. Each pelt is complete and they hang with the head towards the ground. At least half a dozen reed pipe and drum bands produce incessant sierra music that accompanies the dancing. Performing the fiesta, the Alpaca-men dance slowly in a circle, playing their pipes until interrupted by the sudden appearance of the condors. Then squealing in good imitation of a alpaca alarm call, they dance faster as the 'condors' flap into the plaza with great wings and long necks beating towards the 'alpacas'. At Huata, this mime continued until long after dusk, even when most of the dancers were thoroughly drunk, either sprawled on the cobbles or unsteadily pouring more crude alcohol from an apparently undiminished stock of bottles. Similar fiestas are more elaborate and the 'condors' are given away by the onlookers who participate; sometimes dancers represent evil spirits and dress as demons to appear for the witchdoctor to have a chance to act. In the village of Irpichico not far from La Paz, a condor and fox drama is played, and the Condor-man dances within a circle of musicians while other Indians throw dried skins of foxes to the ground. The introduction of a leading figure in Andean folklore – the wily fox and its defeat by the condor – is to show the superior place the bird retains in the mythology of the Indian.

A visitation by condors is greeted with a variety of emotions by communities along the Andean sierras; sometimes the Indians are startled by the presence of the bird and call on the Yatiris, or they will try to capture it and keep it for good luck. By the lakeside, the arrival of a condor before the harvest is taken as a powerful omen of good fortune, and the Aymara firmly believe that the crop will be plentiful. On one occasion at Chijipana Chico, near Achacachi, Bolivia, a condor landed on a carcass near the village and became so gorged that it was unable to take off before the Indians managed to secure a rope to its legs. After some bad years of drought, the presence of the bird started a great fiesta when the entire community expressed gratitude for such an unexpected offering from the upper-earth – their interpretation of heaven. Miraculously the following year was the wettest (and most disastrous) for a long time. The Indians of the Andes have devised several methods for trapping condors and the simplest way that is effectively used has to rely on the heaviness of the bird after feeding, and its inability to take off without a run. Spotting a group of condors feeding (if necessary on bait) two or three Indians creep up quietly until they are within a short distance. At the last moment the men break cover and run at the birds which take fright and are confused. In their hurried attempts to escape by flight, usually one is grabbed. Similarly in Argentina and Chile the farmers have developed this method to a technique whereby a carcass is put into a crude wooden corral roughly thirty yards square. Once the condors arrive and have gorged they are surprised and cannot get into the air because the corral limits their run. The capture is a frantic affair as the huge birds rush at the fences with wings outspread and half in flight, but unable to escape, they are trapped pathetically by their own size and physical limitations.

In central Peru, the Quechuas have used other methods for condor capture, that are more arduous and painstaking though centuries old. Essentially the ruse is similar, and a carcass or cow-skin is used as bait to cover a trap. The Indians dig a pit high in an open mountainside and cover the opening with camouflage of puna grass or tola bushes; the skin or the carcass is spread above the concealed hole and an Indian climbs into the space beneath to wait in silence until the condors come. His vigil may last for days and all the time the fetid carcass becomes a less and less desirable roof, though the Indians' olfactory sense probably is deadened after the first few hours of exposure. If the trap is not perfect or there is the slightest movement, the condors are wary and will not land, but generally the Indians are expert and within two or three days several birds are feeding busily. Underneath the bait, the Indian is well prepared and as soon as a condor gets into a good position above him, he slips a noose of rope quickly through the camouflage and around a leg of the bird. Again, the capture is accompanied by a frenzy of vicious action and the condor makes desperate and powerful efforts to leap free, but the Indian is well prepared and the rope is tied carefully to stakes driven into the ground. A few companions hidden some distance away wait until they see the great flurry of wings when one condor is held firmly on the trap, then they rush down the hillsides and cover the bird with skins or sacking. By capturing a condor, it does not necessarily prove for the Indians that they are superior to the bird they regard so highly, and the captures are taken because for some of the most spectacular Indian rituals a live condor is a vital element, and the mere presence of the bird at some fiestas is a requisite for banishing evil from the village.

The most famous of all Indian festivals is the traditional Inti Raymi (Sun Festival) celebrated in midwinter throughout the central Andes. Dances, sacrifices and libations are non-stop for seven days and though in bastard form, today this fiesta continues to be sacredly connected with Cusco, the one time heart of the Inca Empire. In towns and villages of the region other ceremonies have been aligned with the Catholic calendar: such festivals as those at harvest or sowing, and around the Cusco area, the gathering of the crops soon after Inti Raymi is celebrated by bull fights and dancing. Bull fighting is an introduction from Europe and its place in the highland life stems from days when the region was extremely isolated and Spanish overlords had to provide a sport for themselves. Over the centuries the Indians have copied their masters and with some dances they mimic Spanish costumes, disguising themselves with masks to poke fun at the despised white man. Even now they continue these mocking charades and for some bull fights they mount a live condor on the spine of a large bull to demonstrate the dominance of the ancient Indian god over an alien beast.

Paruro is a famous centre for this strange sport and though condors are not found every year, the spectacle draws crowds from the entire province. If the word gets around that the *Mayordomo* of the fiesta has had the good fortune to capture a condor, Paruro is flooded with visitors and tourists from Cusco. The village square is surrounded by whitewashed adobe houses all roofed with fine, red Spanish tiles and high mountainsides slope gently up to the puna three thousand feet above the plaza. Colour is added by the variety of dress worn by the crowds: ponchos on the Indians, gay sweaters on the Cusceños and the groups of bullfighters in typical costume.

Not much has changed in the style of the fiesta for years and the condor's legs are tied into the hide of the bull, each sewn with long leather thongs. An Indian pierces the skin with a sharp knife and pushes the binding through the holes and back over the talons before passing the leather several times around the legs of the bird. During the preparation a cloth covers the condor's head and with hardly a struggle it submits to the preparation. Everything is made ready quickly, then the cloth is released, the gate opened and a handful of hot pepper – *ají* – is rammed into the anus of the bull. For brief seconds atomic fission could not make a more violent impact on the ring and the maddened beasts cavort in the first moments of surprise. The condor pecks viciously at the neck of the bull and the enraged animal charges around the ring trying to dislodge the unseen irritant. Village matadors are forgotten as a ton of enraged beef hurls against the stockade and when the bull tires, the roar of the crowd begins to have an effect. Out of its blindness, the animal charges again and again and each rush could swipe the huge vulture against rough palings. All the time the condor tries desperately to remain balanced by outstretching its wings with sad, dazed and completely forlorn attempts to fly. If the condor is secured well, the fight lasts until the bull is weary and the bird is released, later to be set free in the hills. At one time the fiesta was finished by killing the bull and offering its heart to the victorious condor, as a gesture implying total Andean superiority over the hated invaders. The barbaric bull and condor fight is not common these days and takes place only once every two or three years in each of the traditional centres for the sport. However, one disturbing development is the interest shown by the local impresarios who are using the spectacle to attract paying tourists and in almost every season in recent years, a fight has been staged in Cusco.

Another and little known fiesta occurs in many of the villages deep in the Callejon de Huaylas of central Peru. When travelling through the region with my wife in 1968, I first encountered the story in Pueblo Libre overlooking the slopes of the incredible mountains of the Cordillera Blanca. We were told that a condor had to be beaten to death each year by the bare hand of the villagers. To avert a bad harvest, floods or other catastrophe they believed they should trap and kill at least one condor at a ritual locally named *Condorachi*.

In June 1970 the people of the Callejon were in the path of the greatest disaster to hit the world for many years. Over fifty thousand dead or injured, as many again were without homes and three towns vanished in a few moments of terror. The Peruvian earthquake had its epicentre between the Callejon and the coast and when the Andes moved they shook a beautiful Indian valley apart. It was not the first time that the people there had experienced sudden, natural danger. In 1941 a glacier-fed lake burst over the town of Huaraz killing ten thousand and in 1962 an avalanche from the slopes of Huascaran wiped out the village of Ranrahirca. The major factor which contributed to the instant, almost total obliteration of the northern towns of the valley was, sadly ... another avalanche from Huascaran, Peru's highest mountain and centrepiece of a wonderfully scenic National Park. High between the mountains are deep glacial valleys, and a number of small lakes, of which Llanganuco is the most beautiful. The dark rocks leading to the snow line are remote eyries for the condor, and there are

ake Titicaca, Looking East toward the Cordillera Real of Bolivia

orrent Ducks with young

Condor

small forests of Polylepis trees with red papery bark, which have been stunted by the high altitude environment. Between the lakes and down the length of the valleys are enormous deposits of debris from the ancient glaciers, and these with tons of fresh ice and mud swept into the Callejon.

The guide books said that the Callejon was the Switzerland of Peru and an annual influx of tourists and mountaineers started in the fine winter months from May to September. Such influence from outside had not changed the Indians very much and once away from the main routes around Huaraz, the villages were undisturbed and as remote as any of the places in the higher, desolate southern puna. It was in the isolated communities that Condorachi meant so much and when looking for the fiesta in 1968, we began our enquiries in Caraz. It was a typically Colonial sierra town with a small plaza and attractive, tiled adobe-houses. With a few questions made quite openly in the local bars and market we soon unearthed the information that led us to three villages where a Condorachi was planned. The date and time could never be precise as the capture of a condor cannot be arranged to schedule, but we were told that the fiesta was held during Carnival and usually on the last day.

Our choice was Huaylas, the tiny village tucked into the side of the sombre Cordillera Negra and the community that gives the name to the entire Callejon. Once away from the main dirt road, the track climbs slowly along the mountainside. At every corner the exposure becomes greater until the slope on the right-hand side is a precipitous two thousand feet to the narrow Huaraz river tumbling towards the Cañon del Pato where its course breaks through the Andes to the coast. The road is never more than Land Rover width and in places seems narrower, particularly in parts where minor landslides, often months old, cover the original surface and give a forty degree camber to tilt the vehicle towards the edge. The view on such occasions was the same as from a banking aircraft and nothing was between the cab and the wide valley far below. At eye level on the far side of the valley the Cordillera Blanca was like a massive wall until white ice-fields merged with the clouds. The great snow slope of Huandoy had a jagged unreal quality, an almost telephoto effect in its nearness, while Huascaran loomed menacingly above the quiet towns spaced along the river. Huaylas nestles in a valley, backed by steep, well cultivated

9

hillsides facing other snow-capped mountains less than fifteen miles away. The three communities which had arranged Condorachi fiestas were beyond the village and we followed one crowd on foot from the *plaza* to a small field a mile beyond the church. Carnival time has the same frivolity over most of Latin America, and by the time we arrived at the open space where Indians were gathering, we had been covered with handfuls of flour and water in a multitude of colours and apart from our extra height, we were unrecognizable among the hundreds of revellers busily dusting each other. Most of the party were spectators and only a few of the villagers stood around in the arena, holding the bridles of horses and getting down to the tough preliminaries.

The condor, alive and anxiously watching every move was suspended on a wire between two tall poles. Cords around the wings held the bird to the main rope, which passed through a pulley on one support so one man could act as 'hangman' and raise or lower the condor. Fire crackers, drums, wild laughing and shouting urged the horsemen to start, and time after time they rushed between the poles to take vicious swipes at the bird with their bare clenched fists. With their bravery spurred on by cane alcohol, a dozen men took turns at making the dash. Sometimes the hangman would lower the condor to the level of the rider's head; then the crowd roared and an Indian seeing his chance would take his hands from the reins and punch with both fists, often falling from the saddle with the impact. The condor with a free beak and talons was able to put up a limited fight and after thirty minutes, most of the horsemen had slashes on their cheeks, hands or forehead. But the condor could never survive such an onslaught and during a barrage of punches, the great crested head suddenly drooped and the Condorachi was over. In the final rite, the Indian who delivered the fatal thrust rode forward and with his teeth, bit out the long yellow tongue of the dismally inert bird. The significance of this final act was that the Indian had undertaken to find a condor and pay for the fiesta at the next Carnival.

In some ways Condorachi is considered as the Spanish way of showing the Indians that they could conquer the local god whenever they wanted to and so they tied the fiesta to the Catholic week of Carnival. Why the Callejon Indians have perpetuated this and now consider the condor death as a good omen is not very clear but perhaps as the area has been a stronghold of Iberian influence since early days of the Conquest, the condor has taken on a different meaning. The 1970 earthquake, the most serious of the disasters to date, is unlikely to change the way of life for the survivors. Once the shock has passed they will get back to their old way of life, a pattern that is deeply rooted in their early history. Undoubtedly the Condorachi will be revived, perhaps with new vigour as evil spirits are clearly about.

Inevitably, the conservation of the condor will be a problem; the numbers taken each year for ceremony probably has not increased in several centuries, but the affect of civilization is serious. In Colombia, the destruction of the habitat in the high Andean forests has led to a serious decline in population and it is feared that the species will soon disappear from the northern ranges. Everywhere the peasant farmers have some type of gun and they have no traditional respect for the bird and shoot for fun without restriction. In Peru where the condors are frequent visitors to the coast the guardians of guano bird sanctuaries have permission to kill those which raid the sea-bird colonies. The vultures are said to take both live and dead chicks and their appearance overhead is believed to upset the cormorants and thus could upset plans to establish some large breeding colonies on the mainland. One guard claimed to have shot fifty condors in three months of the sea-bird nesting season, possibly more than exist in all of Colombia.

I have counted more condors in one hour along the coast of southern Peru than in a month of Andean travelling; they sweep down the arid valleys from the high sierras in long lines effortlessly gliding and ever watchful. There was one day near Paracas in late January when we counted fifteen in one flight and as many more only two days later. High figures were not uncommon, but how can the species survive in the face of senseless persecution by the custodians of the guano birds? Will it be shortsightedness in the death throes of a dying trade that will force the extinction of yet another species? As the condors concentrate along the coast in summer, others seem to arrive from the sierra to fill the ranks after the slaughter, and the destruction has so far continued unabated. Surely with the natural limitations of a long period before maturity and only a single young, any premeditated threat must be heartily condemned?

The Indian fiestas, though barbaric, only affect a small number of birds and after all the legendary King of the Andes has survived in spite of an Aymara legend that says its blood is an infallible rejuvenator. Perhaps it is not the centuries old beliefs that endanger the condor, but the plentiful supply of guns for civilized people who have advanced beyond the simple life and are motivated by less trustworthy ideals.

Lake Above the Clouds

Puno is a small Andean town of growing importance in the southern highlands of Peru and, with neighbouring Juliaca, it has become the centre of development for a region forgotten since the days of the railway age in South America. In many ways Puno is unique. Not only is it the world's highest port but probably vies with very few other places for being either totally uninviting or incredibly romantic within the space of a day. An evening in the dampness of the narrow streets is bitterly cold when fine sleet whips across Lake Titicaca curling over the low mountainsides to gather in deep potholes. Only a few Indians keep a lonely watch in the empty *plazas* or pairs of Guardia Civil, muffled to eye-level, stand slapping their arms to revive a tortured circulation.

Through the main street runs the track of the Southern Peru Railway, which built at the turn of the century is a reminder of the pioneering days, and despite set-backs it faced in the 1960s, there is a chance that it will prosper again after a recent demand for better cargo facilities between land-locked Bolivia and the Pacific. Just as the morning light seems to vitalize the people of Puno, they now feel there is some hope for the future resting in Lake Titicaca, a great inland sea with ports, industry and eventually better communications which will change the life of the region. The lake is the highest navigable water on the earth and according to Aymara Indian legend it is the womb from where their god Viracocha appeared. They say that Viracocha came out of the lake to form an ancient world of giants and darkness, but he was angered by his first children and so he destroyed them under a great flood. Then he tried a second time, rising from the lake again to create the Andean world and the Aymara we see today. The Indians and their legends have hardly changed, but some new pressures are altering

Highlands of southern Bolivia and northern Chile

their place in the life of Titicaca and sadly the same pressures are endangering the lake and wildlife.

Studies of the biology of the region began in earnest in the last century in 1827 with the work of Alcides d'Orbigny who travelled extensively in Bolivia and Argentina, producing the classic volumes of research – 'Voyage dans L'Amerique Meridionale' – in Paris; Von Tschudi followed in 1838 with his travels in Peru, and after him went Bergelund to survey the lake for the Peruvian Corporation which owns the steamer service. The lake and the main outflow through the River Desaguadero were mapped and his reports were published in France in 1903–1904. The work of all the early scientists, excepting the hydrographic survey by Bergelund were of a general nature, and though the American Geographical Society added further data in 1922, it was not until the Percy Sladen Trust Expedition in 1937 that a detailed study was made, concentrating on the flora and fauna. Many of the plants and lower animal forms were classified for the first time and the report of the Expedition has been the basis for research conducted intermittently since 1940. The present condition of the lake is an unfortunate result of haphazard research which can in part be accounted for by the division of ownership, and hence responsibility between neighbouring Peru and Bolivia. A lack of interest and constant friction engendered by political rivalry probably has had considerable effect on the establishment and continuity of projects.

About thirty years ago Peru and Bolivia agreed to stock the lake with Rainbow Trout (Salmo gairdneri) and set up a fish-hatchery and research laboratory at Chucuito a few miles from Puno. At the expense of the remarkable endemic fish population, the introduced species reproduced rapidly and within a few years Lake Titicaca became famous for fine sport-fishing and large catches of excellent fish for the surrounding villages. It seemed that food problems would be solved and that Titicaca faced a booming future. It did, but only for a very short time: the experiment which was apparently so successful has ended in disaster and there is a chance that the damage may be irreparable. Lines of research began as recently as 1965 ground to a halt through a lack of funds and an undercurrent of political bickering within local universities, while on the international level the owners of the lake have had a hard time agreeing on a course of action. By

October 1969 Peru had taken the lead and proposed a commission of specialists to study for the first time, so it was said 'the fisheries potential and general characteristics of the lake'.

There are two native genera of fish in the lake: a catfish (Trichomycterus rivulatus) locally named *suche* or *mauri* and various species of the genus Orestius called *carachi*, *boga*, *ispi* and *umanto*. The sub-family Orestiinae is a branch of the Cyprinidae which includes many of the common freshwater types, the best known being carp, perch and minnows. Most of the Orestines are relatively large and some reach ten inches so they have been an important food source in the region for countless centuries.

However the trout and another exotic species, the Argentinian freshwater pejerrey (Basilichthys bonariensis), introduced in 1958 reduced the endemic fish population and though for a few years the Indians were able to change their techniques and catch the new food fishes which at the time seemed better, the apparent improvement did not last very long and by 1969, the lake was almost empty of all fish. At one time the Indians caught Orestines and Catfish with simple traps of fine nets supported on large hoops. The fish were either fried or turned into soup and any surplus catch was cleaned and dried in the sun. Even in the early 1960s, it was not unusual to see rows of carefully opened fish covering reed mats along the lakeside. One of the aims in 1940 was to help the Indians by increasing their food supply with a species yielding greater weight of protein but though the desired effect was achieved, albeit at the expense of the endemics, commercial exploitation had not been considered carefully enough in the original plan.

By 1967 four fish canneries were operating and the product was aimed at the luxury market in the United States and Europe. The Indian fishermen found a quick source of income by working for the canneries and instead of providing more food for the majority of Indians, a few well-equipped families began to reduce the fish population of the lake. Canning operations started in 1960 and the annual catch was between three and four hundred tons; the 1965 season was good but a decrease of nearly twenty-five per cent occurred in 1966 and for 1967 there was a further twenty-five per cent decrease. By 1968 less than one hundred tons was caught and the canneries started to close down. Peru imposed a two year close-season, a move that Bolivia would not accept and in return suggested a maximum of only a year, though preferring six months. The highly controversial *veda* or close-season was pushed back and forth across Titicaca and in July 1969, Bolivia announced a three month close-season back dated to the first day of the month. Peru was not satisfied and though an argument for good management can be put against a demand for a cessation of fishing for a long period, the Peruvian attitude was to close the lake and study it.

A quick look at the problem would indicate a plain case of overfishing. The trout seem to have reached a climax, and at the same time, while there are very few Orestias caught now, Indian fishermen are lucky to trap more than one or two whereas in the past they returned each day with plenty. The Rainbow Trout being a migratory species ascends rivers around the lake to spawn and by laying nets across the streams it was easy to make a haul. Also, there is a plentiful supply of dynamite in the mining areas of the Andes, and this explosive has been used frequently. A stick or two exploded underwater stuns fish within a large area and they are collected as they float to the surface. The method is not recommended as all fish of every size and species are affected and dynamiting can be likened to instant sterilization of the water. This crude method of fishing is illegal, but very few laws are understood by the Indians, a distressing factor that makes a close-season futile from the outset. In fact many of the fishermen welcome a close-season because it raises the value of fish sold illegally; and though not displayed openly a good customer can find plenty of trout in the La Paz market for a few pence extra per pound.

Short term research projects were undertaken between 1966 and 1968 by British and American volunteer biologists based in Peru, and they were clearly aware of the limited use that could be made of data collected during their brief stay. Their conclusions naturally were guarded, but unquestionably pointed to the need for better management with strictly enforced controls and the commencement of a long-term research programme. In fact, more or less the proposals that were published in 1969. Unfortunately, the paucity of statistics from previous years could make serious difficulties for any programme. There always is a possibility that the fluctuations in the fish population result from seasonal or periodic variations which affect the ecology of the lake; certainly the level of the lake varies considerably and Peruvian Corporation records seem to indicate that these variations are cyclic. In recent years a drought caused a severe drop in 1956 and again in late 1969 the lake level dropped by as much as fifty-five inches by November when the rains are usually expected.

Lake Titicaca is not large by African or North American standards, being only one hundred and ten miles long by forty-six miles wide with a total surface area of 3,141 square miles. The maximum depth probably does not exceed much more than eight hundred feet despite the Indian legends of it being bottomless, and the surface is at an altitude of 12,497 feet above sea level. Several rivers flow in from the surrounding mountains and the River Desaguadero flows out into Lake Poopo, a salty, almost dry lake in the Bolivian Altiplano. (Poopo was stocked with the Argentinian Pejerrey and the fish moved up the Desaguadero into Titicaca.) Though Titicaca is not the highest lake in the world, a steamer service between Puno on the Peruvian shore and Guaqui in Bolivia accounts for a record of the world's highest navigable water. To reach Guaqui steamers leave Puno through a narrow channel which needs constant dredging to keep it open, and once outside the bay, the lake resembles a magnificent inland sea with high mountains on the eastern horizon and low hills to the west. A narrow deep water channel, the Straits of Tiquina, divides the water into two parts and the smaller (or Laguna Pequeño) with an area of approximately seven hundred and fifty square miles is bordered mainly by the Bolivian shore line. The peninsular of Copacabana projecting from the western side carries the border between the two countries and there is a frontier post on the road between Yunguyo in Peru and Copacabana in Bolivia. Another frontier control is on the road bridge across the Desaguadero, while in the north east a road runs south from Moho crossing the border to Puerto Acosta and onwards to La Paz.

The setting of the lake is remarkable with the continuous range of the Bolivian Cordillera Real making an impressive, white-capped backdrop to the east, and a faint, distant hint of the mountains of Azangaro in the north. Each one of the main Bolivian peaks reaches to over 20,000 feet and the hard, white glaciers and high ice-fields are sharply defined against the richly clear blue of the Andean sky. In winter from May to August the sky is almost perpetually cloudless and reflects in the cool water, concentrating in strength and imparting an unbelievable vivid colour. But in springtime when the climate changes and great cumulus clouds pour over the eastern Andes the water is patterned with soft reflections making the hues portray the lighter face of Titicaca: another season and a time for the fields, for the flocks and more fiestas. Storms occasionally sweep across the lake with astonishing rapidity and high winds set the usually still water into short waves; the Andean sky darkens to a dull grey and mountains are lost within a canopy of solid rain, freezing hail and snow. If the thunder god angrily sends lightning around an Indian village the *campesinos* take to their adobe homes, making simple sacrifices to ward off the wrath of evil spirits. Even the hardy Andean sheep dogs are cowed and cur-like in the face of such violence, and they run to shelter under the eaves. For a few hours water beats into the hard Andean ground, baked by the ceaseless sunshine of winter; all the rivers are overflowing, and muddy torrents darkened by tons of precious silt from the hillsides. Each year the Indians have to make a fresh start and clear newly exposed stones and debris from their fields: when the fine topsoil is washed away there is even less hope for the primitive farmer.

Most of the lakeside people are Aymara Indians, who were never fully subjugated by the Quechuas of the strong Inca Empire from the north. They are famous now for their skill of building reed boats, used for fishing and transport, and as a group, the Aymara have fascinated anthropologists searching for a key to the early history of the Andean peoples. Alongside the southern shore, no more than a dozen miles from the lake edge there is the ruined town and temple of Tiahuanaco, where the finest stone carving ever found in South America rests chaotically. The builders of Tiahuanaco are unknown, but they could have been the ancestors of the Collas, the ancient Aymara who inhabited the region long before the expansion of the Inca Empire; and it is thought that they could have been one of the most advanced civilizations in the Andes until disaster overtook them. The catastrophe could have been no more than the pressure from the Inca's armies, but it could have been more cataclysmic. Not very much solid evidence can support theories for a sudden change in the central Andean highlands, but certainly the Altiplano, as this region is named, was once part of a system of much larger lakes. Tiahuanaco could have been an ancient port on the shores of a considerably more extensive Titicaca and the design

as well as the mysterious origin of some of the stones seem to indicate that
the lake came very close. It is believed that most of the massive blocks came
from a quarry five miles away and possibly they were carried on giant reed
rafts. Undoubtedly the Tiahuanaco ruins are among the most megalithic in
South America and certainly they were fashioned with great precision.

Some physical features of the Altiplano can be explained only by the
large-lake theory and extending from fifty miles north of Puno to over two
hundred and fifty miles south of La Paz, ancient shore lines show clearly
that two immense lakes can be plotted on a relief map. They must have
existed in their most extensive form long before man arrived on the continent and the presence of such a large body of water has left a mark on the
Altiplano. Titicaca has the greatest area today but around it there are other
lakes and lagoons of fresh water which at one time were connected. To the
south of Titicaca the Altiplano is colder and more desolate but the remains
of the old sea show clearly and the landscape is dominated by salt lakes and
vast beds of dry salt.

The high plain is permanently inhabited and some villages are sited above
14,000 feet. It is a land starkly barren, inhospitable and cold for much of the
year. In general terms the Bolivian shore of Titicaca marks the southern
limit of uninterrupted human occupation though scattered communities
survive, even in the desolate heights of the Puna de Atacama. Throughout
the Altiplano wildlife is equally sparse and the lakes provide a haven for
water birds, amphibians and small mammals; elsewhere any species has to
be well adapted to the height and cold and as food is scarce there is a limited
number of species and individuals. Lake Titicaca can be considered as the
half-way mark in the high Andes: to the north the climate gets progressively
more temperate and by Riobamba in Ecuador the llamoids, for example, do
not occur, while on the other hand the fauna southwards shows a clear
trend with specialized rodents like viscachas and chinchillas as the most
obvious types.

Titicaca is the largest of the Andean freshwater lakes and taken as a
representative of many habitats from the shore line to the open puna of the
surrounding hillsides: also Titicaca provides a wide cross section of bird
species and adaption. Most of the birds included on a Titicaca list are found
extensively in the northern Andes from Peru to central Ecuador and some

which frequent the shallow pools along the lakeside are representatives of the species occurring on the salt lakes of the south.

An example of a widespread type is the ubiquitous Andean Gull (Larus serranus), a high Andean species common from Ecuador to Chile and seen frequently on the coast in winter time. It is slightly larger than Franklins Gull (a North American migrant) and nests in the small bays of many puna lakes. In many ways the gull is similar to Franklins but whereas the black head-cap of the migrant only partially disappears in winter, the Andean Gull becomes almost totally white. At the extreme of limited distribution are some of the grebes and coots. An unusual species endemic to Titicaca is the strange Flightless Titicaca Grebe (Centropelma micropterum). Grebes are weak fliers but the Titicaca Grebe can only manage a crude paddling flight which fails to lift it from the water. The structure of the bird is not greatly different from its flying relatives, but possibly slight changes in the musculature and wing size have developed, thus keeping the species within the boundary of the lake. A good place to see this interesting bird is in the narrow dredged-channel entering Puno harbour as they retreat in an ungainly struggle to the cover of surrounding reed beds. The main protection for the waterbirds is provided by large areas of a bulrush (Scirpus totora) known locally as *Totora* or collectively the area is the *Totoral*. This tall growth covers extensive sectors of sheltered water in the bays where the depth does not exceed fifteen feet. Often the beds are so dense that the Indians are forced to cut channels from their lakeside villages to the open water.

Most of the birds nesting on Titicaca can be found in the Totoral and the Flightless Titicaca Grebe is no exception; also two other related species are known: the Crested Grebe (Podiceps occipitalis) and the Chilean Grebe (Podiceps chilensis). Of them all, the Chilean Grebe is the smallest and has the widest distribution in South America, being found from Peru, through Chile to Tierra del Fuego and across south west Brazil, while a separate sub species (Podiceps rolland rolland) is found in the Falkland Islands. This tiny grebe is distinguished by darker plumage and the head, neck and back are black. Also, instead of possessing the whitish-grey underparts of the other species, the Chilean Grebe is richly ferruginous. It has slightly different habits which help to distinguish it and is much more timid than the others, diving at the slightest danger. On surfacing only the head and neck show above water until the bird is satisfied that the disturbance has passed; any movement nearby causes it to dive again. Though the Flightless Grebe is confined to Titicaca, other grebes are found on many of the central Andean lakes, often in situations where the reeds are short or entirely absent. In these places the nests are constructed of water plants forming floating platforms, but placed openly some distance from the shore where they are out of reach of most predators other than man. Indians usually rob the nests of waterbirds though this is not a problem on lakes remote from villages. A problem on Titicaca which is becoming serious is habitat destruction and with the inroads made in the breeding season, the combined effect could spell disaster.

For centuries, the Indians around Titicaca have used the Totora for making their reed boats, named *balsas* by the Spanish, but the plant has numerous other uses and it is cut for animal food or occasional human consumption: it has a taste like young celery and pieces are on sale in many village markets. Unfortunately for the birds the recent demand for Totora has increased and better road communications to the coast together with an increasing population there has raised the demand for totora matting, and many tons are sent to the desert region where it is used in simple houses as walls, roofing and beds. Chimu village just outside Puno is a centre of the industry; there the lake shore is lined with stacks of Totora resting in wig-wam fashion to dry in the sun. Each family has a reed bed nearby, with the property boundary defined by a narrow canal, but this Totora has been cut in to severely, leaving only small patches for the cattle and family use. To get the main supply for the industry, the villagers sail to other parts of the lake and cut tons which are piled into the form of a floating hayrick which can be poled or sailed across the lake. This work takes the men and their families away from Chimu for several weeks and it is not unusual to see wives, children, chickens and pigs sitting calmly on a raft moving along slowly many miles from the shore. In some ways the method is a reminder that any possibility of trans-Pacific journeys by ancient Peruvians is not too remote, and as if to prove the quality of Totora the American explorer Gene Savoy sailed his raft the Kuvi Kuyo from Peru to Panama in 1969.

Extensive cutting of the reed beds is reducing cover for the birds and at the same time the practice introduces another hazard because the Indians take all young birds from the nests, and during reed cutting they have the chance to surprise and capture many adults. Taking the birds for food has been traditional, but with the sharp decline of the fish and the slowly developing economy of Indians in the towns, there is now a strong demand for wild birds. During the summer months when most species are nesting, the markets of Puno, Guaqui, Pomata and nearly every lakeside village have many stalls displaying an assortment of grebes, duck, coots and even Glossy Ibis. The Indians cannot be blamed directly, as they have poor education and recently they have experienced an unprecedented change in their subsistence level fishing which has unbalanced their centuries-old Titicaca way of life.

Just as the Totoral has been a refuge for the birds, several groups of Indians have taken to the water in retreat from the shore dwellers. The most distinctive of these groups were the *Urus*, one of the most ancient tribes of the Andes and distinguishable by a dialect entirely different than Aymara or Quechua. At one time the Urus inhabitated the swamps of the Desaguadero, but by 1950 Bolivian anthropologists realized that pressure from the surrounding Aymara had affected the Urus disastrously and now they are extinct. However groups of Indians live on Titicaca in the reeds not far from Puno, and though established today in the local lore as Urus, they are clearly Aymara speaking. Their homes are made entirely from Totora and stand on large rafts cut from reed secured in the Totoral or to rocks on the lake bottom. As well as the advantage of living close to the fish and bird life, the floating colonies have found that their Uru-like existence attracts tourists who are willing to pay to visit their 'islands' and additionally to photograph the people. Paradoxically, despite their continued primitive life on the lake, this group of Indians has one of the largest cooperative credit accounts with the local development bank, and owns property on the mainland. Such admirable exploitation of their own habits has helped these Indians to progress but unhappily they have enough money now to buy shot-guns and have become one of the main suppliers of game for profit: a change that could quickly clear the wildlife from the Bay of Puno and nearby.

Perhaps the most obvious of the birds found on Andean lakes is the Andean Glossy Ibis (Plegadis ridgwayi) and it occurs in small groups on the marshy puna or swamp areas around Titicaca. It is known only in the high altitudes and is commonly seen from northern Peru to the north of Chile and Argentina. Another species, the Common Glossy Ibis (Plegadis falcinellus chihi) is widely distributed in the Americas and yet is absent from the highlands; very frequently it is found in large flocks nesting in colonies among the reeds of coastal lagoons of both temperate and tropical areas. The Black-faced Ibis – the Bandurria (Theristicus caudatus) – occurs as two separate races in Peru: the Common Bandurria (Theristicus c. melanopis) of the coast and a Northern or Andean Bandurria (Theristicus c. branickii) from the high Altiplano. The Bandurrias are typical of marshy ground where they feed on small frogs, insects, worms and aquatic life; they live in flocks and nest communally in groups of ten to thirty pairs. Recognition is simple and not only are their colours extremely fine with greyish wings, marked with black, fawn neck and black underside (the Andean Bandurria is whitish underneath) but the call is a metallic clanking which cannot be mistaken. The distribution of the Black-faced Ibis is widespread in South America, though the Andean race is confined to the highlands. Bandurrias of the lowlands and highlands, with the two species of Glossy Ibis are another clear example of altitude speciation.

Titicaca and the adjacent freshwater lakes, including Laguna de Arapa, Las Lagunillas and Umayo are ideal for the visiting ornithologist and offer a great variety of typical Andean avifauna, and in the summer there are many migrant species. Some of the smallest lakes have good populations of the rare Giant Coot (Fulica gigantea) found only in the Andes. It attains the size of a small turkey but is distinctly coot-like, easily distinguished by size and extremely large feet which support it well on weeds. The nest of this coot is enormous, often three to four feet in diameter and built well away from the shore; once again though secure from most danger, the eggs are large and good eating for the Indians so that even in the high altitude lakes – a favourite haunt – the nests are raided annually. Other, more familiar species are the Slate-coloured Coot or Andean Coot (Fulica ardesiaca) and the American Coot (Fulica americana) while a small gallinule (Gallinula chloropas pauxilla) is the Andean race of the Common gallinule generally occurring from Canada to Chile. A rare high altitude species is Garmans Gallinule (Gallinula chloropas garmani) which is slightly larger

yra *(Eira barbara)*

ar of Uyuni 12,150 feet

Andean Caracara

Female cock of the Rock

being fourteen to fifteen inches and found in some parts of Peru, Bolivia and northern Chile and Argentina. Though there are many representatives of the Rallidae, some like the Giant Coot and Garmans Gallinule are not encountered everywhere, while some species encountered in this hard-to-see category are possibly more numerous than present records indicate. In this group are the Rails, not only shy and nocturnal, but generally accepted as birds of the lowlands: only one or two are listed for the central Andes. There is the high altitude race of the Common Rail (Rallus sanguinolentus tchudii) from central Peru and possibly the Virginian Rail (Rallus limicola) from the mountains of the north.

Many ducks (Anatidae) are common in the Titicaca region and the Ruddy Duck (Oxyura ferruginea) is abundant and closely related to other races found from Colombia and Chile. Intergrades are recognized and for a short while there was a chance that a distinctly new race had been discovered on the Hacienda Checayani near Azangaro, a few miles north of Titicaca. Several specimens of this Ruddy Duck possessed a pure white head and neck giving them a clown-like appearance among their conservative neighbours; however the owner of the land, Dr Hernando de Macedo now working in the Museo Javier Prado in Lima, considers that the ducks on his land are half albino.

From Colombia to Tierra del Fuego or in fact through most of the Andes and the foothills, a number of Dabbling Ducks (Anatini) occur with wide distribution. The Chilean Pintail – Brown Pintail (Anas georgica spinicauda) is both widespread and common and found nesting throughout its range as well as at heights of 14,000 feet. The Andean Teal (Anas flavirostris andium) found in Colombian and Ecuadorian highlands is replaced by other races in the south; and the Sharp-winged Teal (Anas flavirostris oxyptera) occurs around Titicaca and through the highlands to northern Argentina and Chile. At one time this race was generally considered as an Andean species, though A. W. Johnson has noted that it is found in valleys of the Atacama, especially the Huasco and Copiapo regions.

Included in the same group of ducks are some with Andean forms only slightly different to the nominate race, illustrating altitude speciation through long isolation in the mountain habitat. Typical of much of the

10

southern South America is the Argentinian Cinnamon Teal (Anas cyanoptera cyanoptera) and the Andean race (Anas cyanoptera orinomus) differs slightly in colour – the female has a lighter breast and darker head than the lowland race, and also the mountain form possesses slightly larger wings.

The Andean Silver Teal (Anas versicolor puna) called locally the Puna Duck or *Yucsa* is fairly common in Peru, Bolivia and the northern Andes of Chile. It is recognized by distinctive head markings: the sides of the head and throat are a creamy white and the crown, nape and hind-neck black or dark brown forming a cap. Two other races are found at lower altitudes across the southern half of the sub-continent and the Southern Silver or Versicolor Teal (Anas versicolor fretensis) reaches the Falkland Islands.

An interesting genus, the South American Crested Ducks (Lophonetta) is represented only by two sub-species. One is common in the south of Chile and Argentina (Patagonian Crested Duck – L. specularoides specularoides) whilst the other, the Andean Crested Duck (L. specularoides alticola) occurs over a range from Lake Junin to the latitude of Santiago in Chile through the higher Andes. The genus represents a transition between the Shelducks and Dabbling Ducks, and they are recognized by their large size and brownish crests. General coloration is brown, the tail is long and the legs are set well forward. In Peru, the common name is the *Pato Cordillerano* or Mountain Duck and it is usually noticed because it is one of the largest ducks on the mountain lakes. The Andean Crested Duck is common in most of its range and nests in marshy areas, building on tussocks or on the ground, sometimes using the abandoned nest of another waterbird. Not far from Titicaca, the series of lakes or *Lagunillas* on the roadside west of Juliaca are inhabited by this species where they tend to keep to the small islets not far from the shore and well protected by open water.

Local names for the ducks and for most other birds vary considerably from region to region, and the name given usually refers to a characteristic of the bird – often the call, as it is interpreted in the local dialect. As the dialects even between Quechua speaking Indians can be very different, there are many names for each bird. In most instances, I have excluded local names because too frequently when asking an Indian for a particular species, the difficult pronunciation makes the answer misleading. Often an Indian will understand only limited Spanish and the naturalist only limited Quechua, which can lead to one answer – *Pato* meaning 'duck' in Spanish. On one occasion I followed an Indian for some miles in search of Torrent Ducks, armed with a book of illustrations, Spanish and rudimentary Quechua. 'There' he said 'There are the ducks' and pointed happily to where paddling in the river five hundred feet below was a group of some exotic farmyard variety, the pride of his tiny cooperative.

In the area of Lagunillas there is extensive marshy ground and some large bays with shallow water. Often it is an excellent place for observing many species, particularly in the summer when the migrants arrive: Wilsons Phalaropes occupy the smallest pools and there are both the Lesser and Greater Yellowlegs (Tringa flavipes and T. melanoleuca). Occasionally a solitary Stilt (Himantopus himantopus mexicanus) is seen on Titicaca and in many visits I have only twice encountered the species. Though it is known to visit the high lakes, usually the bird is solitary or only in small groups not comparable with the large numbers found in the northern regions of South America in the summer.

The waders and other shore birds can be found easily not far from Puno on the route towards Desaguadero; in this section of the lake the water is shallow and in some seasons extensive mud-flats appear. Flamingos are not uncommon, often gathering in groups of up to twenty birds: they are a sub-species of the Greater Flamingo of Eurasia, Africa and the Caribbean and often referred to as the Chilean Flamingo (Phoenicopterus ruber chilensis). It is the most widespread of the three South American species and also migratory within its range from central Peru to Tierra del Fuego. Unlike the two rarer species which are confined to the southern highlands, the Chilean Flamingo is found on many lakes in the sierra, as well as occasionally on the salt-pans at Huacho not far north of Lima on the coast; also they frequently haunt the wide bay of Paracas near Pisco.

Along the lake shore from Puno southward is a great variety of habitat with open shores or small shallow lagoons held behind old beaches. Many of the birds occupying these zones can be seen easily from the road. Night Herons (Nycticorax mycticorax hoactli), the Common Egret (Casmerodius albus egretta) and Black Cormorant (Phalacrocorax olivaceus olivaceus) are typical though they can be seen in similar habitats throughout the central Andes; but one species common around Titicaca, the Andean Goose

(Chloephaga melanoptera) has a restricted distribution. This handsome Goose is unmistakable: it is large, white and with black areas on the wings and tail. When in flight the upper wing markings are characteristic; not only are the tips black but a central band of black from each wing extends to join the tail coloration. Usually seen in pairs, they inhabit soft, marshy ground near the lake or just as frequently they favour boggy-land high in the mountains as high as the glaciers, or even in the open puna where water collects in shallow basins. This species is the largest of the genus Chloephaga and occurs in the Andes from central Peru to the latitude of Mendoza province of Argentina and to Nuble in Chile; sometimes moving into the lower plains in the southern half of its range.

Of the many birds from the central region to be encountered in the environs of Titicaca and the Altiplano, there is the South American Snipe – Common Snipe (Gallinugo paraguaiae andina); the Andean Snipe (Chubbia jamesoni). Not to be confused with the snipes are the Seed-snipes of a separate family, the Thinocoridae, which are seed eaters but with the rapid zig-zag flight typical of snipe. This family is exclusively Neotropical and species are found high in the Andes as well as along the barren sea coasts. The Pigmy Seed-Snipe (Thinocoras rumicivorus cuneicauda) is coastal from Ecuador to Tierra del Fuego, though a mountain race (T.r. bolivianus) occurs in the highlands of northern Chile, Bolivia and northwestern Argentina. D'Orbigny's Seed-Snipe (T.o. orbignianus, and T. orbignianus ignae) are typically Andean with the latter race occurring in southern Peru and the high plains of Chile, Bolivia and Argentina. A third species, Gays' Seed Snipe (Attagis gayi gayi) inhabits the highest parts of the mountains often only just below the snow line or in semi-desert regions above the level of puna vegetation; it is known from the mountains of Ecuador to southern Chile, where another race, *Attagis gayi simonsi,* is restricted to the province of Jujuy in northern Argentina. All the Seed-snipe are small: seven to eleven inches and well camouflaged with a speckled brown, almost partridge-like plumage. Their colouring sometimes confuses them with the Andean tinamous, though their flight gives them away instantly. Tough, spiky grass, the *paja brava* or *Ichu* (Stipa ichu) is the characteristic vegetation of the high punas of the southern Andes from central Peru to the northern Atacama: it forms hard tussocks and even at the highest levels of the sierra, small clumps manage to grow on the mountainsides. The overall pale-yellow ichu is excellent cover for the smaller birds such as Seed-snipe, or small plovers and lapwings. Here, the Andean Lapwing (Ptiloscelys resplendens), is instantly recognizable by its strident calls alarming all the other birds when danger is close, and in the same habitat a Puna Plover (Charadrius alticola) is common; while the American Golden Plover (Pluvialis d. dominica) can be seen occasionally – it is a rare visitor from the north.

One bird well suited to the puna environment is the Andean Woodpecker or Flicker, locally named *Pito* or *Gargacha* (Colaptes rupicola puna) which lives in an entirely treeless zone, making use of holes in the stony parts of the high pampas. These unusual birds are yellowish-brown, with a lighter yellow underside and are excellently camouflaged so that only when they fly can they be seen easily. Often this Flicker is seen in groups of four or five, and occasionally an individual finds an old fencing post or boulder for a perch where it can be observed from close range.

Not far from Titicaca, the tallest flower spikes in the world grow from solitary stands of a giant Bromeliad, the Puya (Puya raimondi). This plant is endangered by the Indians who cut it for fuel or even set light to it on the hillsides for the fun of making a giant, flaming candle. Each plant is over thirty feet tall when mature, and its growth is reckoned to take more than a hundred years. In its final year it flowers once only and then dies. Believed to be an ice-age relic, the Puyas are found in very few places; some are known in the Callejon de Huaylas in northern Peru, a few are in Azangaro (on the Hacienda Checayani); others are in a valley not far from Pucara north of Titicaca and a good site recently established as a reserve is at Comanche, west of La Paz, Bolivia. When the Puya is in flower, an estimated eight thousand, greenish-yellow inflorescences adorn the upper two thirds of the plant and attract a variety of hummingbirds, including the Giant Hummingbird. For most of the life of the plant, it stands out as the only tree-like growth on the barren, open puna and despite the solitude of a single puya in thousands of square miles, the plants have become the nesting site for some birds which otherwise would use cliffs or rocky places.

The Variable Hawk (Buteo poecilochrous) is one of the usual residents, and any Puya which has been used by the bird contains the dried empty corpses of a variety of small mammals caught on the puna. Also, among the spiky lanceolate leaves are many pathetic shrivelled small birds which rushed into the Puya to take refuge from the marauding hawk, and then could not get out past the sharp spines. The Puya is used for nesting by several other puna birds and at Comanche I noticed the nest of a ground dove, possibly Metriopelia m. melanoptera.

Among other birds of prey occurring abundantly throughout the Titicaca region and Altiplano is the Cinereous Harrier (Circus cinereus) which is widely distributed in temperate South America and has a range including the highland marshes and rivers. Similar in habits to the Harriers of America and Europe, the bird is recognized by a slow flight and grey-blue colour of the male or brownish colour of the female which is larger. The Andean or Mountain Caracara (Phalcobaenus albogularis megalopterus) is found only in the Andes, principally in the higher zones often above 10,000 feet. It possesses fine black and white plumage, with some bare parts around the beak and the legs coloured bright yellow-orange. The coloration gives it a distinctive and handsome appearance that cannot be confused with any other raptor. They feed on small mammals, reptiles and carrion, sometimes finding the best supply along the roadsides where one can count on seeing groups of two or three on most days when travelling in the sierras. Although these birds of prey are typical, their numbers are limited by the relatively small populations of other birds and mammals. Even the Andean Condor is present in greater concentration on the Peruvian coast, a fact that can be related directly to the relative scarcity of carrion in the mountains.

Indians in the high mountains have a limited number of domestic animals, usually a cow, some sheep and a small herd of llamas; in addition there are a number of sheep ranches in the central and southern highlands, even around Titicaca, but the conditions as much as they limit the domesticated and wild mammals, also limit the predators. Like farmers everywhere, the Andean landowners regard carnivores as a pest, and both the puma and the Andean Fox are shot whenever they are seen. However, large mammals are not a feature of the Andes, and apart from the few vicuñas, most other species are tiny and hence insignificant to Andean people. Just a few rodents have been in demand, particularly the chinchillas and the viscacha.

In the southern highlands of Peru and central Andean region in general, the Mountain Viscacha (Lagidium peruanum), a close relative of the chinchilla is the most obvious small mammal. Dull grey-yellow and about the size of a rabbit, viscachas live in warrens, high in the rocky parts of the puna often above 15,000 feet, where they find concealment beneath large stones and boulder-ruckles. They are common on the mountains around Titicaca, despite pressure from hunters, and anywhere well away from civilization they are abundant. The best time of day for observing them is in early morning or late evening, when they are most active, though they are sometimes out during the day or early afternoon, and in winter they sit on the dark rocks absorbing the precious sunlight. Viscachas are classified in the Super Family Chinchilloidea which includes the coypus and chinchillas. Another viscacha, the Plains Viscacha of Argentina and Paraguay is similar and lives in warrens on the pampas, where it is known by the piles of refuse it collects and discards in front of the burrow. Chinchillas on the other hand are truly Andean and as an adaption to combat the extreme cold, they have an incredibly soft fur which has led to their near extinction in the wild. The chinchilla, often called the Royal Chinchilla of Peru (Chinchilla brevi-caudata brevicaudata) has not been recorded for many years and could be extinct. Fortunately two closely related species, also of the genus Chinchilla, may survive in isolated areas, and *Chinchilla lanigera* which has been given a distribution that once included north Chile has been reported from the western Cordillera of the Andes above Iquique. The animals are tiny, about the size of a small hamster, but with a soft, grey pelage and a long furred tail, usually carried in a tight curled form. It seems incredible that such a tiny animal can be hunted to the point of extinction in the inhospitable wastes of the Andean semi-deserts, but Indian trappers, well suited to working at high altitudes use weasel-like grisons (genus Galictis) and smoke to drive the chinchillas from the burrows into nets.

One report mentions that Sicuani and Oruro in the central Andes were great centres of the chinchilla trade and that Lima and Coquimbo were the ports where skins were sorted for export. From customs data in Coquimbo (reference from Bidlingmaier 1937) it can be stated that in 1905 a total of 18,153 dozen skins were exported, valued at between one hundred and one hundred and fifteen dollars (US) per dozen. In 1906, 9,050 dozen were exported and in 1907 the number had fallen to 2,328 dozen, with the inflated value of between four and five hundred dollars (US) per dozen. As the numbers decreased, and the values went sky-high, the demand from the United States and Europe was to buy at whatever the price. Local agents obeyed, and one species has disappeared, the others are very rare and any location where they are known is a jealously kept secret.

In recent times the value of the chinchilla skin has forced the development of an industry which strangely is only just beginning to start in the native land of the species. Near Titicaca, at Lampa, a chinchilla farm has been in operation for five years. What about the re-establishment of the animal in the wild? At present it is too expensive: a male chinchilla in Lampa is worth two hundred and fifty dollars (US) and a female two hundred.

Amongst the smaller mammals of the central highlands are Highland Desert Mice (genus Eligmodontia), the Chinchilla Mouse (Chinchillula), an Andean Swamp Rat (Neotomys) and others adapted to life in the arid semi-deserts or high punas. These tiny mammals are preyed on by the raptors and mountain carnivores, which include skunks and at least two small cats. The Pampas Cat is more typical of the valleys, being found both in the western Andes and on the Amazon side in the ceja de selva zone while another similar species is the Andean Cat (Felis jacobita) which has a more restricted range limited to the high mountains of southern Peru, Bolivia, and north east Chile as far as north west Argentina. Within their area of distribution these cats can be confused with a feral domestic mottled-greyish cat and often they are seen near flocks or viscacha warrens.

Another rare mammal of the Andes is the *Taruca* or Guemal Deer (Hippocamelus antisensis) and it has been persecuted throughout its range from the sierras of Ecuador to northern Argentina. In the mountains of Azangaro a few miles north of Lake Titicaca, a few scattered groups are known to survive on land which has been privately owned for generations. Hunting the Taruca in these places has been strictly controlled or forbidden. Fortuitously the terrain around the Hacienda Checayani owned by Dr Hernando de Macedo suited the taruca and he had counted as many as seventy individuals. Only recently new agrarian reform laws may turn many estates over to the Indians and though in many ways such a move seems to be a step towards improving the status of the Indian, any changes if they take place too soon will harm the wildlife. A taruca is a good hunk of protein in any terms, and from experience it is reasonable to assume that once the Indians own their wildlife, they shoot it. An obvious argument is that good management can control the shooting, but even in a well developed country restrictions are difficult to impose. In the Andes, the taruca lives at 13,000 to 16,000 feet, land which the Indian is well used to; once the slaughter starts in earnest controls will follow, but that could well be too late.

Nowhere within its range is the guemal easy to observe: they move to the higher levels close to the snowline in daytime where they feed on lichens and mosses, but in the early hours of dawn they sometimes can be found in the lusher pasture of the swampy valley-bottoms, and it is in these places that it is best to set up a blind; following a group on foot is impracticable. The first sight of this rare animal can be an anticlimax; at a distance they are similar to a medium-sized antlered deer, coloured greyish-brown and they watch the approaching danger with great concern. The scene could be from somewhere in Europe until the group moves slowly up the hillsides, and the background changes from yellowing puna to high, ice-covered cordilleras, towering against the mountain sky.

These animals occur within a reasonable distance from Titicaca. Azangaro is no more than ninety miles away and the high ranges along the eastern shore ascend steeply to their 20,000 foot summits within fifteen miles from the lake. But for the naturalist without considerable time to spare, it is unfortunately true to say that only the bird-life of the lake and marshes can be seen easily. Most of the mammals are small, and those larger species that should stand out are shy or nocturnal or both, which leaves an impression that the central Andes are virtually devoid of wildlife. Only the rabbit-sized viscachas make a lasting impression on a journey over the sierras and they bound away at the slightest danger, leaping from boulder to boulder with incredible agility, springing powerfully with their hind-legs. In a richly populated warren, any approach causes the entire hillside to come alive and viscachas rush in every direction to find cover, whilst individuals sit unmoving, watching from the rocks like tiny sentinels overlooking a world a long way above the clouds.

Lake Titicaca is a centrepoint for plenty of the wildlife, and almost inevitably, many of the tales of mystery. Legends of sunken cities, lost Inca gold and strange Indian demons are part of the local life and the appeal of the unfathomed depths of the lake has attracted several diving expeditions variously equipped with simple diving suits or more elaborately, the recent exploration by Captain Cousteau used midget submarines. So far nothing new has been discovered, in fact the lower levels of the lake seem remarkably empty: only an extremely unusual frog has become adapted to permanent underwater existence. Locally known as the *quele*, the frog (genus Telmatobius) is found at depths over two metres and reaches a size of forty to sixty centimetres in total length. Whilst most other frogs have rudimentary lungs, and a skin that is highly vascular allowing oxygen absorption over a large surface area, the Telmatobius frogs possess large cavities laterally within the body which is flattened dorso-ventrally. These spaces are shaped by collagen supports and the walls contain abundant capillaries, making it seem probable that this is an adaption to increase the area for oxygen absorption. On land, when the frog is taken from the lake, it is unable to support its own weight and moves sluggishly with none of the agility of its relatives. Undoubtedly, the telmatobius lives a slow life with a metabolism suited to the cold water that has a low oxygen content. So far only a few studies have been made and these are mainly morphological to aid the taxonomists, with some references to the unusual mode of life. Other related species occur in many of the mountain lakes, and have become aquatic or are still semi-aquatic: the genus is at an interesting stage of evolution and possibly one of the greatest rarities of the Andes.

Little data is available to throw any light on their rate of reproduction and suggestions in the local press have hinted at commercial development of a frog industry, perhaps freezing the delicate meat for export or even the home market. Such an industry could work, and already some frogs are sold in the highlands above Lima. But despite an apparent abundance of the Quele in Titicaca, it could have taken a very long time to develop; once again the conservation stoplight should change to red and studies should come before the factories.

Any new research programme must now encompass the entire biology of Titicaca and hopefully it must lead to a greater understanding of the delicately balanced ecology. Changes have occurred slowly in the past and the strange frogs, fish, some insects and the Flightless Grebe are part of a unique fauna. Even the aquatic plants have a characteristic singularity and none of them possess floating leaves, a common feature in more familiar situations. For students the lake offers a host of projects, but the vital question may remain unanswered. Can Titicaca ever return to the pristine condition of Inca times or will the children of the lake now destroy the home of their creator?

Flamingoes and the Red Lake

To the south of Lake Titicaca the Andes change rapidly. In the areas where the southernmost of the two great lakes existed long ago, there is now a high plain, scarred by volcanic activity and left with enormous deserts of salt or borax that form a moonscape probably unequalled anywhere in the world. The limits of this harsh wilderness are the semi-deserts of Carangas between Titicaca and Uyuni, the high cordilleras that border the eastern and western extremes and folds of the Andes in the south where the mountains narrow between Argentina and Chile.

Much of the land is over 12,000 feet, with peaks reaching 21,000 feet or more and some high desert plateaux, among them the highest in the world at over 16,800 feet. Much of the area comprises the southern Altiplano of Bolivia, but it fringes the highest parts of the Chilean Atacama desert and the influence of this dry zone tends to affect the entire region. It is hardly surprising that the wildlife is equally unusual and though extremely limited by the tough conditions of the habitat, this part of the high Andes is the home of the world's rarest flamingoes and a small rhea of a sub species found only on the highest plains. There are tiny rodents belonging to genera unique to the region and the scattered remnants of what were once numerous groups of vicuña and guanaco. Also desert conditions have preserved traces of what could have been the first men of the sub-continent, and is the refuge of one of the most extraordinary tribes of South America.

It is a region where changes seem to have occurred throughout many times in recent history. The Inca expansion touched it only mildly, the Spanish exploited some of the rich silver deposits, and for more than two hundred years it has been forgotten. Some recent exploration has revealed that the Conquistadores were at the surface only when they started more than two thousand mines, and now there is a chance that this region will be opened-up by modern companies intent upon the rich resources of silver, bismuth, borax, sulphur, manganese and a host of others. This projected rape of the southern Altiplano might not come about for many years; profits today depend on the whim of local politicians, but given a stable climate for investment, the face of these untouched Andean wastelands could be altered within a decade. At present any journey undertaken there takes the form of a tough expedition needing the best equipment and expert knowledge, and for most of my own exploration, I was helped by the unequalled experience of a geologist who had the task of conducting a survey for the Bolivian Government.

The list of travel problems is headed by the desert, often waterless, usually uninhabited and only marked by crude tracks linking isolated villages. Gasoline and water have to be carried and food for a month is a standard precaution. Maps are poor and the few that do exist can be dangerously unreliable; in fact a compass and a modest amount of field knowledge is far safer. Within the Bolivian limits, the southern highlands include the sparsely inhabited triangle in the north, mainly the province of Carangas, the almost deserted area from Lake Poopo southwards to the provinces of Lipez in between Argentina and Chile, and a small triangle behind the Cordillera de Lipez but bordering the Argentinian frontier, where the topography is known only from air-photographs and the land is mostly unexplored.

Lake Titicaca drains southwards through the River Desaguadero which is sluggish, seldom very deep and in some sectors no more than a marsh. Over a meandering length of nearly two hundred miles, the river passes the eastern fringe of the arid semi-deserts of Carangas with a course generally to the south east. Finally the water flows into a lake near Oruro. Only a few years ago, most of the Desaguadero water entered the shallow Lake Poopo, but the delta region silted up and the main lagoon formed nearer to the mining town of Oruro. Lake Poopo has almost dried out and in exceptional years disappears completely, leaving a hard mud-flat, glistening white with a thin crust of salt. In 1969, the driest year for more than a quarter of a century, the level of Titicaca fell far below normal, thus reducing the flow of the Desaguadero, which combined with the effect of an extreme drought in the southern Altiplano, caused the new lake Uru Uru to dry out completely. Thousands of flamingoes were caught by the mud as it changed from a glutinous slime to concrete within a few days. One observer watched the beginning of the disaster in late September, and by late October, Uru-Uru was covered with the shrivelled corpses of more than five thousand birds.

Though 1969 was incredibly dry, there is plenty of evidence to show that the Atacama and the southern Bolivian highlands have been steadily drying out for many thousands of years; additionally some features suggest that the rate is probably increasing. Old beach levels encircle the Altiplano, often with many feet separating the marks to indicate stages in drying. The major phase is believed to have occurred not more than 10,000 years ago. Today, obvious traces of this inland sea exist as strongly saline lagoons and salt-flats or *salars*, covering many hundreds of square miles with thick layers of salt or borax. All the deserts and semi-deserts of southern Bolivia are contiguous with the high Atacama and the pressure of the exceptionally dry climate prevents heavy rainfall in this part of the Andes, so much so, that the rainy season is very short in some years with no more than two or three days when it rains. During these years the desert trails remain passable, but sometimes when the highland storms are severe, great tracts of the desert are flooded, outlining the penultimate level of the ancient lakes.

Few Indians live in the region and apart from isolated pockets of Quechua speaking communities, most of the present inhabitants are Aymara. They were there at the time of the Spanish, and enslaved for work in the mines, but in 1767 rebellion and disease spread through the highlands and the workings were abandoned, often leaving large towns complete with cathedrals and churches which are now crumbling and eerily deserted. A few small mining interests were started towards the end of the last century, and a railroad was built from Antofagasta on the Pacific to La Paz between 1873 and 1917. The line crosses the salars and wastelands to connect the Bolivian capital with the coast and provide transportation for minerals. Until quite recently this intrusion of civilization had little effect on the area.

The first naturalists to work amongst the volcanoes and salt-deserts made their way by mule, travelling either from the Chilean side over the passes of Ollague or Siloli. Some journals describe adventures in the biting cold or when wind-driven snow lashes between the peaks, as the sky turns grey, blending with dark basaltic volcanic ash. One expedition backed by Berkeley James, a British businessman, entered the western cordilleras in 1886 and discovered a rare flamingo, said to be the world's rarest and known today as James' Flamingo (Phoenicoparrus jamesi) after the expedition's sponsor. The original specimens taken for identification faded in museums for sixty years and the descriptions made subsequently were frequently inaccurate; this factor as well as the lack of fresh exploration led to the belief that the James' Flamingo had disappeared. For a long time it was assumed that either the species was extinct or its range was confined to some distant habitat, unknown at that time. In 1957 the species was re-discovered by a Chilean expedition organized by A. W. Johnson author of 'The Birds of Chile'; his party covered three thousand miles by truck, horse and mule and eventually encountered P. jamesi on the Laguna Colorada (latitude 22° 5'S. long 64° 9'W.) at an altitude of 14,800 feet.

The rediscovery of the James was an event in ornithological history and Johnson's expedition was followed by a collecting expedition from the Peabody Museum, another from the New York Geographical Society and a visit by Roger Tory Peterson. Now the James' Flamingo is well described. It is small, no more than thirty-six inches bill to tail, with dark brick-red legs and a large area of rich yellow on the bill. It has an extensive red eye mask and often the plumage seems paler than that of the other species it frequently accompanies.

Of the three flamingoes of the Andes, the Chilean (Phoenicopterus ruber chilensis) is distinguished by the stronger pink colour especially on the back, and by the brownish-blue legs with red knee-joints. This species also possesses a lighter, almost white bill, tipped with brownish-black that contrasts strongly with a very pale eye. Chilean Flamingoes are very closely related to the Greater Flamingo, and of the three Andean species they have the widest distribution. The third species, the Greater Andean or Andean Flamingo (Phoenicoparrus andinus) is the largest, with a length of forty-six inches to forty-eight inches bill to tail. This bird is distinguished not only by size, but by the bright yellow legs, primaries that are strongly black and a smaller red eye mask separated slightly from a reddened area at the base of the bill. On close examination the bill is different from the James and it is yellow, but with a larger area of black. In the field, when it is possible to observe the birds feeding, the leg and bill coloration is the simplest way to identify each species, though all three are reported from the same habitats in the high Andes, where the main confusion occurs. Neither the James or Andean have been recorded below 7,500 feet and additionally they are three-toed, lacking the vestigal hind-toe of the American species.

One habit that helps separate the Chilean Flamingo from the other species is the stirring action of the legs which it uses to raise food particles into suspension. Neither of the Andean species have been observed making this twizzle-stick movement in their natural habitat, and A. W. Johnson comments that even when the three species are feeding in the same area, the Chilean stands out clearly. The leg movement is a characteristic of the genus Phoenocoptera.

There is no doubt that each of the three flamingoes occurring in the high Andes is specialized and suited to a particular habitat. This is observable within one lake, and whereas the Andean Flamingo usually feeds in the deeper less saline areas, the James is often in the shallow, very salty pools and the Chilean feeds in the edge-pools where some fresh water meets the salt. Occasionally all three will be found close together, but most frequently the general pattern is reflected in the distribution of the species. The Chilean is widespread from the coast to the high lakes, while the James is the most restricted, with a limited range and virtually is known only from high, alkaline sites, though recent information shows a larger distribution than ornithologists have recognized until now. Andean Flamingoes occur on high altitude lakes only but appear to have a wider altitude range and slightly broader limits of habitat, not always occurring on strongly saline lakes.

Bolivia's Laguna Colorada, or literally 'Red Lake', is coloured brick-red by tiny algae of the genus Alphanocapsa which are heavily pigmented with phycoerythrin. During a dry year, when the water is shallow and the algae are concentrated, the colour is incredibly rich and by late afternoon it seems that a pool of fluorescent-red dye has been poured between the gently sloping volcanic peaks. The strength of colour is enhanced by scattered blocks of salt standing like 'ice-bergs' often ten feet above the water, backed by a white crystalline fringe along the shore line. Between 1965 and 1969 I made visits to the lake in each season of the year, from the relatively mild days of the Andean summer when the night temperature only touched zero C. degrees to some terrible days in June 1967 when the lowest temperature was minus 21°C. The most beautiful effects in the cold months were the frozen pools where ice and salt crystals had mixed with scattered flamingo feathers. The birds were slow in the extreme cold and seldom took flight in the morning; if they were approached suddenly they walked away over the ice, with an unusual gait. Each step was careful, and with their long legs they looked as unsteady as skaters on stilts.

During 1967 the cold at the Laguna Colorada was intense and prolonged. Much of the lake froze despite the concentration of salts in the water – mainly Sodium chloride at fifty-nine grams per litre and Sodium sulphate 21·41 grams per litre. Only a hundred James stayed there, and a small flock of Andean Flamingoes lived permanently in the area of warm water in the north-east corner where hot springs bubble from a mountainside. Snow showers blew fiercely each day, hiding the volcanoes and distant shore and by the afternoon, the normally high wind sent enormous clouds of salt dust whirling across the level eastern side making photography nearly impossible. Flying salt crept into everything, blinding for the eyes and dangerously corrosive in delicate camera gear. Nothing kept it out, but by sunset the wind slackened and the bitter cold of the night attacked savagely, even through heavily quilted Arctic sleeping bags. Water in the Land Rover radiator congealed despite a concentration of anti-freeze well above the recommended level for the temperature and by morning the metal-work of the car body was cold enough to freeze a plate of hot water set down there for a few minutes.

In the same year I made two more visits to the lake, one in September and another in mid-summer. By December all the James' Flamingoes had gone. The Laguna Colorada believed to be the main nesting site of the rarest species, was empty. Other visits made during the nesting season by Joh. son and his colleagues, observant geologists and once personally in 1966, always revealed considerable nesting activities, but the exceptional weather of 1967 changed the pattern. Sightings of the James in that year came from many places; small groups were seen on the Las Salinas lake above Arequipa in southern Peru, five hundred miles north of the Laguna Colorada. They were found on Lake Coipasa in the small area of open water fed by the River

Lauca where it drains into the northern end of the Salar Coipasa; other reports came from one of the few animal collectors in Bolivia, Sr Charles Cordier and he had seen James' Flamingoes on the edge of Lake Poopo where a few shallow pools existed, and at the mouth of the Rio Grande de Lipez where the river drains into the great Salar of Uyuni. Suddenly it seemed that the bird was everywhere but in its usual haunt.

By 1969, some James' Flamingoes had returned to the Laguna Colorada and they were reported there intermittently in 1968, but no accurate survey was conducted in Bolivia to cover all the possible habitats for the James and apart from the known seasonal migration which finds the species on some of the lower lakes of the Atacama in winter, notably the Salar de Atacama, it seems likely that extreme conditions cause wider migrations beyond the usual range. However, before presupposing a pattern that could occur with increasing frequency if the climate changes rapidly in the southern Altiplano, extensive surveys will be needed, especially in view of conservation problems. Unfortunately, in the vicinity of the Laguna Colorada the possible habitats for the species are remote from the Bolivian capital, and reliable observers seldom make visits. It is possible that the James might have alternative nesting sites in the neighbourhood or even that increased human activity near the Laguna Colorada has caused the birds to move away. This is a mystery that is waiting to be solved and the answer will be just as exciting as the re-discovery less than fifteen years ago.

The Andean winter of 1967 was exceptionally hard and totally dry over the southern plateaux. Charles Cordier was stuck at Queteña near the Laguna Colorada for five weeks with a cracked cylinder-block, and three men driving a truck on the contraband route from the Laguna Verde to Chile froze to death, when their vehicle refused to start at 16,000 feet. For five months the cold was incessant, with only a slight warming of the air at noon in spite of sunshine, but on the other hand the Lipez area was strikingly beautiful. All small streams and the Rio Grande de Lipez were solidly frozen and with the thaw, blocks of ice like miniature pack-ice flowed along in the rivers swollen by the melting snow. Throughout this time, there was no rain and the sky above the open plains remained clear day and night.

The wildlife has obvious adaptions to suit the conditions, and the plants are unique, some types being part of a relic flora. Open areas at the 12,000 foot level are covered by low, resinous *Tola* (Lepidophyllum quadrangulare), a tough slow-growing bush, with small leaves coloured dull greyish-green. Thousands of square miles have good tola growth, with the bushes tightly packed in sandy places and more openly spaced where the surface is rocky or hard. The normal height for the Tola is roughly three feet, though in some areas of Carangas, west of Oruro, the bushes are large and almost six feet tall.

A curiously compacted relative of the Parsley, the *Llareta* – yareta – (Azorella glabra) exists in the high cold zones in the most arid places. The plant is tough and forms a weirdly-shaped growth covering the rocks resembling a green exotic fungus. On close examination, the llareta is composed of many tiny plants with pale-yellow flowers no more than two millimetres across, which soften the outline. But the plant, as well as being resinous, is very hard and has great value as a fuel. Usually the main *llareteras* – the Indian name for extensive areas covered by the plant – are worked by a few men who supply nearby villages. Recently the demand has increased and llareta is now 'mined' by dynamiting the large solid masses and carting by truck to towns far afield. This new threat is certain to have a serious effect on the plant because its growth is slow and already the inroads have cleared it from many places.

Similarly and perhaps far more serious is the ever-increasing demand for tola wood. The plant is another good fuel and the bushes are being cleared quickly now truck-transport is available. Land to the west of Oruro is the most seriously affected and in danger; also, the tola pampas southwest of Uyuni, are being exploited relentlessly to supply the town, as well as the capital La Paz. Railway flat-cars are convenient for carrying the precious bushes to the relatively treeless zone three hundred and fifty miles to the north, where municipal laws forbid the felling of any tree – even the introduced eucalyptus which has taken fairly well to some Andean climates. It is most unfortunate that the two areas of tola pampa most in danger of denudation are among the few remaining haunts of the vicuña in Bolivia. Since 1963 I have followed the fortunes of the two small bands in the immense pampas of Lipez, and they have had no chance against the increase in human activity there; once the cover of the tola is taken away they will be even more vulnerable to hunters searching for food.

The bushes form the main protection for many birds, particularly Tinamous and Rheas. Tinamous are widely distributed and occur in many different habitats from Mexico to Chile. They are found in jungle, tropical grasslands and throughout the Andes. Pentlands Tinamotis (Tinamotis pentlandii) is the largest of the high Andean species and is fairly common around Queteña near the Laguna Colorada. Like all tinamous this species has a delightfully melodious call, that echoes in the silence of the early morning and gives it the local Aymara name of *Kiula* – or *Kewla*. Usually it is found above the 13,000-foot level where low tola or ichu grass give protection. It possesses good camouflage with an overall mottled grey appearance and distinctive lines of black and white on the head and neck. Nests are made on the ground and the eggs have the porcelain surface characteristic of all tinamous; the colour of the shell is bright green. Though not confined to the southern Altiplano, as tinamous are common in some parts of the high central Andes, it can be said that both Lipez and Carangas offer undisturbed habitats which is an additional reason for protecting the areas around certain flamingo lakes.

In some regions of the Andean semi-deserts of Chile, southern Peru, Bolivia and north west Argentina, the high altitude race of Darwin's Rhea was present at one time in abundance, but recently, it seems to be on the decline. The race is *Pterocnemia pennata tarapacensis*, and is hard to distinguish from the nominate race which occurs in the south of the sub-continent. Johnson says that it has a greyer back and fewer white feathers than the Magellan race, and furthermore a close examination shows the presence of eight to ten scales in the tarsus as compared with the sixteen to eighteen of the southern form.

Natural enemies of the Rhea include the mountain cats and foxes, but they are threatened now by the destruction of their habitat; they are killed to supply a trade for feathers used to make dusting brushes. With the reduced number of this sub-species, Indian egg collectors present an additional threat, and eggs are sold in Altiplano towns at roughly six times the price of a chicken egg, almost an increase in proportion with the volume. Rheas nest communally with one male taking a harem of up to half a dozen females, which lay their eggs in a rough depression on the ground; it is the male which incubates and looks after the chicks. As many as twenty or thirty eggs are found in one nest, often situated on the higher ground: they are however hard to find as the adult plumage blends well with the cover and the group feeds well away from the nesting area. The Aymara Indians are always watchful and know the likely places. On occasions their children, who act as animal herders in the daytime, have the chance to observe the birds for hours and they notice habits and movements: once the nesting season begins in November, eggs are located without difficulty.

The Spanish name for the Rhea is *Avestruz*, and in the Andes the Aymaras know them as *Suri*. Though large, flightless and primitive with a resemblance to the African Ostrich, they are not closely related and are much smaller with a size of not more than thirty-eight inches. They can run quickly, and on the open pampa they can outdistance a horse. A typical species of the lowland pampas are the related Nandus (Rhea americana), slightly larger than Darwin's Rhea and in great demand for feathers and skin. Hunting the Nandu is a traditional sport of Argentinian gauchos, who in groups and mounted on horseback chase the birds and fell them with skillfully thrown bolasses.

Even in the thin air of the Andes, rheas run surprisingly fast and for long distances. When chased on the pampa by Land Rover, they make quick doubling-back turns which are difficult to follow, and if they are successful in gaining ground over rough terrain, they have the habit of lying flat on the ground and relying on their superb camouflage. Some fine territory for the Andean Darwin's Rhea is the tola covered plain south of Uyuni, where they are seen close to the trail on journeys to south Lipez. If they stand motionless in the pampa they are hard to see, but once running they take on the comic stumble of an old maid with her grey skirts lifted high from the ground. Fortunately, there is nothing old-maidish about their speed if they are pursued and it needs considerable skill at the wheel to keep up with them.

Many of the smaller birds of these cold, southern Andean plains are similar to species occurring in the puna around Lake Titicaca. They include the same seed-snipes, lapwings, plovers, small tinamous and, gathered at fresh water ponds, there are grebes, coots and members of the Family Anatidae, particularly the Andean Crested Duck, Puna Teal and the Andean Goose. However, a few species are rare and have a limited distribution.

Perhaps the least known is the Horned Coot (Fulica cornuta) which occurs in a tiny area of southern Bolivia and the high Chilean Atacama desert. The species is everywhere confined to high altitude levels above 12,000 feet, and at present there are no precise details of the distribution. It is smaller than the Giant Coot, with a size of twenty-five inches and is distinguished easily by a strange 'proboscis' or muscular appendage over the bill. This structure, of unknown function, gives the bird its name, but since its discovery in the middle of the last century no extensive field work on the species was carried out until W. R. Millie of Vallenar spent two seasons observing the nesting behaviour. Sr Millie is a colleague of A. W. Johnson and his studies have been recorded in 'The Birds of Chile'. In the first year of watching the coots, Millie discovered that the large nest built from water weed is anchored to the bottom on a conical pile of stones. The following year he observed the parent birds carrying stones from the shore and adding to the piles established over the years. Later, on weighing the stones, Millie found that each was approximately one pound and he had seen them carried in the beak, though in the general labour of weed collection, he noticed that the 'horn' seemed to be useful for holding the weed that the bird dragged through the water.

Much of this information came from studies of nesting birds on the Laguna Grande in the high Atacama, and later from another population on the Laguna Santa Rosa at the southern end of the Salar de Maricunga accessible from Copiapo.

During my travels in the same area, I found that the northern limit in Bolivia appeared to be between Llica and the western cordilleras near the Salar of Coipasa; also other lakes in the south, near Laguna Colorada and reached from Queteña were nesting sites, though nowhere was the species so strongly represented than on the Laguna Santa Rosa. On this remote lake, the population seems relatively stable, and I was able to observe many of the habits reported by Millie. At least ninety of the coots were engaged in nest building, and the lake can be studied from water level or from a high bank on the southern shore. The surrounding desert is breathtaking, with great distances of light-grey sand totally devoid of any tree or habitation as far as the horizon. To the east, over fifty miles away, the immense Nevado Ojos del Salado marks the Argentinian frontier. It is the highest mountain in

Chile (22,550 feet), only 285 feet lower than the Aconcagua massif in Argentina. Another mountain group, the Nevados de Tres Cruces, stand closer to Maricunga: they form a solid steel-blue wedge in the gentle Atacama sky and a splendid setting for the home of what is probably the rarest bird in the Andes.

Around the foot of the hill fringing the Laguna Santa Rosa, a narrow track follows the shore to the east and it was obvious that it had been used by sportsmen. Cartridge cases of several sizes including rifle ammunition littered the ground, and crude stone-blinds were evident; possibly it was the work of engineers from the great copper mines. However, there is an agelessness about everything in the Atacama and there is no chance of determining whether shooting is practised regularly or even whether the hunters go there for the coots. Other birds are abundant in the open fresh water, and travelling there with my wife in January 1967, we recorded nesting grebes (Podiceps occipitalis junensis), Andean Gulls, Andean Crested Ducks and a small flock of no more than a dozen Chilean Flamingoes. Nearby, there were signs that guanacos were in the region, and later we disturbed two animals in the narrow *quebrada* which carried the road to Copiapo. They were extremely sensitive to the sound of the Land Rover, which can be taken as an indication that they have been chased by jeep-borne hunters and a sign that some protection must be given soon to the wildlife of the Atacama.

Mitchell's Plover (Phegornis mitchelli) is another Andean rarity, found from southern Peru, to Curicó in Chile and to the latitude of Chubut, 46°S. in Argentina. In the south it is found as low as 6,500 feet, but in the Atacama and Lipez regions it occurs in the zone between 10,000 and 16,000 feet. One area where it has been reported is the rarely visited corner of Bolivia east of the Laguna Verde near the Salar de Chalviri, but this is some of the most difficult country to enter, involving a desert journey of nearly three hundred miles from Uyuni, the last stop for stores. Johnson has recorded this plover near Santiago in the upper Yeso valley, and his party was successful in locating the nest; and it is his report that gives the first description of the eggs.

This plover is approximately eight inches and is worth locating as it belongs to the genus Phegornis that includes two other species, *P. cacellatus* of

Christmas Island and Tuamotu Archipeligo, and *P. leucopterus* of the Society Islands. At an early stage Mitchell's Plover became isolated from the main strain of the Holeartic Order and established itself as a high altitude species in the Andes. Even in such a remote habitat, the bird is rare and usually occurs in well-isolated pairs living along the borders of small streams.

The classification may one day be changed, as Mitchell's Plover has some great similarities with sandpipers – originally it was known as the Chilean Short-winged Sandpiper (1888). It is easily identified by the longitudinal white stripe on the side of a dark brown, almost black head; and the chestnut band which extends over the back and part of the sides of the neck. The other plumage gives a brownish-grey general coloration, but the legs and feet are orange-yellow. Though most of these features separate it clearly from any other similar high altitude species, a feature which verifies the identification is the relatively long bill which is dunlin-like, black, slender and slightly curved. Certainly, Mitchell's Plover poses the kind of ornithological problem that taxonomists can wrestle with for years: even Bock in his work on Plovers (1958) decided to retain Phegornis in the Charadriidae, until new evidence is produced to prove otherwise. Field studies of the behaviour may help to enlighten a student, but he would have to be very hardy to spend months camping in the rigorous habitat of this bird.

Avocets and stilts are grouped in the small family Recurvirostridae which is represented in almost every part of the world, though there are only seven species. The Andean Avocet (Recurvirostra andina) is limited to high mountain lakes and bogs, from the extreme south of Peru to the latitude of the Salar de Maricunga in Chile and Catamarca in Argentina. Most frequently they are seen in small groups of up to twenty, though occasionally they occur singly. They are not large (only nineteen inches) and are distinctively black above and white underneath; they have legs shorter than the stilt, and the bill is long and curved upwards. Instead of probing, the Avocet sweeps the bill from side to side and often a line of them seem to march purposefully almost in time across the shallow saline pools.

Once the sun has risen a few degrees above the horizon, the thin desert air warms quickly, though a cloud or the shadowing effect of a mountain in the early morning can keep the temperature to below freezing for many hours. This climate has a marked effect on the number of species represented, and insects among the invertebrates are not strongly evident. A small scorpion occurs in some sandy parts of the Altiplano, even in the deserts of Carangas and I have seen them active at night when the air temperature is below zero C. degrees. In the daytime, tiny lizards are active and one species typical of the Uyuni area, is finely coloured in mottled yellow and black so that it merges well with the light earth and contrasty shadows.

Small mammals include Andean Mice (genus Andinomys), Highland Desert Mice (genus Eligmodontia), the Chinchilla Mouse (Chinchillula sahamae) which are examples of Cricetidae, as well as several better known rodents that are larger. The Mountain Viscacha is encountered in great abundance in remote and little frequented parts, and the warrens on the rocky cliffs around the Laguna Colorada are especially large. Of the same family, but much rarer is the Chinchilla (C. lanigera) which has been reliably reported from isolated regions near Mount Sajama and to the south near San Pablo de Napa. Rat Chinchillas of another rodent family, the Abrocomidae have not received much attention, though locally the occasional fur is sold under the name of Chinchillon. Cabrera lists seven species in the single genus Abrocoma and all of them occur in high, dry areas of Argentina, north Chile and the high altitude deserts of Peru and Bolivia, the typical species from Bolivia being Abrocoma cinerea cinerea.

One of the most annoying yet curious rodents is the Tuco Tuco (Family Ctenomyidae) which is widespread throughout much of the southern half of the sub-continent. Though typically Neotropical, they resemble gophers and frequent dry, often sandy areas where they burrow extensively just below the surface. Gauchos and Patagonian horsemen curse the presence of the animal because horses stumble wherever the tunnelling occurs. In the high Andes, the mountain slopes of the Atacama and Lipez are very sandy, and hiking over these on foot is made doubly laborious by the unstable surface made by energetic Tuco-Tucos. They are active mainly at dusk or early morning, and camping near their territory is disturbing on the first acquaintance with their uncanny call – Tuco Tuco – that seems to come from underground just before dawn. In the stillness of the freezing half-light it takes great determination to move from the warmth of a sleeping bag and investigate, but by daylight the tucos are silent.

Predators are relatively scarce. A few pumas and some small mountain cats occur even in the highest and dryest zones, moving down to the Indian settlements to take a llama or sheep occasionally: also the Andean Fox somehow survives the paucity of prey, living on young birds, eggs and small mammals though a cold year must limit their numbers severely. Camping by the Laguna Colorada in June 1967 the lowest temperature we recorded was minus 20°C. with the shade temperature in the day never above zero. After we had been around for two days we were visited by a lone fox, obviously thin, and completely unafraid. It approached within ten yards of our tents, collected scraps and even when we were working, it sat among the ichu grass only a few yards away. The edge of the lake was iced over and on several occasions we spotted it stalking the wildfowl, apparently without success.

The present status of vicuña and guanaco is poor over the entire range of both species, and in the wild country of the high Atacama or the southern Altiplano, the remoteness is not a guarantee of safety and the pattern is the same as in other places. Protection of animals, which has never been a South American strongpoint cannot extend to distant corners of a country, and the region includes rugged corners of Argentina, Chile and Bolivia. In this no-man's-land, miles from anywhere, the midnight silence is broken by the rumble of heavy traffic as *contrabandistas* drive across ill-defined borders. A small group of hunters can work undetected for months and the last bands of vicuña there could soon be destroyed. Some of the terrain is perfect for a high speed chase, with the open desert as smooth as a race track for long distances. Against the skyline of a high desert plateau, vicuña mirage into easily visible blobs as they run for the cover of the tola, and on many occasions we have followed them over the Pampa Colorada, the fine red mudflats of Uyuni, or across the Planicie de Panizo, the world's highest desert plateau near the Laguna Colorada. Even the recent convention signed by Peru and Bolivia cannot protect the vicuña in this area, and though the Red Lake and surrounding desert is given the title of a National Park, by the time wardens can be afforded by the Government, even assuming that men can be persuaded to stay there, protection will be too late. The main routes into the high deserts lead from the port of Antofagasta via Calama eastwards through the cordilleras, or alternatively in the north of Chile, a road will soon be ready to take traffic from Arica to La Paz following the line of the existing railroad across the northern part of Carangas. Alternatively, in the south from Copiapo, a dirt road passes near the Salar de Maricunga and across the Andes to Argentina, while from Salta and Jujuy the Panamerican highway crosses the Bolivian frontier at Villazon.

From La Paz the trail to Lipez takes three days. The first stage follows the main road to Challapata south of Oruro; the next is a turn westward around the south of the dry Lake Poopo to Salinas de Garcia Mendoza on the edge of the Salar de Uyuni. The scenery changes in this region to the dramatic expanse of the ancient seabed. Rudimentary tracks skirt the Salar, but the convenience of covering one hundred miles in less than two hours adds to the thrill of a high speed journey over the salt. At the edge of the Salar the ground is dangerously soft and the trail crosses a rough causeway of raised stones built by prudent truck-drivers, but the main Salar has a firm surface of pure dry salt. The Uyuni Salar is roughly one hundred miles long by sixty miles wide, and, seen from one side or even half-way, the whiteness extends to the horizon. Shimmering in the mirage, the cones of distant volcanoes seem to float in the sky, and they are the only guides along the route. After taking a rough bearing to check the general direction, it is easy to drive a straight course over the salt, though some local knowledge is useful to ensure arriving at one of the few causeways leading off at the other side. At the beginning of the year, often until March or April, the Salar of Uyuni is covered with water, sometimes only an inch or two but often more. If the water is not too deep for the vehicle, it is possible to make the drive and the only danger is the weird effect of a lost horizon. The salt just below the surface makes the sky and water surface merge perfectly, and the effect must be similar to a 'white-out' in polar regions.

Lipez and the Laguna Colorada are two hundred miles of desert driving to the south and the trail crosses the wide Rio Grande de Lipez, then follows tortuous dry quebradas and narrow passes between giant blocks of volcanic ash that have been eroded into strange forms. At every turn the terrain is more desolate; it could be the face of another planet and from the scarred cones of the dying volcanoes, wisps of smoke are dark against the sky. The eery landscape instils an urge to explore. Some of the mountains have yet to be climbed, some valleys are unknown and the salars are a mystery. On one occasion we were travelling across the Salar of Uyuni with the intention of camping overnight on one of the islands of rock, possibly old mountain-tops, which rise above the surface on the western half of the salt. For many miles the salar was hard, with only hexagonal crystal patterns as a surface feature: they were left when the last pools of water dried out. After sixty-five miles driving, the uniform whiteness was unchanged and our only feeling of progress came from the gradual enlargement of the mountains appearing above the horizon like islands from a lunar sea. At one point fresh water bubbled from under the salt, leaving brackish pools, enclosed in irregular pipes lined with perfect crystal-flowers. In another spot, hot sulphurous vapour poured from holes, and a hideous slurping sound warned of restless power locked below. The rocky landing site we chose was two miles long by half a mile wide and one of the largest islands with a summit more than six hundred feet above the salar; the nearest mainland was thirty miles beyond.

Stopping the Land Rover within thirty yards of the island to be sure of a firm start in case the salt crust was thin at the edge, we walked to the shore and made our camp. We were on a shelf of hard rock, the line of an ancient beach, where the boulders were encrusted with the calcareous remains of algae, in the same fashion as the beaches on the surrounding mainland. Above the first level, there was an indistinct beach, and above that again, roughly two hundred feet above the salar another well defined shore line showed the apparent extent of the old Andean sea. Between the two beaches at a level possibly representing a time between two periods of drying climate, we discovered a small rock shelter. On the floor we found cracked flamingo egg shells scattered about, and in the sand were arrow-heads, proof of some previous human visitor. Each of the arrow-heads was carefully worked from hard stone, either the black basaltish rock common throughout the region, or finely polished obsidian. Obviously, at some time long ago the early inhabitants of the Altiplano had ventured across the salar; or it could have been a lake in those days, a southerly extension of Titicaca which separated the cordilleras and filled the central Andes from end to end. On other parts of the island we found traces of primitive man and surprisingly between the boulders and tall columnar cactus, there were viscachas and foxes. Somehow they had crossed the salt in the years since it dried, even these days they could not make the journey at any time. The islands in the salt are as solitary as those in an ocean, and in the gentle darkness of the Andean night, the starlight reflected from the crystalline surface. From the island summit, the salt, an absolute desert, was like a vast unearthly plain suspended between the dark cordilleras.

Totalling more than ten thousand square miles, the Salars of Uyuni, Chiguiana and Coipasa are the most spectacular feature of the high Andean deserts. In Chile, the Atacama holds the Salars of Atacama and Ascotan, and around each one of them many traces of early hunting tribes lie casually on the ground. Dozens of arrow heads for birds, spear heads for vicuña, tools for shaping the stone and the occasional club for defending the tribe against raiders. The desert might hold some of the secrets of early America: shrines have been discovered on the highest peaks, simple petroglyphs are clear to this day, and recently Padre le Paige, a Belgian priest and archaeologist, believes he has uncovered the oldest remains on the continent. His dating puts some finds at more than 15,000 years B.C., well beyond the age of anything found so far. The work awaits publication and confirmation but Padre le Paige has worked in the Atacama for twenty years and knows it better than anyone.

Today most of the Andean Indians are herders or simple agriculturalists, and past changes in the way of life are seen in the southern Altiplano where arrow heads and crude field systems are side by side. Only two small groups of Andean Indians continue to hunt on a large scale and they are dying tribes clinging to a precarious life in the salt deserts. The dominant tribes of Aymara and Quechua are settled with well-established villages, but long ago Uru-speaking tribes were widespread south of Titicaca, though regarded by the Aymara as beasts of half-human beings from the *chullpas* – the ancient tombs. Consequently they were persecuted and driven into refuge areas in the desert, where they lived on wildfowl and a few primitive crops. One group of marsh-dwellers, the Urus, has disappeared, but a related tribe of Chipaya survives in Carangas, and a smaller sub group of Morato live at the southern end of Lake Poopo near the swamp that feeds the River Lacahahuira.

The Moratos lived in solitude and before Poopo began to dry out they were reported to make frequent hunting expeditions after ducks and grebes on the lake. Walking as a line through the shallow water, the men would drive the wildfowl to the bank where the women and children were ready to club the birds to death. The meat could be salted, and in the cold climate, it kept for a long time. Now that Poopo has dried-up, the Moratos have changed and the surviving families are now herders, possibly integrating with the nearby Aymara.

Only the Chipaya remain as a relic of the early population, and they live in two small villages at the edge of Lake Coipasa one hundred miles west of Oruro. Their homes are distinctive, built in a beehive shape from sods and thatched with grass, they stand isolated in the flat plain around the lake. Twenty miles away, Sabaya, the nearest Aymara village is not far from the Chilean frontier, and yet the Chipayas have rejected most contact with their neighbours. They have taken to herding sheep and growing a few crops but their main trade is provided by their skill at hunting. Flamingo oil is worth the equivalent of three dollars for each tiny bottle as an Indian cure for tuberculosis, and the Chipayas sell it to miners who suffer chronically from the disease. These hunters have at least two ways they use extensively for catching the birds. One form is a simple snare of cord suspended beneath the water level on short stakes, and the nesting flock is driven into the trap at night when the birds are afraid to fly. The second method is an art which the Chipayas practise from childhood, and they are able to knock flamingoes out of the air with a bolas.

In the late evening as the light changes over salt marshes, into gentle tints of pink and purple, the Chipayas work systematically towards the flocks in the shallow water. As the birds move, slowly trailing their large bills in a twisting pattern across the mud, they are unaware of the danger; they see the men approaching and only take flight at the last moment. In groups of five or six, the birds form a skein that moves along the watercourse in the direction of a distant pool. The Chipayas know the pattern well and half a dozen throwers crouch in the flight path. As the flamingoes pass overhead, the Chipayas spring up, uncoiling themselves and their bolasses in one movement. A hiss of weighted cords breaks the silence, and is followed by a dull thud as the whirling missiles hit soft feathers. The flamingoes flying fifty or sixty feet above, suddenly begin to tumble in ungainly masses of legs, necks and useless wings. Death is quick; the Indians grab at the fragile heads and pull them off.

Chipayas have been slaughtering flamingoes for centuries. Feathers, egg shells and other debris left in the ancient tombs clearly tell the history. But the new demands on their skills, in the form of a pressure from a widening market for their product, is leading them to concentrated hunting. They have no discrimination, and the birds are likely to be of any Andean species including the rare James; it is a trade which is bound to be harmful. Alone it might be controlled, but other Indian groups have found that flamingo eggs can be sold as food – a different story from years ago. Many visitors to the Laguna Colorada have reported the Indians' work of robbing the nests, and in recent years increased mobility has led to a widespread exploitation of all nesting sites. In 1967, one estimate suggests that twenty-five thousand eggs were taken from one area near Uyuni where the Rio Grande de Lipez drains into the Salar; and at the beginning of the season, each egg was worth a shilling, though later the price dropped as the market was saturated.

If the hunting and egg-collecting continues, there could be a serious conservation problem within a few years, and until now, there has been no attempt to protect the wildlife in this part of the Andes. The wilderness which should give adequate solitude also conceals the misdeeds of a few, and with the development of new mines and trade, however insignificant, there will be a temptation to live off the wildlife. It is unlikely that the delicate balance of this once useless land can withstand pressure from the modern hunters and the prospect of a greater drought: it may be the time for some protection.

From Deserts to
Darwin's Country

Almost half the Andean chain is south of the Tropic of Capricorn, and from the widest part which is in the Bolivian sector, the mountains narrow to not much more than a single cordillera extending southwards to Tierra del Fuego. The peaks, including Aconcagua, the highest in the Americas, are some of the most spectacular found anywhere, and they conveniently form the frontier between Argentina and Chile. As well as being a barrier that divides the two sides of the tapering continent in the southern latitudes, the Andes separate two very different climates; on the west are the temperate rain forests while to the east there are dry steppe-lands. In this part of the Andes one gets the impression that the spectacular scenery can far surpass the wildlife as an attraction: certainly the fauna is limited and fewer species are recorded. On the other hand, some of the animals are unique and the inhospitable shores around the tip of the continent are richly populated with marine mammals and seabirds. Similarly, the fauna of Patagonia was rich at one time – there existed only relatively few species, but thousands of individuals. Now farming has tamed much of the land and some species face extinction.

Large areas of the southland have been settled by immigrants from Europe and only a few places in the forested interior remain virtually unexplored. Other parts have been set aside as National Parks and have become famous tourist centres. The fiord-like Pacific coast in the south is among the best of the continent's natural wonders; the lake regions of Chile and Argentina attract thousands of visitors each year and in even the Cordillera de Paine, where tower-like the mountains stand as sentinels overlooking Scottish farms, the holiday trade is developing.

There is not much doubt that the Andes in the southern half of the continent are different; they are not any longer the home of the Indian, but

The Spectacled Bear is the only South American bear and occurs only in the Andes, usually in the ested zones.

A Giant Coot. The largest of the Coots which is nd in the high lakes of the central Andes. These s possess enormous feet, an adaptation to enable n to move across floating water-weed.

13. A Tinamou of the high Andes is perfectly camou-flaged for survival in the low *ichu* grass of the punas.

14. The high altitude species of Darwin's Rhea in the high semi-deserts of southern Bolivia.

15. A group of vicuñas on the Pampa Galeras Res central Peru, situated 13,500 feet above sea leve

16. Shearing alpacas in the highlands of southern Peru.

have been taken by Europeans who have pioneered in much the same way as the frontiersmen of the early United States. The first advance took place in the eighteenth and nineteenth centuries when the majority of the Indians were shot or forced to leave the good lands, until only a handful of each tribe survived. The second move was division and fencing, and it was this action which started the decline of wildlife on the pampas. Finally the sportsmen arrived to shoot everything. Sometimes today they work for farmers who are troubled by vermin; it is said that a guanaco eats pasture enough for five sheep. But when Darwin visited Patagonia, the groups of guanaco were a characteristic feature of the landscape, and it was hard to travel a few miles without finding hundreds of them. Darwin was amazed by their abundance and fleetness; they were the only large mammal and the large groups occupied roughly the same ecological position as the Pronghorn Antelope of North America; and sadly the groups went the same way. Guanacos are now both rare and timid and have disappeared from much of the sub-continent, and there are not many left in Patagonia.

The parks are visited for their scenic beauty and can be very easily reached from Santiago or Buenos Aires. Fishing and skiing are good sports, or the people can sail, camp outdoors and walk through the mountains. Not many of the holiday-makers are interested in wildlife, and they cannot be blamed for their attitude as there is nothing very much for them to see that would excite anyone but an enthusiast. It is a bleak picture on the surface, but for weekend naturalists and anyone with an eye on their environment, there are animals to search for, and some rare ones as well. In Chile and Argentina moves for conservation have been made but most odds are against progress. One problem is that only a few people have bothered to find out what exists in the countryside and very few have described the natural history. There has been a long gap between the time of Darwin and Hudson, to the present day; and the field has been left to men like A. W. Johnson in Santiago who with a number of colleagues has produced the standard work on the birds of Chile. Or, in Argentina, there is Francisco Erize, who has travelled extensively and done a lot to pinpoint conservation problems and endangered species. The position is clear; they say that more protection is needed or there will not be much fauna left in a land already possessing severe natural limitations.

12

Darwin said of Patagonia: 'these plains are pronounced by all most wretched and useless' – and yet today they are the land of the shepherd and gaucho. There is plenty of carrion on the farms and birds of prey are relatively common. It is condor country again and perhaps it compares favourably with the Peruvian coast for the numbers of this species that can be seen; although the Condor fly-past at Paracas probably is unique, the Condor often visits the sheep farms near the Andean foothills. Another vulture, the Gallinazo or Turkey Vulture (Cathartes aura) is found in much of South America and is common along the western Andes from Colombia to Tierra del Fuego. It is just over half the size of a condor, and is recognized by the bare red-head and neck which accounts for its common name. This species seldom occurs above 6,000 to 7,000 feet in the south, though it is found around many Andean towns in northern latitudes. The Black Vulture (Coragyps atratus foetens) is a bird of the lowlands with a wide distribution from the southern United States to south central Argentina and Chile; it is common around many towns, particularly in tropical regions and everywhere is associated with carrion and the refuse of human habitation. This vulture is not found in the Andes, though it occurs frequently in towns of the warm foothills.

In a land where mammalian life is generally small and not obvious, the birds command most attention. Predators are outstanding and seem to form part of the rugged scenery; the dark forests would not be the same without hawks and buzzards, just as mountains would be empty without caracaras or the occasional condor. Normally associated with the Andes except in the far south, is the Chilean Eagle (Buzzard) or Grey-backed Buzzard, which is easily distinguished as it is much larger than other predators occurring in the same territory. The favourite prey of this handsome bird includes small mammals – viscacha and cavies – as well as some birds, especially tinamous. It nests in inaccessible places high on cliffs or in tall trees in wooded parts, usually constructing a bulky nest of dry twigs and lined with wool. This species is not uncommon and can be seen in many parts of the Andes, though in populated areas it faces the same persecution as other birds of prey.

The only hawk which approaches the size of the Chilean Eagle is the Osprey (Pandion haliatus carolinensis) which is a regular summer visitor from North America. It occurs along the coast of Peru and south into

Chile, often as far as Valdivia, and locally it is known as an *Aguila Pescadora* – Fish Eagle. Ospreys are not Andean though in spectacularly wild parts of the coast where the mountains reach down to the sea, I have seen Ospreys on many occasions: sometimes as many as five or six at a time. They do not occur in the far south, and typical species with a southern distribution include the Red-backed Buzzard (Buteo p. polysoma); the Red-tailed Buzzard (Buteo ventralis) and the rare Chilean Goshawk (Accipiter chilensis) found usually in the countryside bordering forests. In the same regions there are falcons and caracaras – the Caracaras or Carrion Hawks are scavengers like the vultures. Chimango-Carrion Hawks (Milvago chimango – three races) are the commonest and they are found in fields and towns, where they feed on grubs, insects and detritus on rubbish dumps; in fact, this Carrion hawk has adapted well to the effects of civilization and it is recorded over much of the southern Andean foothills to Tierra del Fuego. Another Carrion hawk which is widespread in the southern temperate regions, even as far as the Falkland Islands, is the Carancho Carrion hawk (Caracara plancus plancus). It is common around sheep stations in the south, though in Chilean territory it is confined to the desert coast near Peru. An Andean, or Mountain Caracara (Phalcobaenus a. albogularis) is very similar to the race found in the puna and mountain regions of the south central Andes except that it has completely white underparts. It usually inhabits the wilder parts of the mountainous regions of the extreme south, though occasionally it is seen on the coast. The habits of this bird are the same as for the northern race and in general terms, the caracaras are not timid nor are they selective feeders; some of them, particularly the Carancho, are known to band together and attack their prey. On the open pampas, rheas and their young are chased by caranchos and the bird is a menace to sheep. Often, caranchos will attack new born lambs and peck out the eyes so that farmers have been paying a bounty on the raptors. Andean Caracaras feed mainly on the limited carrion of the mountains, competing sometimes with condors over the rights to a carcass; they will also take small rodents such as Tuco Tucos and cavies.

Naturalists visiting the extreme southern latitudes around the Beagle Channel are sometimes lucky to see the very rare Forster's Caracara (Phalcobaenus australis), which, though not an Andean species of the mainland, is found among the inhospitable islands south of the Beagle Channel. It is blackish-brown all over and cannot be confused with any other bird of prey in the region; also Forster's Caracara is a resident of the Falkland Islands where it is known locally as the Johnny Rook, a name that has survived since the old sailing days. In a typical caracara way, this bird is not timid and often is very inquisitive. In the Falklands, I have seen it carefully inspect anything left on the ground especially shiny objects like field glasses, buckles on camera straps or pieces of metal foil.

The land of the northern Andes of Chile and Argentina is dry, and usually the few pools or lakes are strongly saline. Much of the landscape is similar to the high deserts surrounding the Laguna Colorada and wildlife has little variety. Far in the south where the climate is temperate and the mountains are lower, there are many lakes and rivers, and the Chilean side is noted for high rainfall. Dense forests of Southern Beech (Nothofagus) are characteristic, and the snow line is very much lower, often nearing sea level. Whereas the puna zone or the upper limit for wildlife is 16,000 feet in Bolivia, the puna zone is at a thousand feet or lower in the south, and in the extreme south can be absent altogether.

The most productive land in Chile is the heartland from Santiago to Puerto Montt; it is a land of farms, vineyards and small towns. Beyond this, to the south, are the main forests and numerous islands separated by narrow channels; there is only a sparse and scattered population until the province of Magellanes in Chilean Patagonia, and communication is by steamship as there are no roads. On the Argentinian side, the land is mostly dry and almost treeless, though forests spread through the mountains to the Andean foothills. Everywhere the terrain is divided by rivers, glaciers and lakes that are a characteristic feature of the central and southern Andean region. Water-birds are abundant and despite clear similarities with forms occurring in the north, the distribution of some species follows a different pattern.

Torrent Ducks (Merganetta) occur along the entire Andean range and I have seen them in most regions where they are listed. The southern race, (Merganetta armata armata) has a distribution from the far south, extending through the Andes of Chile and Argentina to the northern part of the province of Mendoza. One can be certain of finding this duck in very fast flowing streams where the course tumbles over boulders or through canyons. Sometimes it is seen in level-water but nearly always in those places where there is a strong current. Six races are described between Colombia and Tierra del Fuego and the main differences are noticeable in the males. The Colombian race (M. armata colombiana) is the smallest of the six and the male is lighter on the underside. The Chilean Torrent Duck is very much darker underneath and the almost uniform brown is only partly broken by the characteristic white striping, and in the far south this species is known from very low levels of the mountains often nearly at sea-level, a wide distribution that can no doubt be related to the availability of the food supply. In the north of Chile and Argentina, other races occur and on the eastern side is the Berlepsch's or Argentinian Torrent Duck, and on the west there is Turner's Torrent Duck. All of them have similar habits.

Of the widespread genus Anas or Dabbling Ducks, the largest Chilean species is the Bronze-winged Duck (Anas specularis) and it inhabits fast streams and rivers of the forested Andean slopes in the south from Concepción to Tierra del Fuego. It is Mallard-like in size and shape but distinguished by oval-shaped white areas in front of the eyes which suggest a spectacled effect, giving the local name *Pato anteojillo* or Spectacled Duck.

The Chilean Pintail (Anas georgica spinicauda) probably is the commonest and most widespread Chilean duck; also the species is known from Colombia to Tierra del Fuego and sometimes is found as high as 14,000 feet in the northern part of its range. The Red Shoveler (Anas platalea) on the other hand, is not so common and occurs intermittently in parts of the Andes of Peru and Bolivia, and is widely distributed southwards on the eastern side of the mountains through Argentina as far as the Falkland Islands. Locally in Spanish it is known as *Pato Cuchara* – which literally means 'spoon duck' – here once again is a chance for confusion, as in some places east of the Andes, the beautiful Roseate Spoonbill are given the same Spanish name; fortunately the confusion is cleared up easily once the birds are seen.

Other ducks encountered in the south of the continent include Cinnamon Teal, Silver Teal and Green-winged Teal which occur as southern races restricted to the lowlands on either side of the mountains. Also, there is a southern race of the South American Crested Duck (Lophonetta s. specularoides) which nests in boggy areas near mountain lakes or in long grass around lagoons – especially in the south. After breeding, the Spectacled Ducks usually gather in small groups and often can be seen on the sea coast.

Many southern birds are representatives of typically Neotropical families encountered elsewhere in the Andes or generally in South America. For example, Tinamous occur in Chile and Argentina as far as the Straits of Magellan, and they are very similar to those of the puna lands in the north. A southern race of the Chilean Tinamou (Nothoprocta perdecaria sanborni) occurs south of Santiago while other species, including the Elegant Tinamou (Endromia elegans), and Ingoufs Tinamou – or the Patagonian Tinamou – (Tinamotis ingoufi), occur in the southern latitudes on both sides of the mountains. Near civilization all Tinamous are in demand as game (locally they are referred to as Perdices or Partridges) and some species are endangered in the farming areas of Chile and Argentina. In a few cases I have seen Tinamous sold on the streets of large towns where young boys carrying strings of a dozen birds tied together, pass between vehicles waiting at traffic-lights.

For all birds, the smaller species and passerines in particular, the central lands of Chile and the heavily wooded south make a more inviting habitat in fantastic contrast with the deserts and semi-deserts of the north. At one time, some parts of this region were famous for plentiful stands of Chilean Pine or Araucaria (Araucaria imbricata), the monkey-puzzle tree. Unfortunately, a century of concentrated development has cleared many thousands of square miles of this strange forest and there are only a few areas where the pine survives, and these are in the Temuco region, at levels above 5,000 feet. Temuco is an important dairy centre and the main towns are connected with Santiago by road and rail. A few Indians of the Mapoche (Araucanian) tribe survive in isolated communities, but this part is now the tourist centre of Chile with an incomparable lake district, holiday chalets, snow-capped volcanoes and well-advertised hunting and fishing.

On the road journey south to Puerto Montt and then by steamer to Punta Arenas, the scenery changes as the forests become dominant. The trees are mainly different species of Southern Beech, varying according to the latitude, and the streams are lined in places with the giant rhubarb-like leaves of the Guunera plants; there are brilliant fuschias and rare Copihues (Lapageria rosea), Chile's national flower emblem. Here and there small pockets of Antarctic floras, the remnants of a colder period exist in parts of the lake district and particularly the Cordillera de la Costa near Osorno. In this range of hills, the plant species are similar to those found at the foot of the continent where sub-Antarctic conditions persist. The same coastal hills contain many rain forest plants altered in form by the increased altitude.

The forests are the home of the interesting Huet-Huets (genus Pteroptochos), a group of birds that Darwin noticed and recorded in detail during his Beagle voyage. Huet-Huets are similar to the Turcas (also in the same genus), and there are only four species, three uniquely Chilean and the fourth occurring in the Argentinian Andes as well. Huet-Huets are more typical of the southern forests where *Pteroptochos tarnii* spread eastwards whilst the Turcas live in the scrub-covered hillsides of the drier regions where they have been isolated on the western slopes by the desert conditions. Both Huet-Huets and Turcas are related to Tapaculos and are included in the Family Rhinocryptidae. Tapaculos are more widespread and entirely Neotropical. None of the family are large and they are usually between five and ten inches long, but are stout-bodied and possess strong legs. They are generally inconspicuously coloured and live in low undergrowth, but they have most curious habits and are not good fliers. It is believed that they are about the weakest fliers of all the Passerines and their rounded wings are short, with weak musculature. They move by fluttering or running and seldom move out of cover, though when they are seen, they are recognizable by their habits, or their tail which is usually kept upright or even inclined forward over the head. Of all the Neotropical birds they are one of the most difficult to locate, and though they have characteristic calls – Huet Huet is a native name from the call – the sound never seems to come from where the bird is hidden. Nesting habits vary; some like the Turcas burrow; the Huet-Huets burrow or move under fallen trees, or others nest in crevices or old stumps. These birds feed on grubs and insects which they find by scratching among the detritus on the forest floor, and their feet are well adapted and are large and chicken-like.

A curious, small bird of the forests in the south is Des Mur's Wire-Tail, the only representative of the genus Sylviorthorhyncus of the Family Furnariidae which includes Miners (Geositta), Earth Creepers (Upucerthia, Ochetorhynchus and Eremobius), Spinetails (Leptasthenura) and Cinclodes

(Cinclodes). The Wire-Tail is smaller than a housewren and has an incredibly long tail, the central retrices being twice as long as the body. It is another species that is hard to find as it is fond of dense thickets and usually lives in bamboo within a cover of tangled brush. The Family Furnariidae is exclusively South American and most of the species are uncolourful, with only pale or dull brown shades; however, though widespread in the sub-continent, many of the species occur in the Andes and form a large but often unnoticed part of the avifauna.

Some of the birds found in the colder southern latitudes are unexpected, and there are both hummingbirds and parrots. These families are associated frequently with the tropical regions of the continent, and it is surprising to find them around the cool Magellan Straits. Hummingbirds are found exclusively in the western hemisphere, and their main territory is from Panama to Ecuador. In Colombia alone one hundred and thirty five species are recorded. As one would expect, Chile has very few – only seven species – though one of these, the Green-backed Firecrown (Sephanoides sephanoides) is common and found in Tierra del Fuego, thus according it the record of the most southerly occurring member of the Family. This Firecrown occurs in much of southern Argentina and has widespread distribution in Chile; it is a brilliant green on the back, with a small patch of iridescent feathers on the top of the head. Other hummingbirds in the southern Andes are similarly accustomed to cold climates, and the Hillstars in particular occur in mountain regions often above ten thousand feet. The ability to remain torpid overnight or even longer enables these tiny birds to exist in such cold places.

Parrots are traditionally associated with the warmer parts of the world and it is another surpise to find several of the family in the cooler parts of the sub-continent: even on the high punas of Peru, there is a tiny (only eight inches) Andean Parakeet (Balborhyncus andicolus) that is common and seen in groups of twenty to thirty. The individuals are bright green and noisy and they flash across the mountainsides breaking the silence with harsh calls; it is not unusual to find them in rocky places – old quarries or outcrops, or near the snow line.

At almost the extremity of the continent, on Tierra del Fuego, there is the Austral Parakeet (Microsittace ferruginea ferruginea) which is fourteen inches long. It is the only parrot occurring in the far south, and is coloured dark yellowish-green with dark areas of red showing on the underside. Another southern species, but one which has a distribution in the Andes of central Chile and Argentina as well as the nearby areas, is the Burrowing Parrot (Cyanoliseus patagonus). This species, like many other members of the family, builds a nest in a tunnel made in a cliff or bank usually well out of reach, but the pet-trade has severely reduced the numbers despite the difficult climbs that collectors have to face. Parrots are not only in demand outside South America, but there is a large domestic market and there are dealers in most towns.

Although dealers and sportsmen can be blamed for endangering some species, the main threat in Argentina and Chile now comes from habitat destruction and pesticides. The European immigrants with their great resourcefulness and drive, have opened up most of the land they have settled; their farming methods are similar to those of North America and Europe and smaller birds and mammals could be reduced quickly over a wide range in the temperate regions. Certainly, the national parks and reserves will ameliorate the situation, but in the typical countryside, both underbrush and woodlands are being cut back, and fields are divided by wire fencing, instead of hedges. Many birds of familiar families, as well as many less well-known forms live in these areas. There are finches, swallows, swifts, thrushes, owls, tyrants, spinetails, plant-cutters and others; some will adapt well and survive, others unfortunately will face increasing danger from man.

Argentina and Chile are well ahead in the development of national parks, and many of the protected areas are Andean. To the north of Santiago, there is the *Bosque Fray Jorge*, a woodland isolated in the arid semi desert region in a place where a temperate region flora persists in an isolated microclimate. In the way that the lomas of Peru have induced the development of a characteristic fauna, the Fray Jorge woodland is inhabited by some species uncommon in the surrounding territory, and for this reason it has been given protection. Other parts include Lake Llanquihue with its fine back-drop of Volcan Osorno near Puerto Montt, and the park Nahuel Huapí in the same latitude, though in the Andean region. There are parks in the far south incorporating some of Tierra del Fuego, and in Argentina the *Parque*

Las Glaciares is one of the finest scenic and wildlife zones of the southern Andes. Set in the mountains at 50′S., the twin lakes Lago Viedma and Lago Argentina are the main feature of a region that is backed by a central mountain, Murallón nearly 12,000 feet high; from the mountains magnificent glaciers feed the lakes. This Argentinian park is incredibly beautiful with high mountains and scattered trees; on the ground are soft mosses and the rocks are coloured with bright lichens. The area is remote but not too far from the main highway leading south, though tracks into the glacial zones are not for anything but horses or hikers. Among the southern Andes of this part lives some elusive and rare wildlife.

Black-necked Swans (Cygnus melanocoryphus) and Chilean Flamingoes are occasional visitors to the lake, and the Condor is seen frequently. The mammalian predators in this latitude are again familiar, and the puma is the best known. There are small cats including the Chilean Mountain Cat (Felis guigua guigua) and the widely distributed Geoffroys Cat. A Patagonian Fox (Dusicyon culpaeus magellanicus) is similar to the other Dusicyons, the South American foxes. Of the other carnivores, none are large, but a weasel-like Least Grison (Lyncodon patagonicus) is not uncommon and also there is a Skunk (Conepatus humboldtii).

Rodents are well represented with many species, and there is the rare Patagonian Cavy or Mara (Dolichotis patagonum) which is sometimes called the Patagonian Hare because it has a body like a rabbit or hare on stilt-like legs which take it bounding across the pampas. This species is the ecological equivalent of the jack rabbit or hare and occurs only on the pampas and steppe lands. Other rodents have a more widespread distribution, including the genus Microcavia and the Tuco-Tucos (Ctenomys); however the Mountain Viscacha is typically Andean and southern relatives of the Peruvian form occur as far as 50° 50′S. – (Lagidium wolffsoni).

South American mammalian fauna never seems to reach the spectacular proportions found in other parts of the world; it neither attains great size nor is any species present in large groups like antelope or bison. Perhaps the nearest claim in this direction would have come from the guanaco, but sadly the groups have been hunted ruthlessly. It is the tallest wild mammal of the sub-continent and it possesses a relatively good fur; this factor in addition to the pasture problem has accounted for the disappearance of many thousand of the species in Patagonia. At one time they were hunted by horse-men with dogs, and chases went on for miles across the Patagonian plains. The bolas was used often in the days of the first settlers and I have met farmers in Patagonia who remember catching hundreds of guanaco, especially the young in order to take the skins for use in the ranch houses.

Not many other mammals of Neotropica can compare with the guanaco in size and of course, some are far rarer. The deer family (Cervidae) is repre-sented in the southern Andes by the Guemal – or Huemal (Hippocamelus bisulcus) which is now very rare, having suffered greatly from the work of enthusiastic hunters. Guemals are close relatives of the northern species – the Taruca of Peru and Ecuador; and in his definitive work on the distribu-tion of South American mammals, Cabrera states that the species is found in Chile from Chachapoal to the peninsular of Taitao and Wellington Islands, and in Argentina as far south as Santa Cruz. This mammal is strictly Andean and lives close to the snow line, though it moves to lower altitudes in winter. It is known to have disappeared from parts of its former range where at one time it was abundant and now it exists only in remote or well pro-tected areas. The coat of arms of Chile is a shield supported on the right by a condor, and on the left by a guemal.

Another rare deer is the Pudu (Pudu pudu), the southern representative of the genus. Like the northern form which occurs in parts of Bolivia, Peru and Ecuador, the Chilean Pudu is rare and only twelve inches to thirteen inches high. It is an inhabitant of the damp forests in Andean foothills or in the densely wooded passes through the mountains from about the region of the Lago Todos Los Santos to 50′S. Its known distribution also includes the Chilean Islands of Chiloé and the forested land around the River Bio Bio. Pudus are very shy and usually remain within thick cover, and in a few areas forest clearance is affecting the species. This tiny deer (it is the smallest in the world) is rarely seen in zoological collections, though in Santiago de Chile there are two or three at most times in the zoo, located at the foot of Cerro San Cristobal. The Chilean Pudu appears to be slightly more rufous than the species occurring in the north.

Pudus and guemals are not the only Andean Cervidae and some species of Brocket Deer – (Mazama) – inhabit the forested slopes from northern Argentina to Colombia. An introduced Red Deer (Cervus elaphus) occurs in some parts of Argentina and has flourished; where they are found, they are a great attraction for sportsmen.

The Andes have acted as a barrier for many mammalian species and the fauna of Chile tends to demonstrate the isolation caused by the Andes on one side, and the Atacama desert in the north. Monkeys, for example, are not found in Chile and there are no Edentates naturally occurring there. Only two armadillos live on the west of the Andes, south of Tumbes in north Peru, and both species were introduced. One is the Pichy ciego (Zaedyus pichy cavrinus) which occurs on the east of the Andes and is distinguished by its small size – only five inches long – and a carapace with the scutes attached only at the mid-dorsal line. It was introduced into the Nuble (Chillan) region of Chile. The second species, also introduced into central Chile is Euphractus sexcinctus tucumanus, and it has acclimatized fairly well and is seen occasionally – its original habitat was the Andean foothills region around Salta and Tucuman. This species is related to the armadillo found in the high Andean semi-deserts around Oruro in Bolivia.

The southern part of the continent was the home of the early Edentates, the giant sloths and armadillos – like Glyptodonts which became extinct in relatively recent times. Many fossils were exposed in Darwin's time, and since then countless remains of the ancient fauna have been discovered, including the Mylodon in Ultima Esperanza in southern Chile. In Patagonia, along the fringe of the Andes, there are the dried beds of ancient lakes, now no more than mud flats. From these places, collectors have taken many fossil-bones of the early fauna, and the same region has produced many excellent artefacts made by the primitive tribes. Axes and arrow heads made of stone, with finely pressure-flaked surfaces were the weapons used for hunting in the earliest time of man on the continent.

Everywhere in this extremity of South America, the colours are gentle with the dusty skies above windswept pampas or the permanent coppery-tinge of the southern beech giving a year-long autumnal feeling. Sometimes the Magellan Straits are cloud-free, but these are rare occasions, and often it rains or low cloud envelops the wild southlands. It has been a region of dispute, and for many years, Chile and Argentina have stood fast to their rival claims over the Beagle Channel. In this latitude the Andes turn eastwards to the tip of the continent, not fading away simply but disappearing beneath the sea in a jumble of ice-covered peaks all the way to Cape Horn. The large island of Tierra del Fuego is divided, and is part Argentinian and part Chilean; it is a land of sheep stations and holds the record for the southern-most town in the world – Ushuaia; while on the western side are mountains as much as 6,500 feet high. To the south, towards Antarctica, the Andes follow an undersea line and there has always been the fascinating possi-bility of a super continent, or Gondwanaland which at one time might have linked Australia and South America. Recently a fossilized Lystrosaurus, a hippopotamus-like reptile was found in the Antarctic and the discovery could be a major step towards substantiating the continental drift theory.

The idea of a great linking land has been with us for a long time, but it is unlikely that the 'other continent' was there at a time when it would affect the marsupial distribution or even the appearance of an opossum in the remote tip of the Americas. Lestodelphis halli is the world's most southerly-occurring marsupial, and it is found in the coastal region of Patagonia and Tierra del Fuego; it is rat-like, about nine inches long and has a noticeably short head. Not much is known about the habits of this animal, but it pos-sesses large canines and strong molars which seem to be an indication that it is flesh-eating, living on smaller mammals and insects. Other marsupials occur in the south, though not so near the end of the continent as the *Lestodelphis halli*. There are representatives of the genus Dromicops that are known from the low forest undergrowth of central Chile. *Dromicops a. australis* is found around Valdivia and in adjacent parts of Argentina. This opossum is again rat-like with small ears and it is covered with short woolly-hair; not much is recorded of its habits and a close relative *Dromicops a. gliroides* has been found on the Island of Chiloé.

One of the widespread South American marsupial forms, the Marmosas or Mouse Opossums, so named for their small size, have adapted to many habitats ranging from the cold Altiplano (Marmosa pusilla pallidor has been collected near Challapata, at 12,300 feet near Lake Poopo in Bolivia), to tropical forests and grasslands. Mouse opossums are known also from Argentina and Chile: *Marmosa elegans coquimbo* from Coquimbo in the north and *Marmosa e. elegans* from south central Chile around Concepción whilst *Marmosa e. soricina* is known from central Chile to an as yet unknown limit of its distribution somewhere in the rain-soaked forests in the south.

Mouse Opossums, like many of the other South American opossums, are pouchless and the tiny young develop outside the body of the mother, after being born at an extremely early stage. Each young opossum is attached to one of the mother's teats which are on the ventral side and they remain on the mother, clinging to her fur even when they have ceased to hang to the teat. A group of young marmosas, half covering the mother is a most extraordinary sight, and carrying them appears to be a prodigious effort for such a tiny adult.

An unusual distribution is exhibited by the Rat-Opossums, the Caenolestidae. The first specimens came from Ecuador, and others have been found in Peru, but as recently as 1923 a new genus was discovered on Chiloé at about 43′S. Roughly 30° of latitude and extensive deserts separate the genus known from near Cusco and the genus Rhyncolestes of Chiloé (the same species also occurs on the mainland). Not much is known of the Chiloé Rat-opossum (Ryncholestes raphanurus) or any others in the wild, and it is their morphology that has raised many questions about their affinity to Australian forms.

The Andes south of the tropic line offer a challenge today just as Darwin observed more than a hundred years ago. With almost half of the four thousand miles long range in these latitudes, there is an immense change in the climate and fauna; from deserts in the north to windswept plains of Patagonia or the rain-sodden forests in the south. In some parts, civilization is pushing back the frontiers and limiting the wilderness and yet in other places it seems that man has not taken up the challenge and so the land remains as it has done for centuries. Some of the animals are unusual and others are rare. The Horned Coot from the high northern deserts is one of the rarest birds in the world, and few people know of its existence or have seen it; another example is found in the temperate land of Chile and there the strange Darwin's Frog (Rhinoderma darwinii) fosters the developing tadpole in its mouth – it is known from around the River Maule and from Nublé to Aisen. South American animals have a trend towards smallness, but at the same time their biology is not always straightforward.

It was Darwin who started the studies of natural history in the south, and the fauna was interesting enough to heighten his curiosity and make him examine the wildlife with enormous care. He collected fossils, he watched the guanaco, rheas, condors, and foxes; he commented on the botany and met the Indians. Although some features have not changed even slightly, there are others which have disappeared. When Darwin was in Patagonia, the Fuegians, people of the Land of Fire, were there. The name was given by early sailors who saw the warning fires built by terrified tribes when the first sailing ships passed their coast. Today, the fires have been replaced by flaming gases from the new oilfields of Tierra del Fuego and at night the orange glow reflects from the cold water of the Magellan Straits. In a way the twentieth century fires are a warning that even the most barren land can be taken over and utilized successfully by modern man: perhaps national parks and reserves are the only answer to ensure that something of the wilderness is left by the time that the second centenary of Darwinism is reached.

Even parks and reserves present problems in South America at this moment; in fact, conservation is a topic without bargaining power in the turbulent politics of the continent. To see extremes of destruction and protection it is worth looking at Colombia, and crossing nearly seventy degrees of latitude to where high mountains touch the warm Caribbean.

Odd Men Out

Conservation of natural resources seems to be one of the new sciences that is easy to talk about and yet far too entangled with human affairs for very much to get done. Perhaps some examples come to hand without much trouble, so it is simple to point an accusing finger, though it needs a good explanation why, in one instance, some pesticides have been banned in the United States, while leading manufacturers continue to export the stuff non-stop to South America. In most cases when the question of conservation arises over a species or habitat, there can be two sides to any answer, and in South America most politicians have to consider the human angle first. Whether in Bolivia, one of the poorest countries, or in Colombia, one of the richest, the man who puts conservation in front of education or a burgeoning population, is regarded as some kind of dreamer, – he is an odd man out. To see the type of situation that is likely to endanger the ecology in many parts of the sub-continent, including the Andes, several tough problems in Colombia help to pinpoint the difficulties and show how a little effort used today could prevent total disaster for the people as well as the land.

The Sierra Nevada de Santa Marta is the highest mountain group in Colombia, and it stands in isolation on the Caribbean coast entirely unconnected with the Andes. Although much of the wildlife is very similar to neighbouring Andean forms, some of the birds are unique to the Sierra Nevada while some families are absent altogether. At the foot of the mountains, somehow with a foothold between the sea and the forested slopes is Santa Marta, said to be the first town built by the Spanish in Colombia, and subsequently sacked by numerous pirates including Drake and Cole. Later, in 1830, when South America was striving for independence, Simón Bolívar, the Liberator, and visionary, died there. Then for a long time the Sierra Nevada was forgotten; the mountains were left to a few tribes and a handful

The forested slopes of the Sierra Nevada de Santa rta give some idea of the size of the Andes, as foots and ranges extend as far as the horizon.

18. An Aymara Indian on a floating island in Lake Titicaca. Laid on the Totora reed are small species of Orestius being dried out in the sun.

At the fiesta of Condorachi in Huaylas, Peru, echua Indians on horseback fight for the honour of ing the condor.

20. A golden Condor head which was used on the end of an ancient staff from the Colombian Andes. Photographed in the Gold Museum, Bogota.

21. The arid western Andes of Peru above Nasca.

23. Chipaya Indians of the Carangas province Bolivia hunting flamingoes which they catch wit bolas.

22. The high Atacama desert near the mountains of Tres Cruces. The Laguna Santa Rosa is one of the know habitats of the rare Horned Coot.

of coffee-growers, and the main interest in the region was centred on the surrounding lowlands where the land became famous for an enormous banana production.

The next stage came when in the 1950s, the Republic was torn apart by political strife which erupted violently in several of the departments in the heart of the country. Estimates have varied, but it has been said that during the *violencia*, between one hundred thousand and one hundred and fifty thousand people were killed. Fighting between the two political parties was a constant worry to the central government because the banditry in the countryside often reached a terrifying level. Entire villages were razed, loaded buses were dynamited or the people were killed with machetes. As the feud between the Liberals and the Conservatives gathered momentum, many families left the central regions around Bogota and Cali to make their way to the north coast which was relatively quiet, and hundreds of refugees settled in the Sierra Nevada where the territory was almost the same as the Andean home they had left. It did not take the *colonos* – colonists – long to settle, and they began to clear the forests to make way for coffee, which is a mainstay of Colombian agriculture. But their efforts led to new problems. With a high rainfall in the Sierra Nevada during part of the year, it was not long before serious erosion began to affect the hillsides where forest and undergrowth had been cleared. In some places today, all the forest has gone. Nothing but red-brown earth is left and along the south-western slopes there is more scarred land than forest.

The colonos have moved around the Sierra Nevada to new territory, and the same erosion could begin again. The only protection comes from the local Forestry Service – C.V.M. (Corporación Autónomo de los Valles Magdalena y Sinu) which has very limited strength, and wardens have to make journeys by horse or mule for three or four days across the mountains to reach a settlement; once there they have to persuade colonists to move, and that is difficult. On two occasions when travelling in the Sierra, I heard stories from wardens who had been attacked and forced off settled territory: the details seemed exaggerated, but before we left the region, I had seen a battle between poachers and wardens, and another fight when a warden was shot. In searching for peace in the mountains, the colonists are prepared to use force to defend it, even against the law and conservation service.

Pressure from travelling wardens is not the only way used by the C.V.M. to combat the serious condition which is developing in the Sierra Nevada, and already a forestry station has been established at San Lorenzo, at the 9,000-foot level, about one and a half hours from Santa Marta. Experimental planting programmes have been set up to introduce new quick growing trees, which could be put in the badly affected areas and given to the already established colonists to halt the spread of erosion. From another approach, the wardens are attempting to stop new colonists from entering the region, and also the C.V.M. keeps a close check on all trucks transporting wood between forested areas and the major cities of Barranquilla and Cartagena. On the other hand, the colonists need for land is very fair, and the central government is promoting coffee-growers cooperatives and a coffee-bank with loan facilities; also, development agencies plan to integrate the necessary improvements in the agriculture with a workable, controlled exploitation of the remaining virgin forest.

Fauna of all kinds has suffered in the Sierra Nevada, not only has destruction of the habitat forced some species into small areas, but the colonists fed well off the land in the early years of settlement. Hunting has affected species with good pelts as well as those that had a value as protein. Collared Peccaries (Tayassu tajacu), the South American wild pig, the White-tailed Deer (Odocoileus virginianus), the Brocket Deer (Mazama americana) and Tapir (Tapirus terrestris) are now rarely encountered near the settled zones, as they were in great demand for meat. Of the fur-bearing species, the Jaguar and an Otter – Nutria (Lutra sp) – have disappeared from near civilization, though they still occur in some areas. Other mammals are known to occur throughout the region, though their status is in doubt; among these are ocelot, margay, a porcupine and the Tamandua anteater which is relatively common. Most of the mammals keep within the forest or are nocturnal, which makes observation extremely difficult and nearly all my encounters with them were on the mountain roads at night. A good track leads from Santa Márta to the C.V.M. Forestry Station and, on the way up, the vegetation changes from dry scrub to forest, and then to a damp cloud-forest with palms and tree-ferns; higher still there is a narrow paramo and grassland zone before the tundra level near the snow line. The highest peak is Cristobal Colon 18,950 feet, and it is only twenty-one miles from the

Caribbean shore. This steep slope close to a tropical sea offers what must be the most incredible change in climate and vegetation anywhere in the world, and it is possible to look from palm-fringed beaches to snow in a single glance. Some of the finest views of this kind are from the River Buritaca, east of Santa Marta, on the road to the Guajira Peninsular. The road is new and some sections have to be finished, but the highway provides a link with Venezuela, so that a holiday trade and general commerce might develop between the two countries, mainly to the advantage of the economy of the Colombian departments of Magdalena and Atlantico. One investment has come from a company promoting tourism and a superb hotel has been built near Buritaca and it will serve wealthy vacationers.

Hotel developments and roads will help the Santa Marta trade which in past years has leaned heavily on Colombian tourists, but could now begin to attract Americans and Europeans. The Sierra Nevada de Santa Marta which has a reserve status should be extremely attractive with its wonderful forests and mountain scenery, and already the region is receiving publicity in the United States. It is unfortunate that the mammalian fauna has been reduced, but on the other hand birds are prolific and there is an exceptional variety of species, a feature that is induced by the widely different habitats found in the mountains. Of the outstanding families are the Toucans and Toucanets which are seen easily at many levels of the forest. Possibly the most spectacular is the Keel-billed Toucan (Ramphastos sulfuratus); it is a large bird – eighteen to twenty inches – with an immense bill that seems out of all proportion with the body. However, the bill is extremely light and strong, and the Toucan can manipulate soft fruit and berries with surprising dexterity. Keel-billed Toucans are coloured mainly black, tinged with maroon, but the breast and underneck is a striking golden yellow and separated from the black area by a narrow red band. Much of the bill is a pale green, and an area on the upper mandible is orange: – the tip of the bill is crimson. With amazing colours like these, the bird cannot pass unnoticed and they are common at between 2,000 and 3,000 feet. Of the higher cloud forests and well concealed in the foliage are the bright-green Emerald Toucanets (Aulacorhyncus prasinas); they are hard to see as they prefer the uppermost branches of the trees, so the best way to spot them is to find a clearing where either the colonists have been at work or in a place where a large tree has fallen naturally and exposed the surrounding canopy. None of the family are strong fliers and they proceed with a series of rapid wingbeats followed by a glide, giving a characteristic bobbing flight. They generally travel singly or in small noisy flocks, and their calls include a variety of chattering parrot-like grating sounds and from the larger species a deep croaking that is unmistakable: it echoes through the forests, especially where valleys are deep and narrow – typical scenery in many parts of the Sierra Nevada.

Other avifauna from this region is no less distinctive, and innumerable hummingbirds occur between the warm, humid coast and the snow-line. Then there are the Trogons (Family Trogonidae) which number among the vividly coloured birds of the South American tropics. Quetzals are the most famous of the group, and have great significance in the mythology of Central America, but the Quetzal also occurs south of Panama where it inhabits some forests of the Andes. A White-tipped Quetzal (Pharomachrus festatus) is known in the Santa Marta mountains, and is very similar to the Quetzal. Usually they are seen singly, quietly resting in the high forest, or sometimes on trees at the edge of clearings where, if not disturbed, they stay for a long time. They are fruit and insect eaters and nest in holes, often in decayed trees. Although it is an interesting family, on account of the widely separated distribution in the world's tropics – the Americas, Africa and India to the Philippines – it is the superb, brightly coloured plumage that has given Trogons their greatest attraction. The male White-tipped Quetzal (thirteen inches) has a metallic emerald green upper surface, the head is a bronzy-green and the outer tail feathers are black and tipped with white; the under-side is a brilliant crimson except for the upper breast which is similar to the emerald colour of the back. My first sighting of one of these Quetzals was at 9,000 feet in the Sierra Nevada, when with my wife, I was on a three-day journey from the C.V.M. Forestry Station. The trail was deep with mud and we had just moved from shelter after the daily rain had pounded into the trees to cool everything for a few minutes, when one of the wardens pointed to a brilliant green eye-jerking form at the top of a tall palm. His reaction was almost an awed whisper, as even he recognized the Quetzal as the most magnificent of all the local birds. We watched for nearly half an hour and the Quetzal did not show any sign of movement, so we had to press on to reach a good camp site by the end of the day.

At all levels, from lowland to the upper forests, parrots and their relatives are common in the Sierra Nevada; we saw many different species and Macaws, especially, were a characteristic and not easily overlooked part of the fauna. In the morning and late evening they flew around the valley where we were staying, and their noisy, gawdy flocks always moved into the trees not far from the bungalow. Nearby we had a tree with nesting Oropendolas and they have a far more melodious call than the parrots, and are relatives of the American Orioles (Icteridae). They are usually seventeen or eighteen inches, and have black and yellow plumage and possess long pointed bills. Many icterids are gregarious and nest in colonies, and some of the oropendolas build long purse-shaped hanging nests woven from dry grass. Often the nests are in very tall trees and hang far above the ground; they are secured with great care and each anchoring grass is carefully woven into a position so that the upper part of the nest is bound firmly to a branch. We found one Oropendola (a species with a mellow call with a harp-like quality) at the 2,500-foot level in the sierra, but they were not common, and trees with abundant nests were hard to find. Oropendolas are typical of many South American forested regions from the Caribbean to Paraguay, and I have found great nesting colonies at low levels in the Amazon – sometimes with nests built in bushes or over skeleton trees along the rivers. Also, in some of the narrow gorges of the Andean forest regions, oropendola nests hang from lianas draping the rock walls, and the bottom of the purse will reach within inches of the turbulent streams. Strangely, oropendolas and torrent ducks were nesting close together in one low level Andean canyon in Bolivia.

Isolated from the Andes and possessing a variety of fauna, the Sierra Nevada de Santa Marta would seem to be worthy of any good conservation project even at a late stage, when considerable damage has been done. The C.V.M. is a government agency formed to promote development in the northern part of Colombia. The work covers forestry, parks, fisheries, natural-history and conservation as well as commercial applications of research. Like all government departments, it has limitations and critics, but at least it has commenced the planned exploitation of natural resources.

One day the Santa Marta area might well be a showpiece and already it is well ahead in the field of wildlife conservation. The snow-capped sierras and high forests are only some of the habitats and within a radius of thirty miles from Santa Marta, there are two more reserves. To the west is the mangrove swamp and lagoon area of the Isla Salamanca where there are many tropical water birds, and to the east there is the Tayrona Reserve with Caribbean palm-fringed coast, sea-turtles and scrub-forest. Both of these protected areas are patrolled by wardens who face plenty of problems from colonos, but the conservation message might soon get through to the local population, particularly when the tourists begin to arrive.

The Andes appear south of Darien where the Isthmus of Panama meets the Colombian department of Cordoba. In this heavily forested, rain-sodden corner of South America, the mountains are low and stretch finger-like towards the warm Caribbean. It is a land of the tropical fauna, where many monkeys are found in the forest, and the tiniest primates of all, the marmosets, live in the canopy with scores of birds and insects. From this land which has yet to have a road driven through it, the Andes rise just a few hundred feet to become the northern foothills of the Cordillera Occidental (Western Range). Fifty miles to the east, other foothills in the department of Bolívar mark the beginning of the Cordillera Central (Central Range); then eastwards again the wide River Magdalena flows through a plain between the Central and Eastern Ranges (Cordillera Oriental). Each of the cordilleras spreads fan-like to the north, and the easternmost divides with one line towards the Sierra Nevada de Santa Marta and the other into Venezuela.

A gentleness marks the Andes in the north, and the harshness felt in the far south, or the sterility of the high Bolivian deserts gives way to vegetation-covered slopes. Colombian and Ecuadorian highland fields are green and where the land is farmed it is rich. Heavy traffic streams along good asphalt roads from Bogota, down to Cali in the fertile valley of Cauca, and to the east, highways cut through the *llanos* or low grassland on the way to the Orinoco headwaters. Everywhere in the north the Andes are forested to a high level, and above the trees there is *paramo*, a high grassland or shrub zone where the fauna is limited but not so sparse as in the high puna region of similar altitudes in Bolivia and Peru. Characteristic plants of the paramos are the *Espeletias* or frailejones which resemble the senecios of Africa. Some espeletias are tall, others are tree-like and some are not much larger than average herbaceous plants. In certain regions large espeletias grow in forests across the hillsides, and to see these in flower is a very good reason to visit the paramos. As the stem of the plant develops it bears a rosette of leaves which are carried higher and higher. Gradually, the leaves die and they hang downwards around the stem, while above them, a group of flower heads rise to as much as twenty feet. Above the *paramo*, there is often grassland, and if the mountains attain sufficient height, then there is a tundra-type zone with mosses and lichens to the snow line. Most Colombian and Venezuelan mountains are not high enough to be perpetually snow-covered. None of the peaks in the Western Cordillera have snow, and in the Central Cordillera there are the Sierra Nevada of Ruiz and Huila. To the east on the Venezuelan frontier, there is the Sierra Nevada de Cocay that reaches to over 18,000 feet, and among the Venezuelan highlands snow lies permanently on five peaks over 16,000 feet in the Sierra Nevada de Merida. The contrasting climates found in equatorial and northern Andes are amazing and from the *tierra caliente* – the hot lands between the cordilleras where the temperature often touches 100° F., the Andes rise quickly through many zones, sometimes to snow. Possibly Humboldt's experiences as he trekked towards Quito led him to start work on the zonation of plants at different altitudes; he and Bonpland, the botanist, must have taken days to cover the route by horse and now the same distance can be accomplished in a few hours. But today's speed helps to emphasize the differences, and though I have travelled by both Land Rover and mule through these mountain forests, the change in vegetation and fauna in different levels always has been to me one of the most fascinating aspects of Andean natural history. A most striking feature on any expedition following steep river courses from the highlands is the comparative silence in the evening when the sun is low, and cold air chills the paramo, when only an occasional Tinamou gives a clear note across the hillsides. In the lowlands, the evening insects, frogs and some mammals blend into a distinctive hum, jarred only by the honk-honk of a screamer or screeches from macaws.

Some of the mammals of the warmer northern Andes are not found in other regions, though the predominant fauna follows the general Andean pattern. Counted as one of the more unusual forms, the Mountain Paca (Stictomys taczanowski) is known from the Sierra de Merida to Ecuador, at heights between 6,000 and 10,000 feet. Three sub-species are recognized and they are all similar to the Paca, which is the size of a small pig and is the world's second largest rodent. Pacas and Pacaranas (the tailed Paca) have light coloured spots against a brownish hair, and its pattern is the main distinguishing feature. Mountain Pacas are rarely seen, as they keep to the thick undergrowth near water and it is possible that they are endangered by colonists who find they are a good source of meat. The large rodents, Pacas and Pacaranas are related to Agoutis and are grouped in the Superfamily Cavoidea, which also includes the tiny cavies and the largest rodent of all, the Capybara. Agoutis, Pacas and Pacaranas are forest-dwellers usually living on shoots and insects, and the Agoutis, especially, are gregarious and live in small groups. Often they fight fiercely among themselves over food and when kept in captivity, they deliberately bury small tit-bits. When we were staying with some Machiguenga Indians in the forests of eastern Peru, we were amused for many hours by the antics of four semi-domesticated Agoutis which were kept in the village. They were tame enough to return to their small corral even after an absence of several days when they had been foraging in the forest a hundred yards away. Pieces of *Yuca* left over from the cook-pot were regarded as a delicacy, and they would sit on their haunches and nibble daintily. Later they buried some of the scraps, taking great care to cover the spot with jungle debris. Agoutis (genus Dasyprocta) have a uniform, reddish hair that is not flecked and they are common in the forested Andes from Colombia to Bolivia, frequently occurring at levels up to 6,000 feet. A close relative, the Anouchis (genus Myoprocta) are hardly distinguishable, and are widely distributed in northern South America, including the Andes at low level.

Many rodents are found in the Andes and some are familiar, whereas others are curiosities. The Spiny Rats (genus Proechimys), as their name suggests, possess a fur that consists of soft but sharp pointed spines. They are part of the fauna of the forest floor and are inconspicuous; however, they are widely distributed and a few species occur in the Colombian Andes. One is found around Villavicencio not far from Bogota and others are known as far south as Bolivia, where they live in the Yungas valleys.

A larger spiny-rodent group and easily recognized are Porcupines, but the New World forms (Family Erethizontidae) are tree-living and South American species of the genus Coendou have a prehensile tail which is an adaption for their arboreal life. In Colombia, the family is represented also by another genus, and the Red Porcupine – Puerco Espin Rojo (Echinoprocta rufescens) is very similar to the Canadian Porcupine, the typical North American species. South American porcupines are spiny, but not so well armed as their Old World cousins, and Coendus are nocturnal and gentle, a fact that I can verify as I have seen them handled on many occasions.

A group of rodents not so well represented are the Squirrels (Family Sciuridae) and there are only three genera now recognized in South America. Squirrels in Neotropica are usually arboreal and though they are widely distributed across the sub-continent, they are not an obvious part of the jungle fauna. It is possible that the squirrel niche in the forest ecology has been partially filled by the successful marmosets and tamarins – tiny primates that live high in the canopy, and have a varied diet, eating seeds, small fruits and insects.

The forested Andean regions where the climate is warmer are an exceedingly rich hunting ground for the naturalist. There are countless insects including legions of butterflies and moths; some are extremely beautiful and others attain gigantic dimensions. Blue Morphos, nearly seven inches across, seem to flap lazily through the sunlit clearings, moving slowly and seldom settling. Often butterflies collect in thousands in places where the ground is slightly salty – they will even settle on a camera after it has been held in perspiring hands. A good way to attract them is to prepare an open area with a small amount of animal dung and water; then once the sun warms the ground, there is not much doubt that butterflies will gather. Also, the warmer regions are rich with reptiles: there are many snakes, iguanas and other lizards; then there are amphibians including the marsupial frogs, which have a novel way of caring for the eggs, particularly in dry places or where there is a scarcity of pools. The eggs develop on the back of the female, usually protected by folds of skin, and when the transition to fully-formed froglets is complete, the young seem to burst from the mother at a stage when they are able to feed immediately. Marsupial frogs are known from the tropical Andes as well as in a few places among the cooler sierras of the south.

Undoubtedly, the humid forests offer the greatest wealth of fauna, not only by the profusion of species but by the number of individuals. Some of the mammals are considered rare because they are hard to find, and others, especially some monkeys and the jaguar, have been endangered by pressure of hunting. In the future, it seems most likely that the threat will come from a combination of habitat destruction and the hunter, and one such case in Colombia is the Condor which has almost disappeared. As Padre Olivares has pointed out, the forests in some high regions have been felled and the colonos are well armed. The effect has been to reduce the bird to the tens, not hundreds, within the country, and there is only one good region for seeing the bird, and that is near Pasto close to the border with Ecuador.

Of the rare mammals of Colombia, two are in need of protection: the Pudu, the tiny Andean deer does exist in its northern form in parts of Colombia and Ecuador as well as Peru, but the status and exact distribution is not clear. The species is Pudu mesphistopheles, and it occurs in a number of isolated areas including the paramos around the Volcanoes of Puracé, not far from Popayan in the south of Colombia. Only in this region have I encountered the Pudu in the wild, and then the sighting was too brief as the tiny, russet-coloured animal crossed a mountain track in front of our Land Rover. In spite of a careful search we never found another trace, but this is not surprising as the undergrowth is extremely thick and typical of the paramo zone. Later we were shown skins of Pudu shot in the area, and discovered that the animal is one of the most sought after trophies.

Also from the Puracé area, but one hundred years ago, came the report of a strange tapir seen wallowing in a mountain lake. The sighting must have been memorable as most tapirs are inhabitants of the lowland forests or lower Andean slopes. It was a new species and one that was first recorded in 1829, and named Roulins Tapir after the man who described it; later it was known as the Hairy Tapir and now it is more widely referred to as the Mountain Tapir (Tapirus pinchaque). It occurs in only a few areas of the Andes between Colombia and northern Peru, usually at heights between 6,000 and 12,000 feet and is seldom seen outside thick cover. As the early name suggests, this tapir has longer hair than the lowland relatives and the hair is slightly curly. A good specimen is mounted in the Museum of Natural History at Cali. The Mountain Tapir is one of the rarest South American mammals and is the only member of the genus that lives at high altitude. Certain sub-species of the South American Tapir (Tapirus terrestris) are found at low levels of Andean foothills, and in the north, Tapirus t. colombianus is known from heights of 4,000 feet in the tropical zone of Colombia, including the Sierra Nevada de Santa Marta.

Unlike the highlands of Peru, Bolivia and Ecuador, the southern Andes of Colombia do not contain predominant Indian communities and many of the people are clearly a mestizo type, with a strong Spanish influence. Not only the people are more Spanish, but towns like Popayan and Pasto have fine streets, red-tiled houses and many churches; the countryside around seems well advanced agriculturally, due no doubt to the better climate. Farms are neat with fields divided by tall *agaves* and the wilderness is very much reduced. To a great degree, the Puracé volcanoes and the paramos nearby, represent the best example of an Andean habitat in the north, and so the area has been given reserve status. Much of the credit for the government action on Puracé must go to Sr. Carlos Lehmann, Director of the Cali Museum of Natural History, whose constant work in all branches of natural history, including conservation has kept alive both local and international interest for the reserve.

One of the main problems faced by South American conservation movements is the dearth of good magazines or television to carry any conservation news, and Carlos Lehmann has attempted to fill the gap. He has photographed extensively in the Puracé and Cali area, and now, with short films, he lectures at clubs, schools and university classes. The results have been noticeable, and at weekends many visitors drive into the mountains, and Lehmann often leads small groups to explore out of the way sectors of the reserve. Such great enthusiasm shown by one man is reflected in the museum, and though there is not space for a comprehensive collection of live animals, there is a cross section of the local fauna. In the neat gardens there are several Coatis, the Long-nosed Racoons (genus Nasua) which occur in the forests of both the Andes and lowlands of Colombia; there are Brocket Deer (Mazama) and occasionally a Pudu. Perhaps the most interesting mammal kept there is the Andean Spectacled Bear which occurs in Andean forests from Venezuela to Bolivia. Not only is the zoo section useful for newcomers to the area, but the collection of skins and mounted specimens is of excellent quality and often in demand for identification work; without any doubt this small museum is established justly as the best of its kind in the Andes.

On the other side of the cordilleras where the flat *llanos* grasslands meet the Andes, another reserve has been set aside to incorporate the Sierra La Macarena between the headwaters of the Rio Guayabero and Rio Guejar. The area is approximately seventy-five miles south of Villavicencio and is best reached by chartered aircraft from Bogota which can land at Macarena, the C.V.M. post at the southern extremity of the reserve. The situation of the Macarena has afforded it a unique flora and fauna with many endemic species and sub-species; these have developed by the intergrading of Amazon, Orinoco and Andean species. In geological terms, the Sierra La Macarena represents an intermediate position between the Andes and the Guiana Shield, and the main summit ridge is roughly between five thousand and seven thousand feet high. The range is approximately seventy-five miles long extending from north to south, and averages sixteen miles wide, east to west, with the rock formation dipping to the east leaving steep and precipitous western slopes. Forest covers almost seventy per cent of the area and there are a few places in the south where scrub and grass replace tall trees. At the lowest levels, the Sierra are only 1,200 feet above sea level, and the rivers drain eastwards into the Orinoco.

Although the La Macarena reserve is relatively inaccessible for casual visitors, colonos have moved into some regions and the lowland river banks are now well settled; on the other hand the interior is virtually unexplored and estimates seem to indicate that the fauna is relatively undisturbed. Hunters and skin-traders have made inroads on the commercially exploitable species, if they occur near settlements or along the rivers, and protection will have to be enforced quickly. The C.V.M. is responsible for conservation, and wardens patrol the reserve limits hopefully trying to exert some influence in a region where the laws providing the protection have never been published. Unfortunately, the colonos are well-established and there is a high level of illiteracy among them, so a law in written form has no effect and a response can be achieved only through discussion, which in the jungle has to be on the spot between the wardens and settlers.

The Sierra La Macarena is particularly important because of the variety of flora and fauna, and the birds are especially numerous. Padre Antonio

Olivares has listed more than four hundred and twenty different species or sub-species of which twenty are endemic. Of the more familiar, widely distributed species, there are Spoonbills, Horned Screamers, Hoatzins, Jabiru Storks, King Vultures, Ospreys, Jacanas and Toucans. Listed mammals include the Giant Otter (rare in the Macarena), the Spectacled Bear, Red Howler monkeys, Capuchin monkeys, Long-haired Spider monkeys as well as Jaguar, Ocelot, Tapir, White-tailed deer, Brocket deer and some edentates, and many other species. In many ways, the Macarena Reserve is similar to the lower level and intermediate level of the Manu National Park in eastern Peru, but with the attraction of a unique geology and a high proportion of endemics.

Lowland rivers from the Atlantic to the Andes are the home of the crocodilians, turtles and some aquatic mammals, and this fauna is not generally regarded within the limits of the Andes. However, the mountains after sloping steeply, then extend eastwards with shallow foothills, and in places where the rivers are not blocked by rapids, the Dolphin (Inia geoffrensis) occurs at levels of up to 1,200 feet, reached when the rivers are in flood. This animal belongs to the family Platanistidae – the True River Dolphins or Long-beaked Dolphins – and as the name suggests, the members of this family possess small slender beaks, and they have small teeth. The Amazon Dolphin is up to seven feet long and coloured black above, pink below and can be completely greyish or flesh coloured in older specimens. In the Macarena region, this Dolphin is known as *Tonina*, and in other places is often called Bufeo colorado. Another river dolphin (Sotalia fluviatilis – Family Delphinidae) occurs in the upper Amazon and is seen frequently near the Pongo regions where the rivers finally escape from the Andes. These Dolphins are usually less than six feet long and a general name for them is *Bufeo negro*. River Dolphins travel in small groups and swim near the surface; they often make long leaps from the water, and can be heard as they blow air when they come up. In many rivers they are not uncommon, and have not been persecuted to the same extent as Manatees (Sirenia) of the great rivers, with which Bufeos are occasionally confused.

Wildlife occurring in the warmer parts of the Andes is far more typical of the lowlands than the mountains, and yet it is important in any profile taken of the eastern slope anywhere from Venezuela to Bolivia. At some time in the future, the mountains that were once a barrier giving natural protection to the fauna, might become a factor contributing towards its destruction. At one time it was quicker to trade with Europe via the Amazon river system from places such as the Moxos of Bolivia, the Alto Ucayali in Peru and others, than to cross the Andes to La Paz and Lima. Governments of the Andean countries have been trying for many years to open up the eastern lands of their countries, but the efforts have not gained much success. Air communication has helped and recently some major roads and even oil pipelines have been taken over the mountains from the Pacific to the eastern jungle. None of the Andean countries are backward in this latest move, and in Bolivia, one of the less-well developed republics, there has been sufficient finance from international development banks to begin a new road into the Chapare, north east of Cochabamba. Once these access roads to the jungle were planned, most of them running east-west, it was a logical step to consider a linking road that could run the entire route from Venezuela to Bolivia along the eastern side of the Andes. The project which began in earnest less than ten years ago is named the Carretera Marginal – Marginal Highway – and despite a phenomenal cost and many opponents, the work is progressing in some sections.

A leading proponent of the scheme was Fernando Belaunde Terry, President of Peru until 1968, when he was ousted by a military junta. Belaunde was a visionary, and his road schemes were far too costly for the inflation-ridden economy of Peru in the late 1960s, so the Revolutionary Government axed the budget and much of the Marginal Highway work in Peru was stopped. For two years the forest was allowed to return: where bulldozers had once scarred the mountainsides, trees and scrub quickly began to cover the unfinished road. Parts of the route were thickly overgrown by the end of 1969 when work recommenced. The second attempt will be more cautious, and only a few vital connections will be finished; in engineering terms that means several hundred miles could be ready for use within the next five years. One day the full length of the road will be complete; it will carve the way east, north and south through a frontier of the Amazon. In practical terms, and reckoning from past experience, we can see what effect this has on a habitat and the fauna. Hunting for skins and food increases; for example where a settlement or construction company makes a camp, food imported from the outside world is expensive and the most convenient solution is to hire a small team of skilled native-hunters to shoot game for the workers. This system quickly clears mammals and some birds from a large area around the base. Habitat destruction is next on the list, and once colonos have settled, they discover that burning the forest is the quickest way to clear the land. Large trees are felled, then the scrub is burnt and the process is repeated year after year. During the burning season which often conflicts with nesting, everything in the path of the fire is killed. One cannot blame the man who has to make way for a crop, but he can be censured for setting a thousand acres alight when he only farms one or less. These are the dangers that will become more serious with every completed mile of the new road, and the eastern Andes are bound to change.

Colonists settling in the areas now being opened up are not ecologists and cannot be expected to understand the delicacy of the balance affecting their environment. Ranchers in one area east of the Andes complain that the grasslands are affected by ever greater numbers of termite nests. But do they ever wonder if the increase can be equated with the indiscriminate shooting of the Giant Anteater? The strange animal is now rare on some llanos grasslands. Or similarly, do the people of Rurrenabaque or Apolo in the eastern fringes of Bolivia, realize that extensive ocelot hunting could allow rodents to increase? The rodents carry ectoparasites which in turn are believed to be carriers of the dangerous haemorrhagic fever, a disease that has spread despite great international efforts of research and control. More investigation will be required before the ecology of these regions is understood at a level to allow an accurate reason for these increases to be given, but we can be almost one hundred per cent sure that man has some responsibility. With a growing population and the need to take over more land for settlement, the natural balance is bound to be upset in many places. Hopefully, the results will not always be disastrous and settlers will benefit to the extent of a home, food and communications. Accepting this situation, some thought has to be given to future recreation areas and protection of some habitats in a pristine state for research.

One solution, and the logical first step is the planning and establishment of reserves and national parks to be followed by the enforcement of protection for some species and finally, an education that leads to awareness of wildlife.

The Macarena reserve in Colombia is a good start and the Manu of Peru is protected adequately at the moment, as the Marginal Highway was re-routed around the reserved area and work is not scheduled for the next few years. In Bolivia, there are plans for a national park in the Chapare, though at this time, the area is only a hatched patch on a map labelled 'Parque Nacional Isiboro-Securé', and it has been at this stage for many years. An obvious difficulty is finance and to get wardens into the park zone, they would either have to be dropped by parachute, or use the tiresome route along lowland rivers, the way that hunters have been working.

Money for any wildlife project is almost unobtainable, through government funds in the Andes. Even in the wealthier countries, the budget is tightly controlled. Often it needs outside help to get the basic protection started, and the World Wildlife Fund has sponsored study programmes to select good park areas, and the Fund has contributed to park expenses in some cases. Possibly it is unfair to look at the worst examples every time, but in Bolivia, the Laguna Colorada has no protection despite a quoted status as a national park; also, there is the Sajama National Park in the west of Bolivia where a small forest of polylepis trees grows at very high altitude: the trees have been badly cut into and yet they represent the highest forest in the world. Sajama itself is a perfect volcano and the second highest mountain in Bolivia, with chinchillas said to be surviving on the steep slopes. It is worthy of recognition and the surrounding semi-desert is tola-covered and a known habitat of Darwin's Rhea and the vicuña.

The difficulties of finance arise from the weak economies of the Andean countries where the per capita income in some areas is below one hundred and fifty dollars a year. With much of the population earning little, and with a need for education, food and medical help, it is not surprising that government policies are aimed at improving the standard of living. On the other hand, it could be suggested that with low wages, a battalion of game wardens could be hired, and in fact this is the case in Colombia, and on the vicuña reserve at Pampa Galeras. But low-paid wardens, wherever they are, can be tempted to look away when poachers or colonists make it worthwhile. At the simplest level, wardens need food from the land and as most parks are in isolated places, there is no objection made if the hunter or fisherman offers part of his catch in return for cooperation from the warden.

By this means, hunting continues in a semi-restricted form. Other instances include uncontrolled provision of hunting licences and permits to shoot on reserves, the blind-eye to vicuña trading, or export of rare flamingoes in a three country deal to confuse the laws. The list is endless, and though a few men do their best to follow a code of integrity, many are prepared to help traders because, for their own livelihood they depend very much on the deals. I met one warden who had given up school teaching to live an open air life, and he was posted in isolation under terrible conditions with no facilities for his wife and in constant danger from poachers he had previously reported or warned. His income was twenty pounds a month, less than half the sum earned at the school; so within a year he was teaching again. The system, the dangers and low wage had deterred him.

Wardens are usually untrained, though often drawn from country areas where they have a knowledge of the language and Indian ways if they need it. Whenever possible, skilled supervisors are put into the field, but conditions are not comfortable and it takes a dedicated man to remain in the Manu or Macarena for months at a time – the Dirección Forestal post in the Manu is at least three hard days from civilization. At present, therefore, the best result that can be hoped for is a slowing down of illegal hunting and trading that happens within established reserves and parks, as well as some attempt to implement existing laws covering close seasons, protected species or export of wildlife and skins. Conservationists in South America would like to see more action, but the foundations have to be prepared first and with a period of limited protection in some places, there is a chance that ideas can be worked out in readiness for a time when possibly more money will be available.

There is just one disadvantage that will evolve from the protection given today, and it is that within a few years the reserved areas will be the only places where animals will be seen in any significant numbers, or any individual will attain adult size. Already some tourists are being misled with the safari-style operators who quote 'bag a jaguar or tapir – five days in the Amazon forests with guaranteed good hunting – only two thousand dollars'. The bait is good and the sportsmen leave well satisfied, but in at least one notable area, they have been shooting illegally in a wildlife reserve. The actions of the safari organizers are overlooked, or often abetted by government because the work promotes tourism. The dollar is the rallying cry, but they forget that national parks will pay good dividends when they are equipped for visitors, and shooting now can only upset plans for the future.

With the many political complications affecting conservation attempts, there is a hard battle ahead for the few men who realize that action is needed to save park areas for tomorrow. Too frequently there are depressing inter-departmental misunderstandings, as on one occasion when the head of a government tourist corporation announced to the press that a new national park was the best hunting territory in the country. Telephones in his office began to ring immediately and later the advertisement was changed. But the warning was there. Protect the animals and the result is the same as owning a bank and a constant worry that someone is planning to raid it. In South America there will be a hard race to guarantee security before the wildlife vanishes.

Bibliography

BUSHNELL, G. H. S., *Peru (Ancient Peoples and Places)*. Thames and Hudson, 1956

BATES, MARSTON, *The Land and Wildlife of South America*. Time Life, 1964

CUNNINGHAM, ROBERT O., *Notes on the Natural History of the Straits of Magellan*. Edmonston and Douglas, Edinburgh, 1871

CLISSOLD, STEPHEN, *Chilean Scrapbook*. The Cresset Press, 1952

CHAPMAN, F. M., *Distribution of the Birdlife in Ecuador*. Bulletin of the American Museum of Natural History Vol. 56, 1926

CABRERA, ANGEL, *Catálogo de los Mamíferos de America del Sur*. Vols. 1 and 2. Revista del Museo Argentino de Ciencias Naturales (Bernadino Rivadavia). Buenos Aires, 1957

CABRERA, A. and YEPES, J., *Mamíferos Sud Americanos*. Vols 1 and 2. Ediciones Ediar S.A. Buenos Aires, 1960

CARDOZO, ARMANDO G., *Los Auquenidos*. La Paz, 1964.

DARLINGTON, P. J., *Zoogeography*. Wiley, 1957

DORST, JEAN, *South America and Central America*. A Natural History. Hamish Hamilton, 1967

D'ORBIGNY, ALCIDES, *Voyage dans L'Amerique Meridionale*. In various editions

FAWCETT, COL. P. H., *Exploration Fawcett*. Hutchinson, 1953

FITTKAU, ILLIES, KLINGE, SCHWABE, SIOLI, *Biogeography and Ecology in South America*. Dr W. Junk, The Hague, 1968

GRIMWOOD, IAN R., *Notes on the Distribution and Status of Some Peruvian Mammals*. Special Publication No. 21. American Committee for Wildlife Protection and the New York Zoological Society.

GOODSPEED, T., *Plant Hunters of the Andes*. University of California Press, 1961

HEMMING, JOHN, *The Conquest of the Incas*. Macmillan, 1970

HUMBOLDT, VON ALEXANDER, and AIMÉ BONPLAND, *Personal Narrative of the Travels to the Equinoctial Regions of the New Continent*. Various editions.

HARDENBURG, W. E., *The Putumayo* – the Devil's Paradise. T. Fisher Unwin, 1912

HOWELL, MARK, *Journey Through a Forgotten Empire*. Bles, 1964

HERSHKOVITZ, P., *Mammals of Northern Colombia*. Preliminary Report No. 7 Tapirs. Proceedings of the United States National Museum. Vol. 103, 1956

HUXLEY, ANTHONY (ed.), *Standard Encyclopaedia of the World's Mountains*. Weidenfeld and Nicolson Ltd. London

IBARRA, DICK EDGAR, *Prehistoria de Bolivia*. La Paz, 1965

JOHNSON, A. W., *The Birds of Chile – and adjacent regions of Peru, Argentina and Bolivia*. Vols. 1 and 2. Platt Establecimientos Graficos S.A. Buenos Aires, 1967

KOEPCKE, MARIA, *Las Aves del Departmento de Lima*. Lima, 1964. (English translation Livingstone, 1970)

KOFORD, C. B., *The Vicuña and the Puna*. Ecological Society of America. Ecological Monographs. No. 27: 153–219, 1957

LA BARRE, WESTON, *Aymara Indians of the Lake Titicaca Plateau. American Anthropoligical Association*

MEGGARS, B., Ecuador (Ancient Peoples and Places). Thames and Hudson

MASON, ALDEN J., *Ancient Civilisations of Peru*. Penguin Books, 1961

MOSER, BRIAN AND TAYLER, DONALD, *The Cocaine Eaters*. Longmans, 1965

MATTHIESSEN, PETER, *The Cloud Forest*. Deutsch, 1962

OSBORNE, HAROLD, *Indians of the Andes*. Routledge and Kegan Paul Ltd., 1952
     South American Mythology. Paul Hamlyn, 1968

OLROG, C. C., *Las Aves Argentinas*. Instituto Miguel Lillo. Universidad de Tucuman, 1955

OLIVARES, ANTONIO, O.F.M., *Se Esta Extinguiendo el Condor en Colombia*. Revista de La Academia Colombiana de Ciencias Exactas, Fisicas y Naturales. Vol. XII No. 45, 1963

PAREDES, RIGOBERTO M., *Mitos y Supersticiones y Superviviencias Populares de Bolivia*. 3rd Edición. Ediciones Isla, La Paz, 1963

PRESCOTT, W. H., *History of the Conquest of Peru*. 1847 and later editions.

REICHEL-DOLMATOFF, G., *Colombia (Ancient Peoples and Places)*. Thames and Hudson, 1965

STEWARD, J. H. (ed.), *Handbook of South American Indians*. U.S. Government Printing Office, 1948. Reprinted – Cooper Square N.Y.

SQUIER, GEORGE, *Peru. Incidents of Travel and Exploration*. Macmillan, 1877

SCHAUENSEE, MEYER DE R., *The Birds of Colombia*. Livingstone, 1964
     The Birds of South America. Livingstone, 1970

SCOTT, PETER, *Coloured Key to the Wildfowl of the World*. The Wildfowl Trust.

South American Handbook. Pub. annually. Trade and Travel Publications London

Lake Titicaca, *The Percy Sladen Trust Expedition*, 1937. Transactions of the Linnaen Society of London. Vol. I. Part 2. No. VII to XII. London 1940

VEGA, GARCILASO DE LA, *Royal Commentaries of the Incas*, various editions and translations

VERDOORN, FRANS (ed.), *Plants and Plant Science in Latin America*. Chronica Botanica Company, 1945

Whymper, Edward, *Travels Amongst the Great Andes of the Equator*. John Murray, 1892; reprinted Charles Knight, 1972

WALKER, ERNEST P., *Mammals of the World*. Vols. 1, 2 and 3. John Hopkins Press, 1964

Index

Acnistus, 51
Agoutis, 32, 60, 200
Albatross, Galapagos, 39
Algae, 160, 172
Alligators, 43
Alpaca, 85, 89, 91–3, 94, 99, 100, 102, 103; breeds of, 92–3; diseases of, 104; and folklore, 105, 124–5
Amahuaca Indians, *see under* Indians
Amaryllidacea, 51
Amazon, River, 18, 23, 25–6, 29, 33, 56–8, 60, 74, 75, 197, 205, 206
Anacondas, 59
Ani, Groove Billed, 46
Anouchi, 200
Antarctic Ocean, 28, 31, 36, 189
Anteaters, 18, 29–30, 59, 64, 113; Giant (Myrmecophaga tridactyla), 29–30, 64, 207; Pygmy (Cyclopes), 30, 64; Tamandua (Collared), 30, 38, 64, 194
Antofagasta, Chile, 48, 52, 53, 158, 170
Ants: fire, 29; leaf-cutting, 26
Arequipa, Peru, 95, 116, 161
Argentina, 28–9, 89, 166–7; birds, 49, 50, 84, 121–2, 144, 145, 148, 167–8, 178, 181–6; conservation, 97–8, 177, 185–6, 191; fauna, 59, 63, 68, 90, 92, 94, 96, 101, 112, 113, 115, 151, 169, 186–9; flora, 180
Armadillo, 29–30, 59, 111–14; Chaetophractus nationi, 113, 114; Euphractes genus, 114, 188; Fairy (Chlamyphorus truncatus), 112–13; Giant (Priodontes giganteus), 112, 114; Nine-banded (Dasypus novemcinus), 41, 112, 113, 114; Pichy ciego (Zaedyus pichy cavrinus), 188; Tolypeutes genus, 111, 113
Atacama Desert, 39, 46–9, 52, 85, 156, 158,

169, 188; birds, 48–9, 50, 145, 166–7; fauna, 47–8, 94, 100–101, 120, 169; Puna de, Bolivia, 140; Puna de, Chile, 20, 118; Salar de, 162, 173
Atiquipa, Peru, 52, 53
Auraucaria, *see* Pine, Chilean
Australia, 17; marsupial fauna of, 22, 31, 32, 63, 190
Avocet, Andean, 168
Aymara Indians, *see under* Indians
Azangaro, Peru, 145, 149, 153; mountains of, 138, 152–3

Barcroft, Joseph, 81
Barreda, Don Felipe Benavides, 13, 97–8, 100, 102
Barrientos, General Rene, 98
Bates, Henry, 29
Bats, 48
Beagle Channel, 179–80, 188
Bears, 32; Andean Spectacled (Tremarctos ornatus), 53–4, 55, 67–8, 203, 205
Beech, Southern (Nothofagus), 33, 180, 182
Benavides, *see* Barreda
Birds-of-prey, 43, 47, 149–50, 178; *and see* Buzzard, Condor, Hawk, Osprey, Vulture
Board of Trade, British, 97
Boas, 38, 59
Bogota, Col., 23, 27, 71, 77, 120, 193, 198, 204; National University, 71
Bolivar, Simon, 96, 192
Bolivia, 20, 23, 33, 205–6; Altiplano of, 66, 75, 77–82, 106, 113, 138–40, 148, 150, 156–159; birds, 50, 69, 84, 119, 120–5, 140–8, 156–62, 164–6, 197; conservation, 97–8, 99, 135, 136–7, 149, 170, 208; fauna, 53, 67, 89, 92, 94, 96, 97–9, 103, 111–15, 163, 189,

Bolivia—*cont.*
200, 203; flora, 20, 56, 110–11, 119, 148–50, 162–3; Indians, 75, 87, 106, 110–12, 114–15, 120, 123–6, 139, 158; mining, 24, 82, 156–7; *and see* Carangas Province; Colorada, Laguna; La Paz; Lipez; Poopo, Lake; Titicaca, Lake; Uyuni
Bonpland, Aimé, 26–8, 199
Boobies, 37
Borhaenids, 63
Bosque Fray Jorge, Chile, 185
Brazil, 29, 34, 70, 113, 115, 116, 141
Bromeliads, 27, 70, 149
Buenos Aires Museum of Natural History, 30
Bulrush, *see* Totora
Buritca, Col., 195; River, 395
Bushmasters, 58–9
Butterflies, 201; Blue Morphos, 201
Buzzard: Chilean (Buteo f. australis), 124; Great (Aguilucho Grande), 124; Grey-backed (Chilean Eagle), 124, 178; Red-backed (Buteo p. polysoma), 179; Red-tailed (Buteo ventralis), 179

Cabrera, Angel, 48, 67, 100, 169, 187
Cactus, 49–50, 53
Caenolestids, 31–2, 62–3, 190
Caimans, 38, 61; Black (Melanosuchus niger), 58
Cali, Col., 193, 198, 203; Museum of Natural History, 202, 203–4
Callao, Peru, 28
Callejon de Huaylas, Peru, 128–9, 149
Capybara, 27, 32, 60
Caracara: Andean or Mountain (Phalcobaenus albogularis megalopterus), 150; Phalcobaenus a. albogularis, 179; Forsters Phalcobaenus australis), 179–80
Carangas province, Bol., 106, 122–3, 156–7, 163, 164, 169, 171, 173
Carica candicans, 51
Carnivores, 17, 18, 50, 65–6, 68
Carretera Marginal (Marginal Highway), 206, 208
Casement, Roger, 34, 57
Cats, wild, 32, 61, 66–7; Andean (Felis jacobita), 102, 152; Chilean Mountain (Felis guigua guigua), 186; Geoffroys (Felis geoffryi), 66, 186; mountain (Felis coloocolo), 102, 169–70; Otter- (Jaguarundi

(Felis yagouaroundi), 66–7; Pampas or mountain (Felis colocolo), 66, 152; and religion of Incas, 119–20
Catfish, 136
Cauca, River, 27, 198
Cavidae, Family, 68, 115; *and see* Agouti, Capybara, Cavy
Cavoidea, 32, 200
Cavy, 32, 50, 68, 115–17, 178; Cavia porcellus (household guinea pig), 32, 115, 116; Cavia tschudii, 48; Patagonian (Patagonian Hare, Dolichotis patagonum), 115, 186
Caymans, 27
Cecropia trees, 29
Cerro de Pasco Hospital, 82
Chachapoyas region, Peru, 39, 70
Chan Chan, Peru, 41
Chancay, Peru, 37
Chapare, River, Bol., 206, 208
Chiclayo, Peru, 38, 40, 45
Chile, 46, 56, 63; birds, 45, 73, 119, 121–3, 141, 144–6, 148, 159–60, 164, 166–8, 178, 180–5; conservation, 53, 97, 177, 185, 191; fauna, 20, 30, 31, 94, 186–91; flora, 20, 52, 56, 180, 182–3; *and see* Atacama Desert, Santiago
Chiloé Island, 31, 187, 189
Chimborazo, volcano, 19, 25, 27–8, 62
Chimbote, Peru, 53, 54
Chinchilla, 13, 20, 85, 140, 150–2, 208; Chinchilla lanigera, 151, 169; Rat (Abrocomidae), 169; Royal (Chinchilla brevicaudata brevicaudata), 151
Chinchona tree, 25, 29, 110
Chiroptera, 48
Chosica, Peru, 48
Chucuito fish hatchery, Peru, 135
Chumbivilcas, Peru, 87, 106, 107
Civet, Binturong, 65
Coatis, 64–5, 203
Coca (Erythroxlyon coca), 75, 117
Cock-of-the-Rock, 69–70
Coffee, 193, 194
Coipasa, Lake, Bol., 161–2, 174; Salar de, 162, 166, 173
Colla tribes, *see under* Indians
Colombia, 19, 27, 90; agriculture, 75, 193, 203; birds, 33, 70–3, 120, 131, 145, 181, 184, 195–8, 202, 204–5; conservation, 13, 76, 192, 193–4, 197–8, 203–5, 208–9; fauna,

94, 194, 198, 199–205; flora, 18, 20, 195, 198–9, 204; *and see* Bogota, Santa Marta
Colorada, Laguna, Bol., 103, 159, 160–1, 162, 164, 166, 170, 171, 175, 208
Columbus, Christopher, 22
Comanche reserve, Bol., 149, 150
Compositae, dwarf, 85
Condor: Andean (Vultur gryphus), 27, 33, 47, 84, 120–6, 150, 178, 186, 202; Californian (Gymnogyps californius), 121; and folklore, 87, 119, 120, 123–32
Conquistadores, the, 22–4, 27, 33, 56, 78, 89–90, 104, 105, 108, 156, 192; and wildlife, 23, 30–1, 115
Coot, 141, 165–6; American (Fulica americana), 144; Giant (Fulica gigantea), 144, 145; Horned (Fulica cornuta), 166, 190; Slate-coloured or Andean (Fulica ardesica), 144
Copiapo, Chile, 36, 46, 145, 166, 167, 171
Copihues (Lapageria rosea), 182
Coquimbo, Chile, 151, 189
Cordier, Sr Charles, 162
Cordillera Blanca, Peru, 19, 128, 129
Cordillera Real, Bol., 19, 110, 138
Cormorant: Black (Phalacrocax olivaceus olivaceus), 147; Guano (Phalacrocrax bougainvillii), 37, 131
Cotopaxi, volcano, 19, 25, 28
Cougar, *see* Puma
Cousteau, Captain Jacques, 154
Cuckoo, Gray-capped, 51–2
Cundinamarca, Bol., 27, 120
Cusco, Peru, 58, 73, 87, 92, 95, 190; altitude of, 77, 78; and Incas, 23, 33, 56, 105; and Indian festivals, 126–8; zoo, 123
C.V.M. (Corporacion Autonomo de los Valles Magdalena y Sinu), 193–4, 197, 204

Darien, 22, 25, 198
Darwin, Charles, 28–9, 30, 53, 121, 177–8, 183, 188, 190–1
Deer, 32, 68; Brocket (Mazama americana), 187, 194, 203, 205; Dwarf Brocket (Mazama chunyi), 68; Guemal (Taruca) Hippocamelus antisensis), 152–3, 187; Guemal (Hippocamelus bisulcus), 187; Red (Cervus elephas), 187–8; White-tailed (Odocoilcus virginianus), 38, 68, 194; *and see* Pudu

Desaguadero, River, 106, 135, 138, 143, 157
Dippers, White-capped, 50
Dolphin, River, 205
D'Orbigny, Alcides, 28, 34, 135
Doves, 51, 150; Peruvian White-winged (Zenaida asiatica meloda), 46
Ducks, 32, 45; Andean Crested (Lophonetta specularoides alticola), 147, 165, 167; Bronze-Winged (Anas specularis), 181; Dabbling (Anatini), 145, 146, 181; *and see* Pintail, Teal; Patagonian Crested (Lophonetta specularoides specularoides), 147, 181; Ruddy (Oxygura ferruginea), 74, 145; South American, 181; South American Comb (Sarkidiornis melanotos carunculatus), 45; South American Crested (Lophonetta), 147, 181–2; Torrent (genus Merganetta), 50, 73–4, 180–1, 197; Tree (Tribe Dendrocygnini), 74; *and see* Pintail, Teal

Eagle, Chilean (Grey-backed Buzzard), 124, 178
Ecuador, 19, 23, 25, 27–8, 56, 75, 198; birds, 49, 70, 141, 148; fauna, 17, 31, 59, 190, 199–200; flora, 33
Edentates, 16, 29–30, 59, 111, 113, 188, 205; *and see* Anteaters, Armadillo, Sloth
Egrets, 38, 45, 59; Cattle (Bubulcus i. ibis), 45; Common (Casmerodius albus egretta), 147
El Descanso Soltaro, Peru, 95–6
Epiphytes, 51, 62
Erize, Francisco, 177
Espeletia (frailejone), 198–9

Falkland Islands, 44, 94, 141, 180, 181
Fauna Preservation Society, 97
Fawcett, Colonel Percy, 18, 34
Finches, 50, 51, 185
Flamingoes, 20, 117, 147, 156, 158–62, 174–5, 209; Andean or Greater Andean (Phoenicoparrus andinus), 159–60, 161; Chilean (Phoenicopterus ruber chilensis), 147, 159–160, 167, 186; James' (Phoenicoparrus jamesi), 159–60, 161–2, 175
Flicker, *see* Woodpecker, Andean
Flycatcher, 50; Pacific Scarlet, 46, 51
Forbes, 107
fossils, 15–16, 30, 31, 62–3, 64, 188–9
Franklin, Bill, 100, 101

Frigate Birds, 39
Foxes, 32, 37; Andean (Dusicyon culpaeus andinus), 47, 48, 102, 150, 170; Coastal (Dusicyon griseus), 47, (Dusicyon sechurae), 47–8; and folklore, 125; Patagonian (Dusicyon culpaeus magellanicus), 186; South American (genus Dusicyon), 34, 47–8, 66, 186
Frogs, 20, 59; Darwin's (Rhinoderma darwinii), 190; Marsupial, 201; Telmatobius (Quele), 154
Furnariidae family, 183–4

Galapagos Islands, 29, 37
Gallinule: Common (Gallinula chloropas pauxilla), 144; Garmans (Gallinula chloropas garmani), 144–5
Gentians, 85
Geographical Society: American, 135; of New York, 159
Glyptodonts, 15, 30, 188
Goose, Andean, 147–8, 165
Goshawk, Chilean, 179
Gould, John, 70
Grande, Laguna, Peru, 121, 166
Grebe: Chilean (Podiceps chilensis), 141–2; Crested (Podiceps occipitalis), 141, 167; Flightless Titicaca (Centropelma micropterum), 141–2, 154–5
Grimwood, Major Ian, 13, 40, 48, 58, 99
Grison, 66–7, 151; Least (Lyncodon patagonicus), 186
Ground Tyrants, 50
Guanaco (Lama guanicoe), 30, 47, 84, 94–5, 102–3; hybrids of, 93; need for protection, 100–101, 108, 167, 170; rarity of, 52–3, 99, 108, 156, 177, 186–7; wool of, 98–9
Guanera plant, 182
Guano Administration (Empresa Nacional de Fertilizantes), 47
Guano Islands, Peru, 37, 42
Guemal, 152–3, 187
Gull, Andean, 141, 167
Guinea pig, see cavy

Hacienda Cala Cala, Peru, 93–4
Hacienda Calipuy, Peru, 100
Hacienda Checayani, Peru, 145, 149, 152
Harrier, Cinereous, 150

Hawks: Black-chested (Buteo fuscescens), 124; Carrion, see Caracara; Variable (Buteo poecilochrous), 149–50
Heath, River, 34, 72
Heliotrope, Peruvian, 51
herbs, herbalism, 110–11, 115, 117
Herons, 25, 27, 38, 50; Night (Nycitcorax mycticorax hoactli), 147
High Altitude Research Institute, 81
Hoatzin, 205
Honey-Bear, see Kinkajou
Huaraz River, Peru, 129
Huaylas, Peru, 129–30
Hudson, W. H., 43
Huet-Huets, 183
Humboldt, Baron Alexander von, 24, 26–8, 199
Humboldt Current, 28, 33, 36, 41, 42, 48, 51
Hummingbirds, 32, 37, 38, 49, 50, 70–1, 84, 149, 184, 196; and altitude, 84; Andean Hillstar (Oreotrochilus estella), 84, 184; Giant (Patagonia gigas), 49, 149; Green-backed Firecrown (Sephanoides sephanoides), 184; Grey-chinned Hermit (Phaetothornis griseogularis), 70; Magnificent (Loddegesia mirabilis), 70–1; Spangled Coquette (Cophormis stictolopha), 70; Violet-ear (Colibri delphinae), 70

Ibis, 32; Andean Glossy (Plegadis ridgwayi), 143–4; Blackfaced (Theristicus candatus), 144; Common Glossy (Plegadis falcinellus chihi), 144
Ica, Peru, 40, 44
Ichu grass (Stipa ichu), 85, 87, 148–9
Iguanas, 201
Incas: agriculture of, 37, 62; civilization of, 22, 77, 90, 107, 139, 156; conquest of, 22, 23, 36; hunts of, 108–9, 119; religion of, 56, 105, 106, 117, 119–20, 126; remains of, 16, 33, 34, 62, 119–20, 139–40, 153–4; roads of, 54, 75
India, 29, 82, 196
Indians: agriculture of, 139, 163, 173; and altitude, 21, 77, 80–1, 82–3; Amahuaca, 58, 61; ancestors of, 21–2, 23–4, 33, 172–3; Aymara, 91, 105, 106–7, 110, 114–15, 125, 132, 133–5, 139, 143, 158, 165, 173–4; Chipaya, 106, 173–5; Colla, 105, 106, 110, 120, 139; dialects of, 110, 143, 146–7; diet

of, 32, 61, 75, 78, 81, 83, 106, 112, 136; domestic animals of, 115–17, 150, 200; fishing methods of, 136–7; folklore and religion of, 87, 104–7, 110–11, 114–15, 116–17, 119–20, 123–32, 133–5, 138, 153–4; hunting habits of, 60–1, 119, 123, 125–6, 142–3, 150, 151, 152–3, 164–5, 173–5; Kallawaya, 110–11, 115, 117; and llamas, 87, 89, 90–3, 104–8; Machiguenga, 58, 61–2, 200; Mapoche, 182; Morato, 173–4; Quechua, 104–5, 126, 139, 146–7, 158, 173; Uru, 143, 173; use of Totora by, 142–3
Institute of Andean Biology, 81
Institute of Occupational Health, 82
Instituto del Mar, Callao, 42
Iquitos, Peru, 59, 70

Jacana, 27, 59, 205
Jaguar (Leo onca), 29, 38, 66, 67, 194, 205; as Incan deity, 119
Jaguarundi (Otter-Cat, Felis yagouaroundi), 66–7
James, Berkeley, 159
Jesus de Machaca, Bol., 106; vicuna reserve, 99
Johnson, A. W., 44–5, 73, 123, 145, 159, 160, 161, 164, 166, 167, 177

Kallawaya Indians, *see under* Indians
Kinkajou, 65
Koepke, Dra. Maria, 49
Koford, Carl B., 100
Kontiki expedition, 21

La Condamine, Charles Marie de, 24–6, 28
La Libertad Province, Peru, 53–4
La Paz, Bol., 23, 67, 75, 77–80, 84, 92, 97, 98, 106, 114, 138, 163; railroad, 158, 170–1
Lachay, Loma de, Peru, 51–2
Lambayeque, Peru, 40, 45
Lampa, Peru, 152
Lapwing, Andean, 149, 165
Le Paige, Padre, 173
Lehmann, Carlos, 203
Lima, Peru: agriculture, 54–5; altitude, 81; birds, 45, 49, 51–2, 147; chinchilla trade, 151; climate, 36, 41; fauna, 44, 48; flora, 51; Museo Javier Prado, 145; University of San Marcos, 23, 81; Vice Royalty of, 24
Limpkins, 27

Linné, Carl von, 30
Lipez, Bol.: Cordillera de, 157; desert, 85, 167, 171; mountains, 169; pampas, 163–5; province, 157; Rio Grande de, 162, 171, 157
Lizards, 58, 85, 169, 201
Llamas, 23; (Lama glama), 87–91, 92, 94, 102, 104, 108, 150; 'Chancay', 37; and folklore, 104–7, 120; hybrids of, 93
llamoids, 50, 89, 92, 94, 95, 102–3, 140, *and see* Alpaca, Llamas, Vicuña
Llanquihue, Lake, Chile, 185
Llareta, *see* Yareta
Loa, River, 45–6
Loddiges, George, 70
Loma, 51–3, 94
Lucuma obovata, 51
Lupins, 85
Lystrosaurus, 189

Macarena, Sierra, Col., 76, 204–5, 208–9
Macaws, 59, 69, 197
Macedo, Dr Hernando de, 145, 152
McGahan, Gerry, 121, 122–3
Machiguenga tribe, *see under* Indians
Machu Picchu, Peru, 95, 114
Madders, 85
Madre de Dios River, 56, 58, 59, 60, 61
Magdalena: department, Col., 195; River, 27
Mangrove swamps, 38, 198
'Manoa, Lake', 26
Manu: National Park, Peru, 58–61, 65, 68, 74, 75, 205, 208–9; River, 58, 60
Mara (Patagonian Hare), 115, 186
Margay, 66, 67, 194
Maricunga, Salar de, 166, 171
Markham, Sir Clements, 34
Marsupials, 16, 31–2, 59, 63, 189
Mathews, Andrew, 70
Meiggs, Henry, 39
Mexico, 21, 79, 164
Millie, W. R., 166
'Mitla', the, 34
Monge, Dr Carlos, 81
Monkeys, 21, 41, 61, 198; Capuchin (Cebus albifrons), 38, 60, 205; Howler (Alouetta), 38, 60, 205; Humboldt's Woolly (Lagothrix lagothrica-*Humboldt*), 26; marmosets, 198, 201; Smokey Woolly (Lagothrix cana), 60; Spider (Ateles), 41, 60, 205; Uakaris (genus Cacajo), 60

Monkey-puzzle tree, *see* Pine, Chilean
Morosama, Peru, 40, 53
Mouse: Andean (genus Andinomys), 169; Chinchilla (Chinchillula), 152, 169; Highland Desert (genus Eligmodontia), 152; Long-Eared (genus Phyllotis), 48; South American Field (genus Akodon), 48
Moxos, Bol., 19, 56, 206
Murphy, Dr Robert Cushman, 42
Mustelidae Family, 65
Mylodon (Giant Ground Sloth), 15–16, 30, 188

Nahuel Huapi park, 185
Napo River, Ecuador, 56, 75
Nasca, Peru, 36–7, 39, 40, 41, 43, 44, 99; River, 43
National Parks, 176–7, 185–6, 191, 208; *and see* Macarena, Sierra; Manu National Park
Negro, Rio, 25–6
Nevado Ojos del Salado, 166–7
Nordenskiold, Baron von, 34

Ocelot, 38, 40, 66, 67, 194, 205, 207
Oil-birds (Guacharos), 70–2
Olingos, 65
Olivares, Padre, 71, 202, 204–5
Olmos, Peru, 55
Opossum, 30–1, 59; Black-shouldered (Caluromysiops), 59; Common (Didelphis marsupialis), 30–1; Didelphid, 50; Dromicups genus, 189; Lestodelphis halli, 189; Mouse (Marmosa), 63, 189–90; Philander, 59; Rat (Caenolestidae), 31, 62–3, 190; Virginian, 31; Water (Yapok) (genus Chironectes), 59
Orchids, 62
Orellana, Francisco de, 23, 56
Orestiinae, 136–7
Orinoco, River, 18, 26, 56, 198, 204
Oropendola, 69, 197
Oruro, Bol., 151, 157, 163, 188; department, 114
Osprey, 45, 178–9, 205
Otter, 32; Coast (Lutra felina), 48; Giant (Pteronura brasiliensis), 57, 205; Nutria, 194
Ovando, President General, 98

Paca: (Cuniculus genus), 60; Dasyprocta, 32; Mountain (Stictomys taczanowski), 32, 199–200; Myoprocta, 32; Tailed (Pacarana) (Dinomys branikii), 32, 60–1, 200
Pacarana (Tailed Paca), 32, 60–1, 200
Pacasmayo, Peru, 39, 43
Pacific Ocean, 22, 37–8, 44; crossing of, 21, 142
Palpa, Peru, 43
Pampa Galeras vicuña reserve, Peru, 99, 101, 102, 208
Panama, 90, 142, 198
Paracas, Peru, 45, 91, 121–2, 131, 147, 178
Paraguay, 67, 94, 113, 151, 197; River, 30
Parakeets, 185–6
Paramo, 27, 198–9, 203
Paramo de Guanaco, Col., 90, 94
Paredes, Francisco, 93
Parrots, 38, 59, 69, 184–5; Burrowing (Cyanoliscus patagonus), 185; *and see* Parakeets
Paruro, Peru, 127
Passerines, 49, 182–3
Pasto, Col., 27, 121, 202, 203
Patagonia, 15–16, 30, 53, 94, 100, 176, 177, 187–90
Peccary: Collared, 38, 194; genus Tayassu, 60
Pejerrey, Argentinian freshwater, 136, 138
Pelicans, 37, 42
Percy Sladen Trust Expedition, 33, 135
Peru, 20, 29, 36–55; agriculture, 40, 46–7, 52, 54–5, 75, 90; altitudes, 77, 78, 81, 82–3; archaeological remains, 33, 36–7, 41, 62–3; birds, 37–52 *passim*, 59, 69–74, 121–2, 131, 141, 144–50, 167–8, 178–9, 184; climate, 28, 36, 41–4; conservation, 9, 13, 58–9, 76, 97–8, 99–100, 135–7, 170; *and see* Manu National Park, Pampa Galeras reserve; earthquake, 128, 131; fauna, 38–54 *passim*, 57–69 *passim*, 90, 92–109, 116, 151; flora, 39, 50–1, 53, 56–7, 58, 62, 149; Government (1968), 46, 52, 58, 94, 206; Indians, 58, 60–3, 77, 87, 90–1, 104–6, 126–34, 142–143, 152, 200; *and see* Cusco, Lima, Manu National Park, Lima, Paracas, Puno
Peterson, Roger Tory, 159
Phalarope, Wilson's, 44, 45, 147
Pig, South American wild, 194; *and see* Peccary
Pinchincha, volcano, 25, 62
Pine, Chilean (Monkey-puzzle tree, Araucaria imbricata), 33, 182

Pintail: Chilean (Brown) (Anas georgica spinicauda), 145, 181; Greater Bahamian (Anas bahamensis rubrirostris), 45
Pinzón, Vincente, 31
Pisco, Peru, 44, 121
Pit-vipers, 59
Pizarro, Francisco, 22, 23
Pleistocene era, 17, 92, 94
Pliocene era, 17, 63, 64
Plover, 49, 165; American Golden (Pluvialis d. dominica), 149; Mitchell's (Phegornis mitchelli), 167–8; Peruvian Kill-deer (Charadrius vociferus peruvianus), 49; Puna (Chariadrius alticola), 149; Slender-billed (Oreopholus r. ruficolis), 52
Polylepis trees, 53, 129, 208
Polynesia, 21
Poopo, Lake, Bol., 138, 157, 162, 171, 173–4, 189
Porcupine, 194, 200–201
Portugal, 22–3
Potosi, Bol., 23; department, 114
Procyonids, 38, 65
Pudu, 68, 202, 203; Chilean, 187
Puma (Mountain Lion, Felis concolor), 20, 40, 47, 66, 67, 84, 120, 150, 169–70, 186; as Incan deity, 119–20
puna, 27, 68, 70, 84, 87, 102, 108, 140–1, 149–150, 180
Puno, Peru, 95, 133, 138, 141, 142–3, 147; Illpa Stud Farm, 85
Puracé, volcanos, 202, 203
Putumayo, River, 34, 57
Puya, 149–50

Quaqui, Bol., 138
Quechua Indians, *see under* Indians
Quetzal, 196
Quito, Ecuador, 23, 24, 27, 77, 199; zoo, 123

Rabbits, 32; Cotton-tail, 41
Racoon: Coatimundis, 64, 203; Common (Procyon lotor), 65; Crab-eating (Procyon cancrivorus), 38, 65; Ring-tailed Cat (Cacomistle) (Bassariscus asututas), 65
Rail, 145
Raleigh, Sir Walter, 26
Rat: Andean Swamp (Neotomys), 152; Branick, *see* Pacas, Tailed; Cotton (genus Sygmodon), 48; Old World (R. rattus and R. norvegicus), 48; rice- (genus Oryzomys), 43–4, 48; Spiny (genus Proechimys), 200
Revie, John, 85
Rhea, 30, 118, 156, 164–5, 179; Darwin's (Pterocnemia pennata barapacensis), 30, 164–5, 208; Nandus (Rhea americana), 165
Rice, 40, 45
Rimac, River, Peru, 36, 39
Rodents, 16–17, 18, 27, 43, 48, 50, 59, 60–1, 68, 115, 140, 150, 156, 186, 200–1, 207; and altitude, 85; *and see* Cavy, Chinchilla, Mouse, Porcupine, Rabbits, Rat, Squirrel, Tuco Tuco, Viscacha
Rubber, 25, 34, 57

Sajama: Mount, 169; National Park, Bol., 208
Salamanca, Island of, 27, 198
San Andres, Bol., University of, 82
San Lorenzo forestry station, Col., 194
Sanderlings, 45
Sandia Province, Peru, 67
Sandpipers, 45
Santa Marta, Col., 114, 192, 194, 195, 197; Sierra Nevada de, 72, 114, 192–4, 195–8, 203
Santa Rosa, Laguna, Chile, 166–7
Santiago, Chile, 16, 39, 177, 180, 182, 185, 187
Santo Tomas, Peru, 87
Savoy, Gene, 37–8, 142
Scorpions, 37, 85, 169
Screamers, 27; Horned, 205
sea-birds, 37, 39, 40, 42, 43, 44–5, 47, 131
Sea-lions, 40, 47
Sechura Desert, Peru, 38–9, 41
Sheep: Merino, 85; sacrifice of, 106
Shoveler, Red, 181
Shrew, 17
Sicuani, Peru, 92, 151
Skunk, 114; Hog-nosed (genus Conepatus), 48, 66, 186
Slipperwort, 51
Sloth, 29, 59, 113; Giant (Mylodon), 15–16, 30, 188; Ground, 30; Three-toed (Choloepus), 29, 38
Smith, Captain John, 31
Snakes, 38, 58–9, 114, 201; Asiro (Aym), 115; Coral, 38, 59, 114; Fer de Lance (Bothrops atrox), 59, 114
Snipe, 32, 165; Seed-, 49, 148

Southern Peru Railway, 133
Spain, 22–4, 26, 28, 107, 127, 130–1, 158; *and see* Conquistadores
Spinetail, 49, 50, 183
Spoonbill, 205
Spruce, Richard, 24, 29, 75
Squirrel, 201
Stilt, 147, 168
Stork, Jabiru, 59, 205
Surf Birds, 45
Swallows, Blue and White, 49
Swan, Black-necked, 186

Tacna, Peru, 100; department, 40
Talara, Peru, 38
Tamarin, 201
Tamarugal, Chile, 52
Tapaculos, 183
Tapirs, 30, 205; Columbian (Tapirus t. colombianus), 203; Mountain (Tapirus pinchaque), 30, 55, 202–3; Tapirus terrestris, 30, 59–60, 194, 203
Tarapoto, Peru, 29, 75
Taruca (Guemal Deer), 152–3
Tayras, 40–1, 65
Tayrona Reserve, Col., 198
Teal, Andean (Anas flavirostris andium), 145; Andean Cinnamon (Anas cyanoptera orinomus), 146; Andean Silver (Anas versicolorpuna, Puna Duck), 74, 146, 165, 181; Cinnamon, Argentinian (Anas c. cyanoptera), 45, 146, 181; Green-winged, 181; Prairie Blue-winged, 45; Sharp-winged (Anas flavirostris oxyptera), 145; Southern Silver (Anas versicolor fretensis), 146
Temuco, Chile, 182
Terry, President Fernando Belaunde, 206
Thomas, Oldfield, 31
Tiahuanaco, Bol., 33, 119–20, 139–40
Tierra del Fuego, Arg., 44, 56, 94, 141, 145, 147, 176, 178, 181, 184, 185, 189, 191
Tillesandia straminae, 51
Tinamous, 32, 117–19, 117–18, 164, 178, 182
Tingo Maria, Peru, 72–3
Titicaca, Lake (Peru/Bol.), 85, 110, 133–55, 156, 157; birds, 74, 150–3; fauna, 20, 66, 93, 99, 150–3; fish, 135–8; and Inca civilization, 33, 120, 153–4; Indians of, 77, 87, 91, 105–6, 117, 124–5, 133, 136–7, 138, 139, 142–3, 146–7, 149, 173

Tola (Lepidophyllum quadrangulare), 119, 163–4, 208
Torontoy, Peru, 62
Totora (Bulrush) (Scirpus totora), 141–3
Toucanets, Emerald, 195–6
Toucans, 59, 69, 195, 205; Keel-Billed, 195
Trinidad, 71, 72
Trivigiano, 31
Trogons, 196
Trout, Rainbow, 135–7
Trujillo, Peru, 40, 41, 53–4
Tschudi, J. J. von, 29, 34, 135
Tuco Tuco, 169, 179, 186
Tumbes, Peru, 38; Department, 33, 48
Turcas, 183
Turnstones, 45
Turtles, 205; River, 58

Ultima Esperanza, Chile, 30, 188
United States of America, 30, 32, 65, 112, 178; and import of skins, 9, 97, 152; and pesticides, 192
Uru Indians, *see under* Indians
Uru Uru, Lake, Bol., 157–8
Urubamba River, Peru, 61–2
Uruguay, 66
Uyuni, Bol., 156, 162, 163, 165, 169, 170, 175; Salar de, 171–3, 175

Vega, Garcilaso de la, 105, 120
Venezuela, 17, 23, 53, 59, 67, 69, 195, 198, 199–200, 203, 205, 206; Llanos of, 26
Vicanota, River, 114
Vicuña, 84, 89, 95–104, 208; breeding of, 93–94, 100; protection of, 9, 96–100, 170; rarity of, 13, 96, 98–9, 156, 163, 170; wool of, 85, 92, 93, 96, 98–9, 100, 108–9
Vikings, 22
Viscacha, 50, 140, 150–1, 152, 153, 169, 178, 186
Vulture: Black (Coragyps atratus foetens), 178; King, 205; Turkey (Cathartes aura), 121, 178; *and see* Condor

waders, 32, 44, 45, 49, 147
Wallace, Russell, 29
Weasels, 32, 65–6; *and see* Grison
Whymper, Edward, 28
Wire-Tail, Des Murs, 183–4

Wolf: Andean, 34; Tasmanian, 63
Woodpecker, Andean (Flicker), 149
World Wildlife Fund, 13, 97, 208

xerophytes, 53, 66, 85

Yapok (Water opossum), 59
Yareta (Llareta) (Azorella glabra), 85, 163
Yellowlegs, Greater and Lesser, 45, 147
Yungas valleys, Bol., 67, 75, 200

Zamurilla, Peru, 38, 39; Province, 38

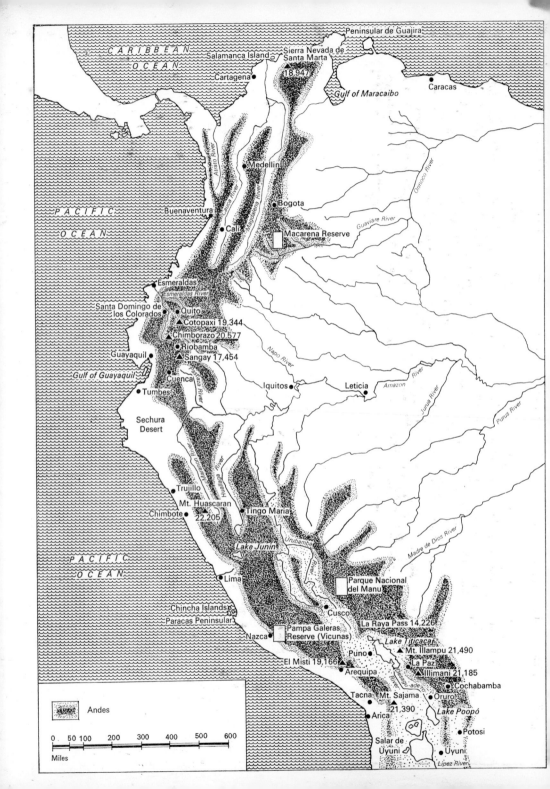